VOICING
AMERICAN
POETRY

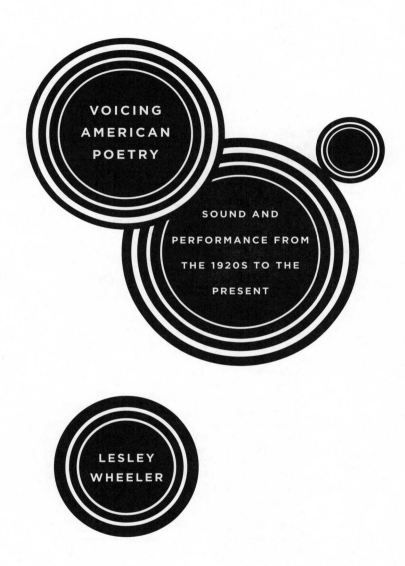

VOICING
AMERICAN
POETRY

SOUND AND
PERFORMANCE FROM
THE 1920S TO THE
PRESENT

LESLEY
WHEELER

CORNELL UNIVERSITY PRESS ⊙ ITHACA AND LONDON

Copyright © 2008 by Cornell University

All rights reserved. Except for brief quotations in a review, this book, or parts thereof, must not be reproduced in any form without permission in writing from the publisher. For information, address Cornell University Press, Sage House, 512 East State Street, Ithaca, New York 14850.

First published 2008 by Cornell University Press
First printing, Cornell Paperbacks, 2008

Printed in the United States of America

Library of Congress Cataloging-in-Publication Data

Wheeler, Lesley.
    Voicing American poetry : sound and performance from the 1920s to the present / Lesley Wheeler.
        p. cm.
    Includes bibliographical references and index.
    ISBN 978-0-8014-4668-9 (cloth : alk. paper) —
    ISBN 978-0-8014-7442-2 (pbk.: alk.paper)
    1. Oral interpretation of poetry—United States—History.   2. Performance poetry—United States—History and citicism.   3. Poetry slams—United States—History.   4. American poetry—20th century—History and criticism.   5. American poetry—21st century—History and criticism.   I. Tilte.
    PN4151.W47   2008
    808.5'45—dc22   2007048430

Cornell University Press strives to use environmentally responsible suppliers and materials to the fullest extent possible in the publishing of its books. Such materials include vegetable-based, low-VOC inks and acid-free papers that are recycled, totally chlorine-free, or partly composed of nonwood fibers. For further information, visit our website at www.cornellpress.cornell.edu.

Cloth printing   10 9 8 7 6 5 4 3 2 1
Paperback printing   10 9 8 7 6 5 4 3 2 1

FOR MADELEINE AND CAMERON GAVALER

CONTENTS

ACKNOWLEDGMENTS

No Muse has ever called me to writing with an audible voice, and yet this book is a record of many conversations in many media. Cynthia Hogue, Julia Spicher Kasdorf, and Chris Gavaler reviewed the manuscript and gave me valuable advice. Many other colleagues assisted me with the initial proposal, read portions of the book at various stages, suggested research leads, or listened generously as I puzzled my argument out aloud: Marsha Bryant, Suzanne Churchill, Ed Craun, Severn Duvall, Helen Emmett, Beth Frost, Derek Furr, Janet Gray, Paul Hanstedt, Suzanne Keen, Linda Kinnahan, Janet McAdams, Cristanne Miller, Deborah Miranda, Dee Morris, Scott Nicolay, John Shoptaw, Rod Smith, and Jim Warren. The Millay chapter owes much to the editorial comments of Michael Coyle, Debra Rae Cohen, and Jane Alison Lewty. Sarah Kennedy, Ellen Mayock, Christopher Matthews, Margo Solod, Jeanine Stewart, and Asali Solomon sang feminist back-up through years of composition, with a catchy chorus about finding time for one's own work. Denise Duhamel, Maureen Seaton, and Marilyn Johnson responded generously to my queries about their work. Without the team from Four Corners, New Mexico, I would have heard a far more limited band of slam poetry. I am very grateful to all of them, and to Peter Potter, whose fine ear helped me regulate my pitch.

Current and former students framed questions and discovered answers with me, especially John Rumin and Courtney Harrison. Discussions with Jeanne Dillon, John Melillo, Brandon Waddell, Michael Wagoner, and many others similarly started in the classroom but resonated beyond that wonderfully noisy space. I am grateful to the staff, librarians, and curators of Leyburn Library at Washington and Lee University and of the Yale

Collection of American Literature, Beinecke Rare Book and Manuscript Library, Yale University. Sandy O'Connell supported my work in myriad ways and I hope she won't quit anytime soon.

I could not have written this book without timely funds from the National Endowment for the Humanities and from Washington and Lee University's Glenn Grant Program. Two other communities were crucial to me during the research and writing process: the Modernist Studies Association and the Women's Poetry List (WOM-PO).

I owe my whole orchestra and its first tuning to the wonderfully clashing accents of Pat, Bill, and Will Wheeler and Claire Kerr. Chris, Madeleine, and Cameron Gavaler kept the radio playing, the needle in its groove, the timbres true. I thank them most of all.

"Voice" copyright © by Ron Padgett reprinted by permission of the author from his *New & Selected Poems* (Godine, 1995).

"Last night I heard upon the Air" quoted by permission of the Edna St. Vincent Millay Society.

Part of chapter 3 appears as an essay in *Fieldnotes* 3.3 (Fall 2007).

Poems and correspondence from Zoey Benally, Amy Mullen, DJ Mydas, Scott Nicolay, and Tish Ramirez appear with their permission.

L.W.

VOICING
AMERICAN
POETRY

VOICE IDENTIFICATION

I have always laughed
when someone spoke of a young writer
"finding his voice." I took it
literally: had he lost his voice?
Had he thrown it and had it
not returned? Or perhaps they
were referring to his newspaper
the *Village Voice?* He's trying
to find his *Voice.*
   What isn't
funny is that so many young writers
seem to have found this notion
credible: they set off in search
of their voice, as if it were
a single thing, a treasure
difficult to find but worth
the effort. I never thought
such a thing existed. Until
recently. Now I know it does.
I hope I never find mine. I
wish to remain a phony the rest of my life.
   —Ron Padgett, "Voice," *The Straight Line*

Any book about poetic voice must involve an array of media problems.
First, do I mean voice in a literal or metaphorical way?—am I writing about

performance or print? This question points to a dilemma of definition: What *is* poetic voice? Different communities within and adjacent to literary studies use variations on this phrase constantly, but no consensus exists on its meaning, and further, no consensus has existed in recent literary history. Writing about voice is also risky because the word invites suspicion from many of poetry's best readers. The phrase "voice-based lyric," for example, can be a term of intense opprobrium. Ron Padgett's poem, quoted above, demonstrates how vulnerable voice is to demolition.

The idea of voice in poetry, however, deserves sustained investigation precisely because of its ambiguity and because of the range of esthetic, cultural, political, and even spiritual attitudes the word so often encodes. What does poetic voice mean and how has its meaning evolved? What remains useful or at least interesting about the concept? Two terms used throughout this book help to clarify these problems. *Textual voice* refers to voice as a metaphor employed by poets and critics in and about works in print. In contrast I refer to *voiced texts;* these include poems recited, read aloud, performed by authors, actors, students, and others. What is the relationship between voice as performance and voice as figure? Poets and scholars often link voice to another fraught but resonant term, lyric; these two words share fluctuating fortunes in this book and elsewhere. Tropes of voice in poems often mark challenges to how lyric poetry is defined, and, paradoxically, references to voice in critical writing can signify a resistance to the rational processes of criticism itself. I premise this study on voice's multiplicity of meanings—not its emptiness or speciousness, but its fascinating excess of connotations.

Voicing American Poetry examines the shifting significance of voice and sound for U.S. poets and audiences from the early twentieth century, when modernism's coteries accumulated power, to the present. Because lyric poetry is traditionally defined in relation to music, voice and sound are key elements of the genre. Voice and sound suggest new complications, however, for twentieth- and twenty-first-century poets and their audiences because of changing sound technologies and their profound influence on U.S. culture. This study begins with the 1920s because of radio's sudden expansion during this decade; the resultant revolutions in American life include the decline of amateur and professional poetry recitation and the rise of new poetry performance conventions. Other developments in distancing technologies—recording, television broadcast, the internet, the relative cheapness of book and magazine printing—continue to affect poetry's formal possibilities and the ways it can reach audiences. Voice, which variously indicates poetry's source, medium, style, availability, and effect, has therefore become an increasingly tricky term in poetry studies.

In its foremost sense, voice implies poetry's reliance on sound, a first principle for poets of various affiliations, including much ethnic American writing, New Formalism, and many species of performance and sound-directed poetry—both mainstream and avant-garde. However, voice is also a metaphor for originality, personality, and the illusion of authorial presence within printed poetry—meanings that have been particularly useful and/or provocative in some sectors of literary criticism and creative writing. Voice in the political sense, as the right or ability to speak or write, also intersects with literary studies, particularly through the fields of composition and feminist studies. The word voice encapsulates these poetic conflicts but also suggests the common interests underlying them. One syllable thereby signals many of the issues that have obsessed American poets for a century.

The poetry of the United States has long flourished in multiple media including print publication, live oral performance, and more recently, broadcasting and recording. Of all these poetic incarnations, published books possess the most prestige, endure the longest, and constitute the most convenient objects of study. In books, voice and sound are tropes—sometimes master metaphors with power to define poetry itself, but still metaphors for the physical processes that occur when human beings listen and read.

Because, however, so many poets in the United States, not least the ones treated here, have been deeply concerned with live, broadcast, and recorded performances, voiced texts are as important as textual voices. The comparison between the two media rests on a surprisingly difficult question to answer: Where do the conventions of contemporary poetry readings come from, and how were texts voiced in the modernist period?

The Platforms of Modern Poetry

Modernist poetry performance deserves a book of its own. The sites and methods of sounding poetry shifted in significant ways during this period and highly various approaches and attitudes coexisted even in single cities. Most practices, further, are hard to track and describe, because live readings are inherently ephemeral events. However, even though a full and detailed account of poetry performance practices in these decades does not exist, many reports of individual readings and tours are readily accessible in memoirs, biographies, and, increasingly, literary criticism. Newspapers and other popular media reported on and reviewed such recitals far more often than they do in the twenty-first century. Less available, but also crucial, are archival documents, especially correspondence, that cast light on these short-lived events. What emerges through these materials is an increasing trend during the modernist period to conflate the performer of poetry with the poet herself—figures that were mainly separate in the nineteenth-century United States, but have since become so fused that we fail to remember the history of the change. Recent books by Laura Severin, Peter Middleton, Adalaide Morris, Joan Shelley Rubin, and others are finally rendering the contexts of modern poetry audible.[1]

These sources, in addition to recordings made from the 1930s onward, indicate several different kinds of poetry performance occurring in the twenties and thirties. In the first part of the twentieth century, poetry was sounded in an enormous variety of spaces, including drawing rooms and salons, clubs, churches, cabarets and cafés, universities and schools of all levels, libraries, bookshops, and concert halls. One kind of poetic sounding in one segment of the modern era is of particular interest here: the public recitation of poems by their authors in the 1920s and 1930s. This short history cannot account for all the figures who gave readings, nor all the kinds of readings they gave, but it does attempt to make general sense of the poetic soundscape with reference to a few interesting examples. Such performances drew on significant resources that are now unavailable to United States poets and audiences. Edna St. Vincent Millay, for instance, as well as her peers and audiences, were trained in an educational system that emphasized poetry recitation; this rich environment for speaking and hearing involved a set of expectations and conventions that has since faded. In particular, many modernist-era poets were schooled in the presumption that the poet would rarely be the best oral interpreter of her own poetry, and that superior recitation required unusual skill and sensitivity in the performer.

One of the most important contexts for the sounding of modern poetry was the prevalence of recitation by non-poets. Often this was a private activity, entertaining a family or a small circle of friends, but it could also be a highly public exercise.[2] For instance, actors, public figures, and other poets read each other's works aloud at a range of literary and publishing events. Often these performances were promotional. Robert Frost's "first reading," for example, featured the poet's work read by a supporter to a banquet of a Men's League, while Frost "cowered" in a corner, but the event led to a handy job offer (Parini 93). In 1927, Macmillan arranged a "preview" of Edwin Arlington Robinson's *Tristram* by actress Eleanor Robson just prior to the book's publication; this glitzy reading and reception, held at Manhattan's Little Theater, barely even involved the author, who only made a brief appearance at evening's end (Rubin 75–77). Ambivalence and reclusion on the author's part during such performances were normal.

When someone other than the author recited poems in the presence of the author, the act could also signify social bonds and/or respect for the poet's proper introversion. Although Frost would transcend his initial nervousness and become a particularly winning performer, other poets detested formal readings, as did Elinor Wylie (Stanley Olson 250). Sara Teasdale was also too shy, and sometimes too ill, for such spectacle. At a Poetry Society of America meeting, Witter Bynner read Teasdale's poems aloud for discussion (Carpenter 140); at another date Amy Lowell demonstrated no such modesty and presented her own poems to the same group. Even Millay, precursor of contemporary performers of presence, devoted at least one public reading to another poet's work—Wylie's, when Millay learned of her friend's death just before assuming the stage at the Brooklyn Academy of Music in 1928 (Milford 307).

Far more commonly, no relationship existed between the author of a piece and its performer. The most important site of this kind of recitation was the school. Rubin describes the shifting and sometimes contradictory roles poetry recitation played in American education in the late nineteenth and early twentieth centuries: it was supposed to enhance patriotism, "instill virtue," convey "the value of discipline," and with the advent of progressive education in the thirties, encourage self-expression (107–64). Many books of recitation pieces and so-called "memory gems" survive, as well as published curricula, testifying to the ubiquity of memorization and recitation as requirements. Further, the canon of elocution—the most famous and most admired poems for recitation—is remarkably different from the literary canon that survived recitation's ubiquity. Rubin observes, for instance, the mixing of nineteenth-century and early modernist poems in recitation curricula (124–25). Race and gender also played an important role in the elocutionist's repertoire. African Americans were regarded as "natural elocutionists" and pieces by Frances Harper and Paul Laurence Dunbar were frequently recommended for recitation (Loeffelholz 121–24).[3] Mary Loeffelholz argues that the schoolroom, an important location for poetry, was also one of the few public sites often dominated by women. Elocution was therefore a gendered and racially inflected art, characteristics that probably contributed to its decreasing cachet in the twentieth century.

In this educational practice, students did not always recite publicly the poems they had learned. Sometimes they wrote them out to strengthen memorization, spelling, and handwriting skills. Nonetheless, recitation itself was frequently scheduled on Friday afternoons as a festive activity, and "both schools and civic organizations sponsored competitions" that enlarged the social worlds and opportunities of many children (Rubin 109–10). Decades afterwards, children schooled by these techniques often remembered poetry recitation as a family activity and a source of community identity; indeed, generations memorized the same poems, sometimes from the same school books.

Of course, the oral performance of written works did not begin in the nineteenth century. However, the nineteenth-century art of elocution was one of the traditions most immediately influential on modernism, although effaced by a "deliberate amnesia" (Middleton 92). People from all classes voiced poems in domestic settings as well as in public settings such as clubs, reading circles, schools, and competitions. Actors even gave poetry readings to paying audiences. While these practices were not hospitable to the challenges of modernist verse—as an example, Middleton describes William Carlos Williams' "disappointing reception" by reading circles and Williams' eventual recourse to an "emergent college reading platform"—they do form an important context for modernist innovation.[4] For example, "the young Charles Olson was trained in these traditions as a successful school debater and drew on them unacknowledged in his 'Projective Verse' essay" (Middleton 81, 91).

Nearly everyone, it seems, sounded poetry in nineteenth-century North America and Britain. Recitation was, in fact, a participatory entertainment, although "poetry readings" in the twenty-first century tend not to be. Many groups fostered recitation as a means of education and social uplift as well as amusement; sometimes competition was part of the fun, as in the poetry slams that proliferated a hundred years later. "Penny Readings" were a British phenomenon of the nineteenth century sponsored by a group called the Public Reading Association (Sivier, "Penny Readings" 224). They occurred across England from the 1860s until World War I, although their very popularity led to parody by the nineties. When amateur and professional reciters began using musical accompaniment, the satire became especially merciless (Sivier, "Penny Readings" 228–29). William Butler Yeats, in fact, inspired by Florence Farr, was an ardent proponent of chanting poetry to the accompaniment of a twelve-stringed instrument called a "psaltery" (Foster 250, 257); his turn-of-the-century enthusiasm, needless to say, did not prosper.

Although the elocutionary manner died slowly and ignominiously, its aims did not. For example, the British verse speaking movement of the 1920s, inspired by Yeats and led by poet John Masefield and teachers Elsie Fogerty and Marjorie Gullen, led to a series of festivals, based primarily at Oxford, in which verse speakers competed for prizes (Sivier, "English Poets" 282–300). The practice of choral verse-speaking also became prevalent. For instance, Gullen's Glasgow Verse-Speaking Choir emphasized groups reciting poetry in unison (137); this practice became commonplace in the United States and in the 1930s was especially popular in East Coast women's colleges.

Such cultural developments emphasized the talent and skill of the reciter: choirs and festival competitors did not perform their own compositions. Nevertheless, some judges of the Oxford festivals were also poets and supported the performance of authorial presence in other contexts. Harold Monro and Alida Klementaski (later Monro), proprietors of the Poetry Bookshop, were deeply involved in both models: poetry recitation as an exhibition of skill, and poetry reading as a manifestation or spectacle of authority. At their London establishment, readings by diverse poets were scheduled weekly during the teens, twenties, and thirties. These readings, the best modern-era analog to the contemporary academic poetry reading, lasted about forty minutes and attracted average crowds of thirty-five during the series' apex (Grant 75–79). The Poetry Bookshop was contemporary with the verse speaking movement, which encouraged imaginative surrender to the poet's words, and in fact some poets' works were only heard there when recited by another (Millay is an example). Nevertheless, Monro and Klementaski promoted "true authorial presence" with certain reservations (Morrisson 76). Monro in particular felt disturbed that curiosity about the poet rather than about the poetry might draw audiences (Grant 2). The Poetry Bookshop, in fact, was instrumental in a "fundamental historical shift in the relationship of English poets to their public" (Morrisson 77).

Platform conventions in the nineteenth century United States were similar to those in Britain—not surprisingly, since groundbreaking reader Charles Dickens toured on both sides of the Atlantic, not to mention reader and author Fanny Kemble, whose solo performances centered on Shakespeare but sometimes included lyric poetry by other writers, such as Longfellow (Furnas 333).[5] Poetry readings by the authors themselves were not in vogue in either Britain or the United States. Instead, this was the age of the lecture, and a few poets did take to the stage for this very different mode of performance. The lyceum circuit in both countries and the chautauqua movement in the United States emphasized aurality as a means of reaching mass audiences.[6] Many of the stars and agents of this system—such as Bayard Taylor and James Redpath—are not well known today. Among the heavyweights of the present canon, Edgar Allan Poe and Ralph Waldo Emerson were successful on the lecture circuit, but poetry recitation played a minor role in their performances. Walt Whitman gave a few readings of single poems at public events and closed his popular lectures on the death of Lincoln with a rendition of his elegy, "O Captain! My Captain!" (Reynolds 502, 513–14, 531). These figures were succeeded in the twentieth-century by other accomplished poet-lecturers: T. S. Eliot, Wallace Stevens, Gertrude Stein, and Countee Cullen, for example.[7]

Women of color provide the main examples of nineteenth-century poet-performers who entertained by reciting their own work as much as, or more than, lecturing. Frances Ellen Watkins Harper, very much in demand for her lectures on equal rights, quoted her own poetry more liberally in her orations than Whitman or Poe did, thus building an audience across the nation. She also, in her very presence as an eloquent black woman using perfect elocution, testified for abolition, and after the war represented the struggles of reconstruction through the folk voices of poetic characters such as "Aunt Chloe."[8] In Canada and England, E. Pauline Johnson, half Mohawk in descent and half Euro-Canadian, was a frequent platform entertainer and the clearest American precursor in stage style to Millay. By the mid 1890s, Johnson began each recitation (including poetry and skits) in buckskins, fascinating audiences with a spectacle of Indianness, and then changed at intermission into Victorian evening wear (Leighton 148).[9] For these poets, words were utterly grounded in bodies and hence in culture and politics; their self-presentations emphasized these connections. Performing presence meant engaging stereotypes, whether to reinforce or challenge them, and could result in financial and/or political gain.[10]

This model of mixing lecture with recitation persisted well into the twentieth century. Carl Sandburg's success as a platform entertainer is a primary example. In the first part of the twentieth century, Sandburg attempted to build a career as an orator, lecturing on Whitman and Lincoln on the chautauqua and lyceum circuits, and then stumping for socialism. He found more financial success as a journalist, however, until the late teens, when his reputation as a poet began to soar. With his friend and fellow poet Lew Sarrett, Sandburg approached the Pond Lecture Bureau in 1919 with a plan to create a joint "lecture-recital" tour. Sandburg's populist mixture of poetry, commentary, and American folk songs "sung to his own guitar accompaniment" held enormous appeal for audiences (Niven 346–47). By the early twenties he was traveling and performing on a grueling schedule all over the country (Niven 386). As one of his biographers, Penelope Niven, puts it, Sandburg had "discovered a new way to express himself and make money at the same time" (348).

It is tempting to extrapolate from this that the modernist poetry reading occupied a middle space between the nineteenth-century lecture interspersed with a little bit of voiced poetry and the late twentieth-century sequence of voiced poems interspersed with a little bit of lecture. For some, such as Sandburg, this may have been true. Like Sandburg, Robert Frost was a famous platform charmer and also veered between lecture and reading, although, as Louis Untermeyer remarked, "He never lectured. He talked . . . He never 'recited' his poems, he 'said' them" (quoted in Parini 164). Certainly some of Frost's strategies would be unusual now. Several listeners describe Frost's habit of reading a short or new piece twice; he also quipped in epigrams between poems (Parini 164, 270). Frost did not possess Sandburg's oratorical experience, but he projected a distinct personality through his performances, literally banking on his charisma. Frost's "barding around" is in many ways analogous to popular lecture tours of the nineteenth century. Amy Lowell also "traveled extensively on reading-lecture tours—once as far as Omaha" (Benvenuto 19). Like Frost and Sandburg, Lowell often performed to capacity crowds, eventually reaching many thousands of fans and proving the viability of the lecture circuit well into the twentieth century (Lowell died in 1925).

However, while some poet-performers in the twenties and thirties drew on the lyceum tradition and offered "lecture-recitals" or "reading-lectures," this was only one mode for the aural transmission of poetry—and relatively few poets managed it. Even Lowell, in fact, borrowed as much from the conventions of theater as from the lyceum. As the poet herself humbly put it, "I enjoy reading poetry as I should enjoy acting a play to an audience, because it is one side of my genius" (quoted in Gould 258). Lowell's partner was an actress who helped coach her vocal delivery as well as her use of gesture, props, and costuming. Bradshaw recounts how, at the start of one of these reading-lectures, Lowell's entourage would dramatically remove the lectern in favor of a large table, upon which they installed a powerful reading lamp. Then, "during the course of a reading Lowell went through a series of increasingly strong, color-coded pince-nez, which she carried with her in a basket" ("Let Us Shout it Lustily" xix–xx). Her most infamous props were the cigars she smoked before and after the events. An often-told legend about Lowell the platform entertainer involves a 1914 recital at the Steinhart Hall in Boston. Lowell read fourteen poems, and for "The Bombardment" concocted a "demonstration of a cannonade": at the moments corresponding with the word "Boom!" in the printed poem, Lowell's friend, composer Carl Engel, pounded on a bass drum while concealed behind a backdrop (Gregory 122). These extra-literary elements allied Lowell with theatrical traditions that also influenced Millay, Edith Sitwell, and other poet-performers during this era.[11]

For literary entrepreneurs like Langston Hughes, any number of performance models came into play. Hughes was expert at manipulating the expectations of very different audiences. Speaking to blacks in the South, Hughes assumed a role familiar to these audiences: the traveling preacher (Davey 225). Elsewhere, he used the conventions of cabaret, salon, recital, and other kinds of spectacle. Hughes alone, in fact, could represent the diversity of modernist poetry readings. His performance practices are also better recorded than those of many others. Among biographies of modernist poets, Arnold Rampersad's life of Langston Hughes is particularly rich in the details of his readings. While Hughes occasionally read for free at a bookshop or dinner, promoting his own publications or supporting other artists, he more often read for money at social clubs, such as the Penguin Club and the Civic Club in New York City (115, 228). Hughes was relieved when grants eased his overloaded performance schedule; it could be exhausting to read his poetry to an endless series of "ladies clubs, YWCA, and the leading literary societies in places like Columbus" (quoted in Rampersad 158). Nevertheless, he was very good at it and unusually adventurous in his eagerness to perform with blues musicians and gospel choirs. Most exceptionally, he strove to build audiences among southern blacks through poetry performance. Hughes contacted black colleges and schools to set up readings, sometimes in academic spaces and sometimes at other public sites like clubs and churches. He also printed an inexpensive pamphlet of "recitation pieces" as well as broadsides to sell to his audiences, many of whose members could not afford books (Davey 223–43). The second part of his two-volume autobiography, *I Wonder as I Wander*, describes the pragmatic details of this tour. The chapter "Making Poetry Pay," in particular, recounts how he structured readings around autobiography and anecdote to win over audiences (56–60). In fact, a full typescript of the poems Hughes read and his framing comments is archived at the Beinecke Library (Langston Hughes Papers 479.11913).[12]

However, the "platform" was not always literal, nor especially public, in the modern era. During the teens and twenties, rich literary women and artistic couples held salons in New York, London, and Paris. Many poets found responsive audiences there. These elite groups fostered community among the avant-garde and connected poets with each other, with editors, and with supporters and collaborators of all kinds. In Greenwich Village in the teens, Mabel Dodge hosted a salon that brought artists of various kinds and affiliations together with intellectuals, socialists, suffragettes, entertainers, and many others; one Poet's Evening included, for example, Robinson and Lowell (Westzeon 20; Rosenstone 142).[13] Dodge's salon was succeeded by more intimate nightly gatherings hosted by Walter and Louise Arensberg, at which Stevens and Williams met Mina Loy and Marcel Duchamp, newly arrived from the continent. Carolyn Burke's biography of Loy describes these evenings in some detail, comparing them to their Parisian counterpart in the salon of Gertrude Stein (213). In the early twenties Loy visited "Lola Ridge's ascetic rooms, where poets read their work and anyone from the fiery Russian Mayakovsky to reserved Marianne Moore might show up" (288). Georgia Douglass Johnson was also an important organizer of "literary soirees" (Schwarz 26), and Arna Bontemps offers a memorable description of a party held by Regina Anderson and Ethel Ray at which Langston Hughes read from his travel journals; Jessie Fauset, Charles S. Johnson, and many other figures instrumental to the Harlem Renaissance attended and heard new poems about jazz and Hughes' sea voyages (18–19).

In *Cultures of Modernism*, Cristanne Miller provides a partial list of such salons, emphasizing the centrality of women to the organization of American modernism:

> In New York, influential salons were held by Mabel Dodge, Gertrude Whitney, Regina Anderson, Marguerite and William Zorach, Bill and Margaret Sanger, Elinor Wylie and William Rose Benet, and Walter and Louise Arensberg. Anderson also made the 135th Street branch of the New York Public Library a key gathering place for Harlem intellectuals. (40)[14]

Salons—a quintessentially urban venue—also fostered artistic community in London (Catherine "Sappho" Dawson Scott, Virginia Woolf) and Paris (Natalie Barney as well as Stein), although not in Berlin, where the public, neutral spaces of cafés were far more important (Miller, *Cultures of Modernism* 32–33).[15] Poetry readings were not the chief occupation of such gatherings, but these sites gathered sympathetic audiences for poets performing at the forward edge of their art. In these and other semi-public, semi-private spaces, such as the offices of *Poetry* in Chicago, poets could sound their work for small groups of appreciative listeners.[16]

The salon reading, while it paid hungry bohemians only in food, drink, and company, was an important alternative model for poets who would not or could not give populist lecture-recitals. Lyndall Gordon provides a glimpse of one of these London institutions in his biography of Eliot:

> By December 1917 Eliot was reading his poems under the auspices of the Red Cross to fashionable society in the Mayfair drawing-room of Lady Colefax. Also giving readings were troops of nervous Sitwells, Robert Graves, Siegfried Sassoon, Aldous Huxley, a writer called Bob Nichols who hooted and moaned war poetry, and Viola Tree, who declaimed in a voice cloyed with syrup. (143–44)

Gordon's mocking tone reflects a common anxiety about the voicing of poetry. Even when the poems themselves allude to and sometimes express yearning for the audible world, the poets themselves, their critics, and some audiences resist the mixing of poetry and mass culture. To read aloud is to hawk not only the words but one's very body in public marketplaces. Salons mediate between this desire for a listening public and horror of mass culture the way contemporary university readings do. In the latter, honoraria are small for all but the most celebrated, yet the network-building potential is important; the events are open to all interested parties, but in fact draw mainly coterie crowds of university insiders. These venues are absolutely crucial for the development and dissemination of some kinds of poetries, yet a complex world of very different models and traditions thrives outside them.

The 1920s and 1930s saw the word "elocution" fade from school curricula in favor of "interpretation" (Middleton 91). At the same time, the soundscape of American culture shifted with the booming popularity of radio. These changes may have promoted the poetry reading as we now understand it: the poet herself reading aloud or reciting a series of her own works. Oral performers of the very best skill and talent became audible to everyone over mass media, while presence was a rarer commodity. As its audience shrank, poetry became even more intensely an art of authenticity, representing the opposite of the polished, distant televised world. This authentic poet-performer emerged as if suddenly in the 1950s, when, to cite the most famous example, Allen Ginsberg awed crowds with his chanting of "Howl"; that generation's revulsion against modernist impersonality demonstrated itself partly through oral performance, in which the person of the poet, passionately rebellious, is salient (even naked in a few infamous cases). The increasing professionalization of literary studies, followed by the professionalization of creative writing, also played a major role in the history of the American poetry reading. Those poets who attempted to make a living from their art needed cash, and they found sponsors and audiences increasingly willing to hear and see them deliver their poetry. The latter forces coincided suggestively with technological shifts to encourage poets to assume the stage.

Experiments with sound, presence, and poetry's possible media define much of the new poetry of the early twentieth century, linking writers such as Lowell, Sandburg, Eliot, Millay, and Hughes who did not otherwise identify with one another's work. This unlikely canon suggests new lines of influence and connection, and it emphasizes different kinds of mastery than anthologies produced later in the twentieth century would seem to suggest. Moreover, as the performers' poetics of presence competed with the high modernists' theories of impersonality, the performers exerted an influence that is not yet fully recognized. Poetry readings as manifestations of authentic authorial presence, rather than as demonstrations of vocal skill, would become the mainstream mode of aural dissemination. Personality would become central as distancing technologies otherwise took hold of American culture.

A Sound Spectrograph

Because performance and print are both crucial to the meanings of poetic voice, this book offers a spectrograph, a visible document, of its complex resonances. It alternates between accounts of multiple media in twentieth-century American poetry, sounding the relationships among page, stage, broadcast, and to a lesser extent, recording. These intersecting approaches demonstrate that lyric poetry remains a far more flexible genre than the usual definitions allow. The theory, in short, does not match the practice: received geniuses disbelieve in originality; poets identified with music and speech are visual artists; traditional versifiers share goals with avant-garde poet-scholars. All of the very different American poets I gather here are deeply interested in voice, yet none of them understands voice or the lyric as a treasure or as singularly truthful (to use Padgett's wry terms). All of them are innovators, seeking to test the limits of what poetry is and what it can do.

Chapter 1 is the only chapter not centered on a set of poetic texts, whether books or performances. Instead, "Sounding Voice" explores the meanings of poetic voice for literary studies, finding that while poetic voice is a resonant metaphor, it is not *only* a figure. Voice is a medium for poetry, a physical phenomenon, and a force for social and political change. Writings about voice, further, are often characterized by a rhetoric of haunting, as if voice encompasses presence, spirit, or divinity. The meanings of poetic voice in literary criticism and theory overlap with, and are influenced powerfully by, the discourses of composition studies, creative writing, and feminism.

Chapter 2, "Edna St. Vincent Millay's Performance of Presence," addresses how voice in Millay's printed and performed poetry springs from and reinforces an illusion of authorial presence. Millay played a key role in a period of esthetic transition, not least through her contributions to radio broadcasting. Millay manifested ambivalence about distancing technologies—not only the new medium of radio, but the older technology of print. Nevertheless, she valued the capacity of both modes to deliver an illusion of presence, and hence of intimacy between the poet and her audiences. Millay's work collapses stage and page as if to materialize a speaking body. Millay's poetic tropes of voice intersect with her voiced poems, so that her apparently formal, conservative approach to poetry actually poses fresh and urgent problems for lyric definition. Performance and trope are interdependent, and no one medium, even print, can offer the single, "real" poem.

In print, however, voice must be represented through visual strategies. Chapter 3 examines Langston Hughes's efforts to translate sound into textual form. The most insightful critics of Hughes' poetry have rightly emphasized its aurality, its commitment to folk sources, and its conversation with musical forms, especially blues and jazz. However, scholars have largely overlooked how Hughes teases out the relative roles of music and visual design. The figure of voice—and the problems it raises about sound and transcription, the expression or construction of poetic selves—becomes paramount in these negotiations. One consequence of this interest in sound, was, perhaps paradoxically, Hughes's development of poetry as a visual art. "Voice and the Visual Poetics of Langston Hughes" demonstrates how Hughes understood poetry as a mode that appeals both to the eye and to the ear. He both invokes and challenges the trope of voice at the center of African American poetry, and of lyric generally.

Voice seems to imply an expressive self who speaks through the poem in a unique way, using a set of markers as recognizable as the whorls of a fingerprint. However, even poetry that seems to possess a strongly individual voice, like the work of James Merrill, is, as the poet warns, not as original as we like to think. Chapter 4 argues for poetic voice as intrinsically choral, multiple, and allusive by focusing on two lyric sequences—one single-author work that uses collaboration as its material, and a second that is the product of overt coauthorship. The former series, "The Book of Ephraim," may be a monument to Merrill's singular genius, but this séance-based sequence obsesses over the boundaries of authorship and presents its lyric speaker as a fragile piece of artifice. The poems, in fact, emerge from and reflect a sort of supernatural literary salon, with Merrill and his partner David Jackson playing host. In *Oyl*, a coauthored chapbook collection of poems based on a cartoon character, Denise Duhamel and Maureen Seaton also conceive of the lyric as a social rather than a private form. Like "Ephraim," *Oyl* blurs literary genres, bringing a virtuosic array of inherited forms into potential conflict with a dialogic method. The result does not dismantle voice as a trope, but reveals voice as inherently dissonant or haunted, even when a work lays claim to unity. Poetic voice, seemingly singular, can help to stage profound encounters.

This refusal of solitude is even more pronounced in poetry slams. These are competitive performances in which poetry readings become a kind of team sport. Chapter 5, "Voice Activated," begins with the evolution of the contemporary academic poetry reading, epitomized by the 2006 meeting of the Association of Writers and Writing Programs. The National Poetry Slam of 2005, and in particular a novice team of poet-competitors from Four Corners, shows by contrast how slam dismantles inherited associations of the lyric with privacy by conceptualizing poetry as a site of conversation. While this kind of art might appear to depend on the literalness of poetic voice and presence, slam poetry actually tends to reflect considerable anxiety over authority, authenticity, and identity.

My aim is not to tell a story of the development of voice as a term, although this book has narrative elements. Instead, the chapters of *Voicing American Poetry* address aspects or connotations of poetic voice: performance and presence; the relationship between sound and text; the fiction of originality; the lyric as a social form. However, the meanings of voice overlap continually for the writers and theorists at hand. To use a visual metaphor, focusing on definition means perpetual blurriness. I am especially aware of such blurriness and overlap because of the complexity of my own professional identity. I am a scholar who was credentialed in the mid-nineties by a traditionally structured English Ph.D. program, but I am also a publishing poet and a professor at a teaching-focused liberal arts college (and an occasional poetry performer whose research dooms her to increasing self-consciousness in front of the microphone). For the most part, these roles enrich rather than divide my life and work. My thesis is rooted in personal experience as well as intellectual process. The idea of voice has been useful to so many readers and writers in part because of its very resistance to stable definition.

The term voice mediates between poetic communities with varying agendas. This study clarifies the terms of the debate. Poetic culture in the United States can seem splintered into several hostile universes: (1) the world of academic poetry, supported by M.F.A. programs, university-affiliated magazines and presses, and professional conferences; (2) avant-garde scholar-practitioners, identified with independent presses and a smaller range of academic resources; (3) communities of ethnic minority poets, such as American-Indian and African American writers, who must often create parallel institutions in order to reach audiences; and (4) the populism of spoken word, manifested in poetry slams, jams, hip-hop, cowboy poetry, and diverse local scenes. Voice highlights not only the tensions but the commonalities among poets affiliated with a wide variety of aesthetics. In showing that wildly different poets share a motivating concern with a cluster of problems, I argue that American poetry itself remains a vital, coherent enterprise.

SOUNDING POETIC VOICE

The second quality that a good poetic voice must have is difficult to characterize, it's something like vividness, actual presence of the live poet in the dead words on the page—the poem is
very little without that, and very few, comparatively, poems have
that. To make that transference is a mysterious thing to do and
no one who can do it can teach the skill to another person.
   —Alice Notley, "Voice," *Coming After*

Out of all the creative writing patois, the phrase "finding your
voice" rankles me the most. . . . What an obnoxious aspiration!
The EPA should send fleets of crop dusters above the poetry
summer camps to spray for this menace.
   —Peter Campion, "Grasshoppers: A Notebook," *Poetry*

The term "voiceprint," meaning a graph of the frequency and intensity of a
person's speech plotted against time, was first used in a *Scientific American*
article in 1962. It arose from the optimistic assumption that spectrographic
analysis of any human voice would one day identify an individual as surely
as a fingerprint. Voice identification has improved, but even digital technology does not render it fully reliable. Poetic voice, a common phrase in
literary criticism, rests on the same assumption of uniqueness and presents
similar problems in practical use. While it connotes originality and the
continuity of identity over time, even poems that aspire to coherence or
self-expression often turn out to be choral, haunted, or disjointed, as many

readers have observed.[1] Voice can be poetry's medium in live or recorded performance, and even as a figure it calls attention to affinities between lyric poetry and sound and music. However, most critical discussions of poetic voice concern not oral performances but printed texts. Ultimately, the phrase encompasses such a contradictory range of referents that it frustrates definition, let alone critical practice. It is perfectly possible for a writer or a reader to "find" allusion, the use of iambic pentameter, or apostrophe in a poem, but "finding a voice" in the same text is impracticable. Poets and critics close-read poems for characteristic stylistic traits all the time, or make arguments about a poem's tone, or interpret a work's sound structures, but while these activities have something to do with poetic voice as most people understand it, the parameters of the term are fundamentally unclear. Even within relatively small literary communities, there is little agreement on what textual voice means, what it looks and sounds like, how to identify it, or how to create it, although in many of these communities the word carries strong positive or negative associations.

The phrase poetic voice, in fact, often signals resistance to the rational processes of close-reading. Nonetheless, American poetry of the twentieth century and beyond keeps returning to voice as an idea. The most interesting tensions of the period, in fact, intersect in this one fraught term: conflicts between experiment and tradition; between poetry's claims to privacy and the lyric as a public, even a political, forum; among competing definitions of identity and language. Voice is so important precisely because both poets and poetry-explainers invoke it to argue for poetry's power.

The history of the phrase "poetic voice," even when limited to writing in the United States since the 1920s, is not linear. Artists and scholars can use the term quite differently; voice features in poetic, political, and pedagogical works as well as theoretical ones; voice has a complex history in narrative theory as well as in poetry studies.[2] Further, literary criticism overlaps considerably with other fields and has been enriched enormously through interventions by philosophers, linguists, and others. This chapter, therefore, presents several clusters of possible answers to my guiding query: What is poetic voice and when, where, and why does the answer matter? I am particularly interested in who has tackled this question and from what vantage, and in how the meanings of voice for poetry have shifted over time.

What follows these introductory remarks is divided into four sections. The first, "Voice as Medium," concerns the relationship between speech and writing as literary theorists have discussed it, with special attention to how Jacques Derrida, Walter J. Ong, and others have addressed this issue since the 1960s. "Physical Voice, Silent Reading, and Sound in Print" centers on scientific explanations of voice—what happens in our bodies as we speak, listen, and read. "Voice as Pedagogy and Politics" treats composition studies, creative writing, and feminist studies. The phrase "finding a voice" has distinct but overlapping meanings for these intersecting constituencies, many members of which emphasize the social and political ramifications of speaking and writing. Finally, "Voice as Genre" returns to a more sustained study of *poetic* voice. Defining voice often entails delimiting genre: voice and lyric poetry, in particular, are often used to define one another. The word "lyric" most commonly refers to words composed to be sung; however, within contemporary poetry criticism the association between music and lyric as a poetic genre is loose and metaphoric. Definitions of this kind of literary art place at least as much emphasis on brevity and first-person expression as they do on latent musicality. Whether voice refers to textual voices or voiced texts, therefore, it coincides with the category of lyric.

While poetic voice is a metaphor, it also exceeds metaphor—this phrase evokes a physical process, a medium for art, and a means to social change. The term voice in its multiple, overlapping meanings encompasses a range of possibilities for what poetry is and what it can do. Finally, and most paradoxically, voice as a critical term simultaneously frustrates and enables analysis because of its ambiguity and irrationality. Rather than specifying critical procedures, it advocates for poetry's value. Voice reveals the political, social, and spiritual meanings of poetry for various readers and writers.

Voice as Medium

If voice is a medium for poetry as well as a metaphor for poetry's origins and effects, how does the uttered, broadcast, or recorded poem relate to various digital, print and/or manuscript versions? Is one of them the real poem, prior to or more important than the others? Does the answer vary from author to author or work to work? If all poetry has a "fundamentally plural existence" (Bernstein, *Close Listening* 9)—what are the implications for poetry scholarship? Printed discussions of poetic voice as a medium tend to be entangled with such questions and particularly with heated debates since the 1960s over spoken versus written language.

The theory of voice as a poetic medium intersects with the history of voice as a poetic medium, but the two topics also differ significantly. Technologies of presence—especially radio broadcast in the early part of the twentieth-century—altered the cultural role of poetry recitation in American life; later in the century, the centralization of poetry in universities instigated other models for performance, such as slam and the academic reading. The development of poetry readings by authors themselves as an academic institution in the 1950s and 1960s—and the challenges posed to this institution by Black Arts, feminist poetry, ethnopoetics, and other movements—coincide temporally with lively scholarly and theoretical arguments about voice as an idea. As the media for poetry evolved, intense arguments sprang up about poetry's proper venues, uses, and status. In particular, poets, critics, and theorists took sides in abstract contests between literary and oral art.

Literary theoretical debates about voice in the 1960s, 1970s, and early 1980s cast oral and written cultures into competitive relation with one another. In these decades, extended treatments of voice as a medium often celebrate one mode at the expense of the other. Ong and Derrida epitomize the latter approaches. More recently—since the late 1980s—several studies speak to voice as a term in literary criticism. Some of these books and articles analyze oral media, while others speculate about how sound and voice persist in print. In the latter group of texts, voice as medium shades into voice as figure. This is a crucial point about the significance of voice: while categorization and definition are fundamental procedures in any argument, the meanings of poetic voice are particularly resistant to tidy classifications.

Writings on voice as a medium that date from the early 1960s until the early 1980s often suggest the inadequacy of writing as a technology. Walter Ong's *Orality and Literacy* (1981) argues for the priority of sound in a temporal sense—because, he asserts, spoken language preceded the technology of writing in human culture—and in an intellectual sense, because "the basic orality of language is permanent" and cross-cultural (7).[3] Ong observes that both the term "literature" and the vocabulary and strategies of literary analysis are inadequate to oral art (10–11).[4] Ong's position echoes Marshall McLuhan's in *Understanding Media* (1964), in which McLuhan states that "the content of writing is speech, just as the written word is the content of print" (23–24). Oral language is a technology that creates and reflects human estrangement from experience, but written language, according to these sources, is more belated and more estranging. As a medium, according to McLuhan, speech is more inclusive and participatory than writing (81–85).

In *Ferocious Alphabets*, originally published in the same year as *Orality and Literacy*, Denis Donoghue unfolds a similar comparison but focuses on strategies for reading, rather than the media of artistic presentation. Epireaders, according to Donoghue, understand texts as voices and reading as personal encounters; the epireader "wants to restore the words to a source" (98–100). Donoghue allies himself with the "humanism of voice and epireading"

rather than the deconstructive play of graphireading, which he characterizes by its distrust of interpretation (152, 200, 206). Presence may be an illusion, argues Donoghue, but like Ong he values voice for its associations with
community, stable meaning, and empowerment.

Donoghue, Ong, and McLuhan analyze literary media in an age of
rapid technological change, registering major shifts in how literary art is
transmitted and consumed. All of their arguments rely on a traditional association between literature and speech. Jonathan Culler, in contrast, emphasizes and interrogates this connection in a 1985 essay, "Changes in the
Study of the Lyric." Culler begins by quoting Northrop Frye's famous
definition of lyric as overheard utterance (Frye 249) and goes on to comment, "it as is if every lyric began with the invisible words, 'For example, I
(or someone) could say . . . .'" (38–39). This presumption—that texts
should be treated as voices—troubles Culler because of the prevalence of
"awkward and embarrassing" instances of apostrophe in lyric poetry, in
canonical Romanticism in particular. "It is difficult to see these apostro-
phes as fictional representations of plausible historical speech acts," he
observes (39). Apostrophe is only one among many poetic strategies that
can disrupt the simple equation of textual poetry with voice, but modes of
address including apostrophe have been particularly interesting to scholars who treat voice not as a medium but as a potent, recurring, definitive
figure.[5]

The poststructuralist emphasis on visual technologies, indeed, has promoted suspicion of voice as a medium—even though many of poststructur-
alism's seminal texts are careful not to instate a reversed hierarchy. Derrida
most influentially debunks "the strange prerogative of the vocal medium"
(*Speech and Phenomena* 70). In *Of Grammatology*, in particular, Derrida objects to the consignment of writing to "a secondary and instrumental function" (8), as if it always lags behind voice in its belated relation to
presence—consisting merely of "a mediation of a mediation," an echo of an
echo (12–13). Derrida's own tone, as conveyed by Gayatri Spivak's translation, is often exuberant as he describes writing as a site of meaning's endless
"play" (7), but his propositions have provoked a great deal of anxiety and
hostility in other writers on literary voice. His troping on Christian theol-
ogy may be part of what disturbs some American readers. According to
Derrida, voice and presence have often been invested with Christian divinity and an aspiration for spiritual unity with God; he rejects these associations and refuses to dismiss writing as a kind of "fall" from grace or truth
(*Of Grammatology* 12–17).

Many champions of voice as a term of literary analysis, in fact, do attribute transcendence and spiritual power to its manifestations. This rhetoric

of haunting also occurs—with plenty of post-Derridean irony—in several recent studies that return to voice as a channel or medium. Again, it is difficult to discuss sound in poetry without invoking someone's body, and the attendant implications of presence and identity are troubling for readers schooled in poststructuralist critique. As Peter Middleton writes (in mock-gothic voice), "A specter is haunting poetry readings. The 'dead author,' risen from the text again and trailing the rags of the intentional fallacy, claims to be the originating subject from which poetry is issuing right in front of your eyes" (*Distant Reading* 33). Such metaphors suggest that listening to poetry is at best an exercise in nostalgia for old ways of reading, at worst a dangerous invocation of unruly spirits. Middleton and others break the taboo, but in doing so work against what has been the grain of lyric theory and criticism.

Derrida's injunction to understand writing as writing, and not a transcription of voice, has been highly influential on both poetry and its interpreters.[6] Since the late-1990s, however, John M. Picker, Yopie Prins, Adalaide Morris, Charles Bernstein, and others have published books and essays that attend to oral media and contemplate lost soundscapes.[7] The complicated status of sound in print media has also preoccupied many poets and poetry scholars. Eric Griffiths argues for the act of reading as an effort to "inform writing with a sense of the writer . . . an ideal body, a plausible voice." In his influential study of Victorian poetry, Griffiths focuses on writing yet argues that the printed lyric possesses a "double nature," "a text of hints and voicing, whose centre in utterance lies outside itself" (60). Almost contemporaneously, in *Reading Voices* (1990), Garrett Stewart explores the role of sound in silent reading with particular interest in "lexical juncture," or the suggestive slippages between syllables, and how readers process such phonemic juxtapositions (19). This important book also develops the useful terms "phonotext" and "graphotext" to refer to, on one hand, a text's "silent sounding," and, on the other, its scriptive aspect (28).[8] The term voice haunts these very different studies, demonstrating how it speaks to a wide range of approaches.[9]

Most of these recent works either draw their examples from pretwentieth-century poetry or concentrate on contemporary writing from outside of the M.F.A. mainstream, such as Language Poetry, ethnic American and Caribbean poetry, and various kinds of performance poetry. In fact, the affiliation between scholarly research into poetic sound and counter-cultural poetries is quite marked, and this book owes a great debt to such studies. Nevertheless, I resist the idea that avant-garde poetry is necessarily more complex and interesting in its engagement with sound and voice than academic or popular poetry; to measure the impact of acoustical technologies on literature, too, one has to consider mass audiences, or at least a wide array of coteries. Work labeled "academic," "mainstream," and "populist" worries at the meanings of sound and voice just as often, in equally fascinating ways, as the work grouped under the loose rubric of "innovative poetries." Such categories, in fact, are notoriously slippery; binary oppositions (obscure vs. accessible, innovative vs. derivative) do not describe American poetry persuasively. Nevertheless, it remains true that the pioneers of this new work on sound culture and poetry performance are often poet-scholars who identify strongly with various avant-gardes. Bernstein, a cofounder of the online archive PennSound and the editor of *Close Listening*, is a prominent example. As I find in chapter 5 of this book, the institutions of creative writing remain relatively inhospitable to discussions of voice as a medium.

Creative writers have depended on poetic voice as a figure, as a pedagogy, and as a way of defining lyric power, as I discuss below. Within creative writing scholarship, however—especially the body of writings that Tim Mayers refers to as "craft criticism" (29–64)—poets and teachers rarely discuss voice as a medium. Exceptions arise from two related fields. First, as I discuss in chapter 5, the ideologically contrary worlds of spoken word poetry and academic poetry have begun a rapprochement (which may or may not survive beyond a few crossover stars). Second, poets and critics with abiding interests in poetic forms, whether inherited or recently devised, never stopped listening to poetry, and many of these writers possess influence over the sphere Bernstein refers to as "official verse culture," whether or not they personally depend on university paychecks. For instance, Dana Gioia may not be entirely convincing when he compares new formalism to rap, but these dissimilar modes do share allegiance to the aural strategies of rhythm and rhyme; Gioia himself is an example of a poet with intellectual commitments to voice as a medium (13). Indeed, these commitments are also professional: as chairman of the National Endowment for the Arts he has instituted a national poetry recitation contest for secondary students. Feminist formalists like Annie Finch and Kathrine Varnes, positioned squarely within creative writing's institutions, also give meaningful attention to the intersections between poetic sound and performance.[10] These instances may turn out to be unsuccessful attempts to bridge disparate literary communities, building on common preoccupations. However, universities, including creative writing departments, may be resourceful and capacious enough to assimilate performance poetries fully and/or become more receptive over time to non-print poetry publication. In any case, the current critical fascination with voice as a medium does not yet seem to have peaked in any of poetry's microclimates.

Physical Voice, Silent Reading, and Sound in Print

To address sound in poetry is to invoke a body—whether the body belongs to the poet, the audience, or both. This sense of the physicality of language permeates many influential writings about poetry, even when their authors focus on the page rather than the stage. Charles Olson's essay "Projective Verse" (1950), for example, argues urgently for the relationship between breath and the poetic line, as well as "the full relevance of the human voice" (*Collected Prose* 248). In this well-known manifesto, Olson compares printed poetry to a musical score, as a script for vocal performance. For Olson, voice is not a figure but poetry's primary element. Likewise, British professor and poet Francis Berry, although writing from a different tradition, argues for voice as medium in *Poetry and the Physical Voice* (1962). Berry understands the printed poem as a script, defines poetry as "essentially a spoken form," and characterizes reading as an effort to imagine, to hear inwardly, the "personal voice" of the poet as a human being who is changing over time (34, 8). He refers to this skill as "aural empathy" or "vocal imagination" (3, 182). He even posits that "women . . . do not become poets" because they do not begin adulthood with the radical experience of having their personal voices change during puberty (38).

Much of my book addresses textual voice, meaning voice as a metaphor in literary texts. The human voice, however, is also a bodily phenomenon, produced and received via a sequence of physical processes. In order to speak, an individual pushes air from her lungs through her vocal cords, which are muscular folds in the larynx. The quality of the sound is affected by various parts of her vocal tract including the throat, mouth, and nasal cavities. The lips, teeth, and tongue also shape speech sounds. Sound itself consists of mechanical waves propagated through a medium such as air. These "audible variations in air pressure" may be characterized by periodic rhythms (frequency); we register the difference in pressure between compressed and rarified patches of air as intensity (Bear, Connors, Paradiso 351–52). In a listener, in turn, complex mechanisms in the ear and brain translate these speech sounds into perception through neural signals.

Physical voice and auditory processing are important to poetry's composition, circulation, and reception. Are physical and biological definitions, however, relevant to literary discussions of voice? When literary critics, creative writers, and composition theorists deploy voice as a term of analysis, after all, they generally mean it as a metaphor for some quality within a printed text. A manuscript poem, a newspaper column, or a paperback novel might arguably possess a voice in some figurative sense, but not in a physical way unless someone converts the medium by reading it aloud.

Silent reading, nevertheless, is at least partly a physical process. Evidence suggests that even when we read silently, subvocalization occurs. In other words, this seemingly mental activity involves multiple regions of the body, and not only through the visual processing of written language: muscles in the tongue, lips, and larynx may move, sometimes almost imperceptibly. Research in the social and natural sciences, encompassing very different methodologies, technologies, and research goals, supports these points. There are, therefore, conflicts and gaps in the literature. Within just neuroscience studies, for example, approaches are highly various. In the early years of cognitive science, researchers concerned with language studied brain abnormalities and the patterns of impairment that accompany lesions; more recent investigations often involve functional imaging studies that monitor blood flow in the brains of normal individuals while they read and/or listen to words. Even in their variety, however, such studies support my working hypothesis that sound and voice are not purely metaphorical for the silent reader—that the term poetic voice is meaningful even for poems in print media.

Observations of muscular movements during silent reading preceded neuroscience experiments by decades. Åke W. Edfeldt published a study in 1960, *Silent Speech and Silent Reading*, that positions his own investigations of these phenomena against nineteenth- and early twentieth-century research. Edfeldt, a Swedish professor of education at Stockholm University, frames his project in practical terms, with frequent reference to its implications for instruction. He defines "silent speech" as "movements in the speech musculature in accompaniment with reading or other forms of mental activity" (13) and finds that "silent speech *probably* occurs during all reading," although signs of it decrease when the reader is proficient or the text is easily comprehensible. Edfeldt also cites various early experiments showing such muscle activity whenever individuals concentrate on numbers or words, although the subjects or others observing them are rarely aware of such "unconscious whispering" (15). Lips, tongue, and larynx move, and some results suggest that the silent reading of metrical poetry (in this case, *Hiawatha*) produces particularly marked results (15–17). Edfeldt's goal is to prove that all kinds of readers practice subvocalization to some degree and that reducing such behaviors, as some educators sought to do, would not improve student reading skills.

Recent developments in neuroscience also offer partial and provocative explanations for what happens in the brain when we read. I approached the field with the following questions:

1. Can poetry have sound in any meaningful way when we read silently? Does the silent reading of a ballad affect a person differently than the silent reading of a textbook?

2. What happens to our bodies when we listen to poetry read aloud? People demonstrate physiological responses to many kinds of sounds, such as music or a baby's wail. Do we have physical responses to rhythmical language?

3. What happens when we voice poetry, meaning read it aloud ourselves? Is this question the same as number two?

I found only fragmentary answers and discovered, further, that my very way of posing problems did not correspond easily with the existing research.[11] The crux, however, is this: there is some scientific evidence that even when we read silently, our bodies respond as if we are preparing to read aloud. Again, silent reading is a physical act.

One of the first premises of the relevant research is that silent reading and active listening are fundamentally different as far as the brain is concerned. As M. T. Banich explains, "The portions of the neurological system that support processing of written language functions are distinct from those that support auditory language functions, although in the right-handers both reside within the left hemisphere" (295). Spoken language activates the primary auditory cortex, and written language activates primary visual cortex. The processing of written language seems to differ according to a range of variables, including reading proficiency and the kind of attention brought to the task. At the heart of the problem is whether readers convert the visual word directly into meaning, or whether phonological coding intervenes—that is, whether a silent reader translates grapheme into phoneme before understanding it semantically. The scientific literature debates whether or not direct semantic processing is the primary route for silent reading, eventually concluding that both processes (the phonetic and the directly semantic) probably occur to varying degrees. For example, Jared and Seidenberg demonstrate that readers use phonology to access word meaning only for "low-frequency words," that is, words they rarely encounter. However, subjects can access the meaning of a highly familiar word directly, without using the phonological route. They note, further, that written languages differ in the extent to which they encode phonological information, and cross-cultural variations must therefore exist in the brain's processing of written language.

Still more recent studies suggest that some kind of inner voicing does occur during silent reading. Silent reading, in fact, can activate the premotor cortex, as if the brain is priming the body to speak. Nicole A. E. Dietz et al. analyze the processing of real and pseudowords in monolingual, right-handed men and women, asking them to read these sets of "words" both aloud and silently (the visual words were always before the subjects, so this study does not address what happens when listening to words without a text). The experimenters use blood oxygenation-level dependent (BOLD) contrast with functional MRI to determine patterns of brain activation during each task. They find that the premotor cortex is activated during all reading conditions.[12] The premotor cortex helps control voluntary movement, in essence devising and storing movement strategies in advance of actual muscle activity. Its involvement implies that "word reading in general entails some amount of subvocalization, or internal speech" (Dietz et al. 87).[13] J.-F. Demonet et al. (1992), similarly, demonstrate that Brodmann's area 44 (the premotor cortex associated with the production of language) responds to the presentation of phonemes as opposed to semantically empty auditory tones, such as a single musical note. Further, subjects may not have to pay focused attention for this precortical priming activity to occur. Multiple studies have shown that "the presentation of familiar words or repeating tasks will automatically activate semantic and phonological representations even when subjects are not instructed to access these processes explicitly" (Price et al. 62).

It seems likely that phonological coding and the brain areas associated with it come into play when readers are asked to pay attention to sound elements, whether or not these readers are proficient or whether the words are familiar. Reading or listening to poetry could, in fact, involve even more complex neural pathways, as Julie Kane argues in "Poetry as Right-Hemispheric Language." Reviewing a wide array of studies on the processing of poetic devices, brain development in relation to literacy, and the relation between brain laterality and affective disorders, Kane concludes that "right-hemispheric involvement" distinguishes poetry from other kinds of language (22). Lyric poetry's strong association with feeling, for example, suggests the role of the right hemisphere in its comprehension. K. M. Heilman et al. demonstrate that patients with lesions on their right-brain speech centers struggle to identify the emotional qualities of spoken language, or "have a defect in the comprehension of affective speech" (69). However, although many poets and readers identify poetry with emotion—Philip Larkin in an essay, "The Pleasure Principle," regards a poem as a transferal device for feeling (80)—affect does not define poetry and, further, audiences don't always encounter poetry in aural forms. Whether or not the right brain plays a role in the processing of visual language, when that visual language also prompts or conveys emotion, is untested.

Other researchers work near the intersections of literary criticism and neuroscience in fields such as cognitive linguistics and cognitive poetics. Reuven Tsur's concern with poetry and sound, in particular, parallels this book's investigations of voice.[14] Speech therapy is another ready ground for disciplinary crossover. For example, experimenters show that when healthy subjects recite hexameter poetry, it affects their heart rates (Betterman et al. 78). The science of the brain, further, fascinates some poets. Julian Jaynes's *The Origin of Consciousness in the Breakdown of the Bicameral Mind* (1976) is a powerful example that has intrigued poets including James Merrill and Annie Finch, not least because it proposes a physical and evolutionary explanation for the voices that haunt poets, mystics, and schizophrenics.[15]

Applying science to humanism is, of course, a tricky proposition; the very terminology and search protocols can differ radically. No team of neuroscientists has obliged poetry scholarship by examining patterns of blood flow in the brain among individuals listening to sonnets versus prose poems and then repeated the study during silent reading. Nevertheless, a few experiments reinforce the subjective experience of so many poets, teachers, and readers. Sound and voice exist, not in closed poetry collections, but in the act of reading silently. Any act of silent reading engages our physical selves, but poetry's strategies of sound saturation, and the very expectations of sound saturation we bring to poetry, may intensify how the silent reading of poetry involves our bodies.

Voice as Pedagogy and as Politics

Among the resources that the Academy of American Poets web site provides to educators, there is a set of lesson plans for ninth- and tenth-graders entitled "Voice." [16] This unit, created by New York City teacher Gigi Goshko, begins by defining voice as a medium but increasingly develops its political meanings. The initial session involves rap lyrics and a discussion of the performed versus the printed word. Subsequent lessons introduce literary poetry through selections that emphasize "social commentary." Poetry, according to Goshko, is a way of speaking back to power. In the final event of the unit, a student poetry slam, students must "vocalize their feelings in an original poem." Her unit returns, in other words, to defining voice as a medium, but ensures through intervening lessons that students will also understand voice as a channel for social and political participation. In this lesson plan, poetic voice merges with voice in the political sense: having the right and the ability to speak, and especially to dissent.

Goshko's lesson plans orchestrate and harmonize multiple meanings of poetic voice. Her synthetic approach, with its dual emphasis on performance and power, is typical of contemporary treatments of the term, even those that spring from widely separated corners of literary studies.[17]

Certainly it is difficult for poets, literary critics, and theorists to disentangle the various senses of the term. When, for instance, the poem under discussion is a printed text, the metaphor of voice can intersect with imagined or remembered sound and can even stimulate the physical processes of subvocalization. The straightforward question of how sound can exist in a printed poem, therefore, does not have a single, straightforward answer. Here I am similarly investigating a cluster of meanings rather than a single definition of poetic voice. In particular, the overlapping discourses of composition studies, creative writing, and feminist studies employ voice as an instrumental idea.[18] Voice, according to these disciplines, can be taught and/or developed in writers, and the achievement of voice in writing can have social repercussions. Voice serves as a metaphor for power in writing. Rhetorical power, in turn, can be both a metonym and a vehicle for socio-political power. The connection between voice and empowerment has been tremendously important to feminist studies—especially as that field developed in the seventies and eighties, contemporaneously with the expressivist movement in composition and the dramatic expansion of creative writing as an academic field.

A particularly useful resource on the meanings of voice for composition studies is the anthology *Voices on Voice*, edited by Kathleen Blake Yancey. Yancey's introductory essay gives an overview of its significance within the field. She begins by matter-of-factly identifying voice as a "metaphor" that signals "competing references," many of them incompatible (vii). She finds, surveying the literature, that voice can be a figure for the writer, the seeming presence of the writer in the text, or the act of composition. It can be a code for authenticity or the mysterious power within a text that confers its authority. It can be a synonym for style, discourse, or the resonance a text generates in a reader. It indicates the right to speak (or write) and the ability to speak (or write). She finds, further, that voice is dependent on the interaction of writer, reader, language, and the culture that language embodies. While sometimes it signals individuality in an arhetorical, ahistorical way, in other contexts it is implicitly choral, expressing not only complex selves but other people and nature, or is created by the appropriation or approximation of previous voices. For many, finally, voice is a myth or a fiction (vii–xix).[19] These definitions of voice in composition studies intersect substantially with the collection of definitions for poetic voice that I assemble in this chapter and in *Voicing American Poetry* generally. However, for some composition theorists and creative writing teachers, voice is not only a medium or a defining figure for lyric poetry. Voice is also, and perhaps primarily, a quality of fluency, authority, or personality that one seeks to foster in student writing through innovative teaching.

Voice became a particularly important idea during the boom in composition studies during the 1960s, when college students enrolled in high numbers and government funding flowed into universities more generously than before. At this time, Ken Macrorie, Peter Elbow, and others advocated pedagogical approaches such as freewriting that became popular in university classrooms.[20] Randall R. Freisinger refers to this movement as "Authentic Voice pedagogy" (242). Certainly many expressivists, especially Elbow, stress voice as a near-mystical force pervading good writing. In *Writing with Power*, for instance, he discusses how to encourage voice in student prose and in one's own. Fostering voice involves long practice, according to Elbow, who compares this exercise to yoga or meditation; he locates voice in a text by "intuition" and defines it vaguely as "juice" or "power" (285–86). Despite the pseudo-magical language in these passages, Elbow's approach to voice resonates in interesting ways with how literary critics use the term. In both contexts, the term voice appears frequently but resists explication. Its persistence and its power rest in the way voice connects speech to writing, despite the poststructuralist critique of this association, which Elbow addresses thoughtfully. Introducing a subsequent book, *Landmark Essays on Voice in Writing*, Elbow acknowledges widespread "fear and avoidance of the term" and recommends that writing instructors "apply the term with more care and discrimination" (xiii, xx).

The recurrent word "power" in such discussions has a distinctly political resonance for Elbow and others, as James Berlin observes, although it primarily refers to a forceful prose style (486). "Voice" became a charged word in university composition classrooms in the 1960s and 1970s because of its association with dissent from authority at a time when universities were drawing fire, literally and figuratively, as sites of antiwar activism. Paradoxically, the democratic ethos of "Authentic Voice pedagogy"—the idea that anyone can learn to write cogently and with the full authority of his or her knowledge and experience—is rooted in a refusal to define voice narrowly. Voice becomes a metonym not just for the body, but for the soul.

The meanings of voice for composition and creative writing overlap significantly, and not accidentally, because these fields share certain goals, values, and institutional histories. In the United States, as D. G. Myers proves, composition and creative writing were not originally separate disciplines (37).[21] The teaching of composition in college-level courses at the end of the nineteenth century encompassed many kinds of writing beyond exposition and argument. Together, in fact, these intersecting pedagogies were attractive to students and exerted reformist pressure on English as an academic field. More specifically, the teaching of writing challenged dominant theories of literary study. Writing teachers approached literature not as an object of knowledge but as an art, urging that the ultimate purpose of literary study should be the production of more literature. In the early part of the twentieth century, however, composition courses became more narrowly focused on the writing skills most basic to business, while creative writing was reconceived as a natural ally of the New Criticism. Creative writing, in other words, eventually aligned itself with a scholarly discipline but was originally developed as a pedagogical one. This effaced history may partly explain creative writing's persistent resistance to fully professional status (Myers 5–7).

Today, as many have observed, "English" or "English studies" consists of an uneasy coalition among literary studies, composition, and creative writing. While literary studies possesses the most prestige by far in this asymmetrical triad, composition and creative writing were instrumental in the expansion of English departments in the 1960s and remain extremely important in the economics of service teaching, general education, enrollments, and allocated faculty positions. Composition and creative writing, therefore, might seem like natural allies. As Andrew Levy demonstrates, both fields intersect with an emerging genre of handbook literature that is both capitalist and populist, purporting to teach anyone how to create and market literature—that is, they share not only a history but an ideology of access and empowerment (79–82). While in recent decades creative writing professionals have defined themselves as "writers who teach" and composition professionals have been far more concerned with pedagogy as an end in itself, their purposes and even their rhetoric has at times overlapped. In particular, the term "voice" has been important in both fields.

While there exists very little scholarship on creative writing pedagogy, many of the poets who work in creative writing programs publish teaching-related essays, meditations, and inspirational prose in industry publications and non-peer-reviewed journals.[22] Some of these essays address voice, often while meditating on the sources of poetry or its force, and in doing so share many emphases with composition studies. Donald Hall's essay "The Vatic Voice," for example, based on a lecture given in 1968, clearly resonates with the expressivist ethos. He bases his argument on "a premise: within every human being there is a vatic voice," casting writing as a kind of *listening*, an essentially "passive" activity (1, 3). Like Elbow, Hall approaches writing instruction with democratic zeal, offering "vatic voice" as the best phrase for a source of inspiration that is available to everyone.

More recent essays in this vein also use voice as a term for poetry's sources but without the populist fervor (or the cogency) of Elbow or Hall. Chard deNiord's "The Nature of Voice," for example, an essay from the *AWP Chronicle* in the fall of 1991, opens by defining poetic voice as "the emanation of the poet's complex spiritual energy" (7). DeNiord mystifies voice by accounting for it with religious and magical language, although he also links it loosely with meter, diction, and syntax.[23] As Mayers observes, a key piece of "institutional-conventional wisdom" in the discipline of creative writing is that "creativity is individual, intrinsic, even 'mysterious'" and cannot, in fact, be taught (16). This is often the status of voice in creative writing—it refers to inspiration and/or a magical quality within a poem or prose work that gives it power. Craft can be taught, but unlike voice, craft concerns only the formal aspects of a text. Hence, creative writing programs help writers to "find" or "develop" their voices, but not to invent them.

Variations on the phrases "finding your voice," "inner voice," and "writer's voice" remain ubiquitous in many popular guidebooks for aspiring, blocked, or stalled creative writers. A survey of two kinds of documents—advertisements for writers' workshops, conferences, and residencies and the promotional materials of degree-granting creative writing programs—illuminates the changing significance of these terms.[24] Although the word "voice" and the phrase "finding your voice" do recur in these materials, more common marketing buzzwords are "community" and "craft." Creative writing program directors, apparently, are not entirely convinced that "voice" encodes a service they can sell. However, the warm presence of other writers signaled by "community" and the practical skills implied by "craft" are far more definite and probably more attractive to prospective applicants. Voice mystifies a process that writing programs are invested in elucidating.

Graduate creative writing programs do sometimes use the word in their print- and web-based promotional literature. In 2003, the twenty-five top-ranked programs (as rated by *U.S. News and World Report*) used the word "voice" occasionally in such materials.[25] For example, the University of Michigan advertised teachers who can "allow you to find your own voice," New York University printed the word prominently on the front flap of its brochure (floating beside "poetry," "image," "craft," "invent," and "fiction"), and Columbia University in New York advised in an on-line "Message from the Chair" that "those who join us must possess the creative force to find and develop a distinct voice and vision." The phrases "new voices" and "individual voice" were also common in course descriptions and elsewhere. However, the words "craft" and "community" occurred more than twice as often in the same materials. Finding one's misplaced voice, perhaps, implies a certain amount of serendipity—better to advertise a sturdy, practical apprenticeship in "craft" to all those lonely writers longing for conversation with their fellows.

Magazine advertisements, which are far more economically written than brochures and web pages, also provide a useful index to creative writing's shifting vocabulary. A survey of advertisements for creative writing programs, writers conferences, festivals, and workshops in one particularly successful magazine reveals that voice was an important term for this field in the 1990s but has since faded from its former ubiquity. *Poets & Writers*, which promotes itself to professional and would-be professional authors, was founded in 1970 and therefore reflects the explosion of creative writing as a discipline. In February/March 1982, for instance, when *Poets & Writers* was a newsletter, five advertisements for such events and programs used the word "voice" in its twenty-four pages of newsprint. In February/March 1992, when it was a glossy, eighty-eight-page magazine, thirty-one advertisements used the word "voice" and the word "craft" also appeared frequently. The March/April 2002 issue is much larger, at one hundred and fifty two pages, and contains a total of eighty advertisements for academic programs, conferences, festivals, and workshops, not including classifieds and spots that occupy less than a quarter-page. These promotions tend to emphasize the names of distinguished teachers and give relatively little space to descriptive text. However, the word "community" appears in eleven and "craft" in seven. "Voice" only occurs in five ads, and in three of those cases, "voice" is part of the workshop's title. These snapshots seem to indicate a vogue for the idea of writerly voice in the early 1990s. Afterwards, the term loses cachet. In the twenty-first century, programs promote themselves not on the effectiveness of their curricula but on the fame of their teachers. Poststructuralist critiques probably helped to turn down the volume on voice as a literary term, but economics and a changed political climate have also influenced its use.

Feminist studies seems like the odd term in this section, less related to composition and creative writing than the latter two fields are to each other. However, feminist approaches to composition studies have been an active and influential part of that field, and as historians of creative writing attest, the latter discipline has been intertwined with the education of women for most of its existence.[26] More importantly for my purposes, voice has been an instrumental concept in feminist thinking since the inauguration of women's studies departments and programs across the United States in the 1970s and afterwards. The meaning of voice for feminist studies is very like the meaning of voice in composition studies: it signifies both rhetorical and political power.

Voice occurs as a metaphor in works of and about women writers that predate the women's liberation movement. The term became even more common in the 1970s. The goal of "giving voice" to silent and oppressed multitudes motivates a great deal of feminist poetry, ethnic American literature, and antiwar poetry of that era. Further, in various liberation movements of the 1960s and 1970s, writing and performing poetry are deeply interdependent acts. Poetic voice can therefore refer to an action, getting up on a platform to speak verse, as well as serving as a literary trope—it can be effective as well as expressive.

Various researchers and writers promoted the term and shaped its meanings, but Carol Gilligan is one of the most salient. Throughout *In a Different Voice*, voice is synonymous with expressed perspective. Because Gilligan's research is based on interviews, when she refers to women's voices the connotation of speech is also strong. Her controlling metaphor of voice also conveys a political stance, given that in this book Gilligan redresses the gaps and failures of her own discipline in representing or "giving voice" to women's experiences. Upon the reissue of this influential book in 1993, Gilligan adds a preface that meditates upon this word, among other subjects. While voice, for Gilligan, encompasses legal rights, internalized compulsions, self-expression, and even desire, she sums up the term's significance to her as follows: "by voice I mean something like what people mean when they speak of the core of the self" (ix–xvi). For Gilligan, as for Elbow, voice means something like soul or spirit, although she does not use religious language. Voice is internal, if not eternal; resistant to definition, if not ineffable.

The four coauthors of *Women's Ways of Knowing* (1986) also use voice in Gilligan's primary sense, as "academic shorthand for a person's point of view." However, Belenky, Clinchy, Goldberger, and Tarule also make the point that voice is a valuable term for women's studies, because voice is an important concept for many women. "We adopted the metaphor of voice and silence as our own," they write, because "we found that women repeatedly used the metaphor of voice to depict their intellectual and ethical development" (18–19). In writing and in political awareness, voice can suggest a teleology: to come to voice or find a voice is to discover one's right and ability to speak. Bell Hooks, for example, emphasizes such empowerment when in *Talking Back* she describes voice as a "metaphor for self-transformation" (12). She brings voice's literary and political meanings into resonance when she describes "coming to voice" as a black woman writer (10–18). Notions of voice and subjectivity continue to engage women poets, even those who identify with Language Poetry's challenges to those concepts, as Clair Wills (34–35) and Linda Kinnahan demonstrate (19–23).

The voice of feminism is often most powerfully representative—one "I" speaking for many silent selves—or even collective. The coauthors of

Women's Ways of Knowing make this point in a preface that describes their collaborative endeavor.

> In collaborating on this book we searched for a single voice—a way of sub-merging our individual perspectives for the sake of the collective "we." Not that we denied our individual convictions or squelched our objections to one another's points of view—we argued, tried to persuade, even cried at times when we reached an impasse of understanding—but we learned to listen to each other, to build on each other's insights and eventually to arrive at a way of communicating as a collective about what we believe. (ix)

This investment in collectivity is the biggest difference between feminist rhetoric and the discourses of creative writing (unlike creative writing as an academic discipline, composition and rhetoric is well-informed by collabo-ration studies). Feminist works of the 1970s and 1980s do emphasize the "core self" and individual transformation, but they also listen for consen-sus, recognizing that a chorus may be more socially powerful than many separate arias. Feminist studies, then and now, is as riven by fault lines as any other discipline, but it remains more interested than most in the pos-sibilities of collective voice.[27]

Voice as Genre

One of the most-cited essays on voice, T. S. Eliot's "The Three Voices of Poetry," discusses voice as a determinant of verse genre. "The first voice is the voice of the poet talking to himself—or to nobody," the piece begins (96); for Eliot, this mode of address is quintessentially lyric, although he prefers the term "meditative verse" (106). He identifies the second voice "with the poet addressing an audience, whether large or small" (96) in dra-matic monologue or any work that has "a conscious social purpose" (104). The third voice, finally, belongs to dramatic verse, in which the poet is subsumed into characters: "the world of a great poetic dramatist is a world in which the creator is everywhere present, and everywhere hidden" (112). According to Eliot, these voices spring from authorial intention and the process of composition, and often intermingle. Their flux may be discerned by readers and listeners. Although Eliot does not give specific directions on how to distinguish them, he does suggest that one might be able to hear the first or second voice behind the third under certain circumstances: "Per-haps, if it is a great play, and you do not try too hard to hear them, you may discern the other voices too" (112). Otherwise, Eliot defines voice by genre—not the three large classes of lyric, epic/narrative, and drama de-fined by Plato and Aristotle, but a similar tripartite arrangement likewise characterized by distinctive modes of address.

Eliot's influential essay, delivered as a lecture in 1953 and published shortly after, resembles many other literary critical works on voice through its em-phasis on literary kinds. In "The Three Voices of Poetry," Eliot argues that "the term 'lyric' itself is unsatisfactory," because it confuses verse meant to be sung with poetry of expression or meditation—characteristics that do not necessarily overlap (105–6). Nevertheless, for Eliot and for many other writ-ers, voice intersects with the lyric as a genre.[28] Voice, for all its ambiguities as a critical term, remains one of the defining problems of twentieth century poetry—one of its most "vexed issue[s]," as Patricia Parker puts it in her in-troduction to *Lyric Poetry: Beyond New Criticism* (16).

John Stuart Mill's influential definition of 1833 has strongly shaped sub-sequent discussion of lyric poetry in characterizing reading as a sort of eavesdropping on the private monologues of a sequestered poet. His meta-phor underlies most recent references to poetry as voice, even or perhaps especially when the poet or scholar criticizes this equation. Mill empha-sizes the solitude, expressive function, and aural appeal of the genre: "Elo-quence is *heard*, poetry is *overheard*. Eloquence supposes an audience; the peculiarity of poetry appears to us to lie in the poet's utter unconsciousness of a listener. Poetry is feeling confessing itself to itself, in moments of soli-tude" (348). Later theorists, continuing to negotiate the relative positions of poet and audience, shift their attention away from sound towards the printed text. In 1957, Northrop Frye invokes Mill in describing "the con-cealment of the poet's audience from the poet" (249), but also examines the lyric's visual design as well as its music. Jonathan Culler in 1975 stresses poetry's crucial difference from speech by analyzing the defining expecta-tions of its readers (*not* listeners): "It is the form that most clearly asserts the specificity of literature, its difference from ordinary discourse . . . the spe-cific features of poetry have the function of differentiating it from speech and altering the circuit of communication within which it is inscribed" (*Structuralist Poetics* 162). These lyric definitions increasingly treat voice as a metaphor, a fiction of presence created by a printed object.

The received definition of lyric as an expressive form, and voice as its medium of expression, certainly persists, although many invoke this mean-ing to announce lyric's extinction. Marjorie Perloff categorizes the latter kind of poem as a "Romantic lyric" and celebrates postmodernism's expan-sion of poetry's possibilities, although in a later piece she discusses the prob-lems with using "Romantic lyric" as a "derogatory term" (*Dance of the Intellect* 175; "A Response" 246). In fact, the poets of the Language Writing movement have generated some of most powerful and influential critiques of voice in the lyric. As Perloff puts it, "One of the cardinal principles—perhaps *the* cardinal principle—of American Language poetries . . . has been the dismissal of 'voice' as the foundational principle of lyric poetry" (*Differentials* 129). Even in her latest book, as Perloff reconsiders the role of the subject in Language Poetry, she rejects voice as a term because it "implies, quite inaccurately, that *speech* is primary and prior to writing and that hence a poem is simply the outward sign of a spoken self-presence" (*Differentials* 135). While Perloff's work is prominent among recent interrogations of lyric and voice, moreover, many others also contest the term. William Doreski identifies poetry's "modern voice" as an escape from stifling lyric purity (xiii). In his study of modernism's "borrowed voices," Leonard Diepeveen finds that strategies of quotation undermine a sense of voice, a term he defines as "unity" (95–97).[29] When Tilottama Rajan and Herbert F. Tucker characterize the "pure lyric" as monologic (Rajan 196) or remark on its "sublime idiocy" (Tucker 230), they do so to champion what they argue are more sophisticated lyric varieties—the Romantic "interdiscursive lyric" and dramatic monologue, respectively.

As Kinnahan observes, however, "a plethora of critical reassessments of the lyric appeared in the mid- to late nineties," exploring its "slipperiness of meaning" (13). Elizabeth Willis, Mark Jeffreys, and others argue for a more capacious definition of lyric as a mode that can and does place subjectivity under stress (Willis 228–29; Jeffreys xix).[30] I argue that even lyric subgenres like the sonnet can fracture, layer, and challenge the ideal of a stable, coherent consciousness apart from the world, expressing its thoughts and feelings—despite powerful arguments to the contrary by Rachel Blau DuPlessis and others.[31] In her practice with such received forms, Millay, for example, proves herself a theorist of lyric voice, teasing out rather than being controlled by the lyric's inherent tensions between voice and silence, absence and presence, nature and culture, the gaze and the beautiful object.[32] My approach emerges from the conviction that despite the tremendous poetic innovations of the twentieth century, poets have not moved utterly beyond engagement with lyric definitions. Lyric has remained a central structure even for many poets who challenge its supposed boundaries, and this means that many poets display a persistent interest in the fiction of voice.

Approaching lyric's apparently lone and overheard voice as a figure enables nuanced discussions of its operation. When Paul de Man, for example, refers to the lyric itself as "the instance of represented voice" (*Rhetoric of Romanticism*, 261), he not only indicates voice's crucial role in generic considerations but also highlights its fictive character. "What comes out of a mouth is a voice," Ira Sadoff likewise insists, "what we extract from the page is a series of inscriptions analogous to a voice" (221); voice as "workshop cliché," he continues, "assumes myths of constancy, coherence, and universality," and these myths enable the reader's desirable illusion of intimacy with the poet (222).

This understanding of voice as trope often coexists with arguments for voice as medium. De Man, for example, argues that these two definitions must remain interwoven. "It is essential that the status of the voice not be reduced to being a mere figure of speech or play of the letter," de Man asserts, "for this would deprive it of the attribute of aesthetic presence that determines the hermeneutics of the lyric" ("Lyrical Voice" 55). Charles Altieri, writing in 1984 about the "scenic style" dominating American poetry at the time (11), identifies the proximity between the "representing self" and the "dramatized actor" in such poetry as key to creating a valued appearance of sincerity, his dramatic diction suggesting performance and presence as lyric attributes (16–17). Poetry may enact, according to Altieri, an "interplay between a desire to be personal and a desire to acknowledge the multiple rhetorics through which a person may be glimpsed" (17). Kinereth Meyer similarly argues that "some poems invite us to read voice as oral, others as figure" (using confessional in contrast to impersonal modes); these are always interdependent impulses, according to Meyer, but one can be highlighted by various features of the poem (134). Meyer offers a lyric I "not as timeless and stable, but as fluid process, place, or meeting ground," evoking oral presence and trope interdependently (131).

Meyer's multiple references, in fact, to a "ghost of orality" in the lyric coincide with a rhetoric of haunting in many discussions of poetic voice. In "The Three Voices of Poetry," Eliot explains why someone might address a poem only "to himself—or to nobody" (96): "he is haunted by a demon, a demon against which he feels powerless, because in its first manifestation it has no face, no name, nothing; and the words, the poem he makes, are a kind of form of exorcism of this demon" (107). Rajan, more recently and less gothically, describes how Romanticism's "interdiscursive lyric . . . reveal[s] the traces of another voice within the seemingly autonomous lyric voice" (200, 195). Mary Jacobus analyzes how voice, apparently creating unity, can "take on the daemonic aspect of possession," threatening the poet's wholeness. For Wordsworth, she says, "voice comes to imply all the destabilizing multiplicity of plural (or ancestral) voices" (174–75). Parker likewise refers to "the haunting or inhabiting of an apparently autonomous voice by traces of alien voices or texts" (17).[33]

Many of the poets and theorists who address voice, in fact, employ a supernaturally inflected vocabulary to describe its function; a sense of mystery thereby seeps into their diction, if not their overt arguments. Voice may have receded from presence in guidebooks and literary glossaries because of its irritating vagueness; the epigraph from Peter Campion at the beginning of this chapter is a vivid example of the frustration it inspires. Nevertheless, the term poetic voice retains force for some poets and critics because it asserts literature's power. Lyric poetry is the literary genre in which authors can seem to be both most intimately present and, ironically, most cut off from historical context. Voice as a term invokes the eeriness of such encounters, the aspect of presence resulting from but also somehow exceeding elements of style. Semi-technical and semi-magical, the word allows objective scholarly language to register the joy secretly animating all kinds of poetic work, including not only writing but analyzing the lyric. A problematic formal term such as voice can, in fact, issue an important counter-challenge to the "eclipse of stylistics" that troubles Garrett Stewart and others. In short, voice registers the weird sexiness of reading poetry, the illusion it enables of a private tryst between author and reader.

Poetic voice is, among other things, a metaphor: it refers to literary qualities that evoke physical qualities. Specifically, the syntax, vocabulary, and visual characteristics of a printed poem may suggest the timber/pitch/ volume/ intonational rhythms of a specific person's voice, often the poet's own, but sometimes the imagined voice of a persona or character. No exact or even approximate method exists for identifying voice in a poem. Yet, as Alice Notley suggests in the epigraph I pair with Campion's complaint, many poems seem to manifest voice, a quality of sound and presence that somehow exceeds its component factors. This excess, the multiplicity of meanings and arguments that voice can mobilize, reverberates through twentieth-century American poetry. This book cannot record all of its echoes, nor encompass even a significant fraction of the poets for whom voice is a motivating idea. Through a few strategically chosen poets and movements, however, *Voicing American Poetry* does chart how far and powerfully poetic voice carries.

EDNA ST. VINCENT MILLAY'S
PERFORMANCE OF PRESENCE

Last Night I heard upon the Air
A little man who wasn't there.
He wasn't there again today
I hope he'll never go away.
　　　　—Edna St. Vincent Millay

Edgar Bergen, the famous ventriloquist, and his dummy, Charlie McCarthy, made their radio debut in 1936, a few years after Edna St. Vincent Millay began performing in that medium. The miracles of broadcasting and ventriloquism might, from a twenty-first century perspective, seem to cancel out one another, but Millay and others appreciated the play of voices Bergen created.[1] The fragment of occasional verse above is evidence of her enchantment with radio as a technology. Most importantly, it manifests her delight in radio's illusions. The poet was, for instance, "a Charlie McCarthy fan [and] once expressed her appreciation to Edgar Bergen" in the quatrain quoted above (Cuthbert 62).[2]

Radio delivers a version of human presence through voice, despite the paradoxical absence of the speaking or singing body. The "Air" constitutes a medium for uncanny meetings; the broadcast voice enables an unlikely intimacy despite physical distance. For Millay, such phenomena were entirely welcome. In fact, Millay recognized that in these qualities radio possesses an inherent likeness to the printed lyric poem—a medium similarly haunted by impossible presence. While broadcasting draws on the skills a poet develops on reading tours, its effects resemble those of print media.

For Millay, this new medium offered a fresh approach to a very familiar idea: despite the inherent alienations of performance, print, and broadcasting, the lyric in all its forms remains a site of human connection.

Millay's innovations helped shape two important methods of poetic transmission that were developing in the 1920s and 1930s: live and broadcast poetry readings. Even her print work displays a persistent concern with authorial presence, the way a poet is "there" and "not there" at once, and how deeply the lyric depends on this tension. Presence and absence, further, are a central problem for poetry in this period generally, because American culture was changing rapidly. As broadcasting and other technologies of distance developed, the public sounding of poetry underwent a significant transformation. While public recitations had formerly been displays of elocutionary skill, mostly by speakers other than the author, they increasingly became spectacles of authority. Instead of demonstrating talent and training for the stage (which most poets, then and now, do not have), readings began to manifest the authentic presence of the poet for audiences. Analogously, private recitation, or reading aloud in homes, was increasingly displaced by the voices of radio announcers and performers. Any study of poetic voice must address these shifts, because the textual voice coexists with its literal counterpart, the voiced text. Millay's work suits this discussion so perfectly because she refuses to prioritize one medium over another; sound is embodied in text and vice versa.

When poets, readers, and critics identify voice in a printed poem, they often mean that it creates an illusion of authorial presence. Poems in books, magazines, letters, and other print and manuscript sources often seem to resonate aurally, but they do not have "voices" in the most common sense: no physical sound occurs during silent reading. The poet is absent, although he or she has shaped voice textually, both through how the poem is printed and through diction, punctuation, rhetorical figures, pattern and other elements. One result of such strategies can be the sense that the poet is somehow present in the language, that the printed object is imbued with a real person's distinct character and verbal mannerisms. This impression of personal contact is, for many audiences, at the heart of poetry's appeal.

How does this sense of poetic voice, as a presence mysteriously generated by the interaction of text and reader, relate to the physical voicing of poetry? An answer lies partly in the relative benefits and disadvantages of different media. In the 1920s and the 1930s, poetry could be publicly transmitted in at least four ways: live readings, broadcast readings, recorded readings, and print. Live readings are immediate; they involve the bodies and senses more vividly than print media and allow poets and audiences to respond to one another instantly.[3] However, the number of people involved in such a recital must be relatively small and performed poems are ephemeral. Broadcast poetry, a practice that began during this period, is similarly fleeting. Network radio shuts down the instant feedback loop between poet and audience, but it can reach many more people at greater physical distance than live readings. Recording technologies, which were available late in the nineteenth century but improved radically in later decades, can deliver versions of presence to even larger numbers of people over temporal and geographical gaps. Finally, the technology of print carries poetry over distance and time in a way live readings never can. Print exchanges presence for longevity, voice for script, and therefore textual poetry sometimes exhibits a nostalgia for presence or a preoccupation with the ideas of voice and body.

In response to this increasingly complex and noisy aural culture, sound symbolism and tropes of speech and song pervade poetry from the modernist era. These strategies emerge strongly in the works of Edna St. Vincent Millay and Langston Hughes, whose experiments I study in chapter 3. Sound, a defining metaphor of the printed lyric in English, remains vital to twentieth-century poetic practice even during the literary upheavals of the period, and even though so much modern poetry engages the visual arts. Further, Hughes and Millay were highly deliberate in how they physically sounded verse for various audiences. Although their performances are less available to contemporary readers than their printed poems, the relations among these media were vital to how the poets conceived of their arts and identities. For both of these writers, poetry has a "fundamentally plural existence" (Bernstein 9); among a poem's manifestations, book printing may survive best, but it represents just a facet of the whole work as it might appear in various textual and oral performances.

Millay's distinguished performing career intersects in fascinating ways with her work in another aural medium—American broadcasting. Millay was among the first to explore radio's possibilities as a medium of poetic dissemination. Many other American poets showed, or would soon show, keen interest in acoustical technologies. T. S. Eliot and Ezra Pound, for instance, recorded work at the Harvard Vocarium in this period,[4] and many influential writers would eventually create radio plays, including Millay and Hughes. According to Michael Coyle, Eliot broadcast at least eighty-one talks over the BBC and was "resolved to help shape its future" ("T. S. Eliot on the Air" 141–43). Millay, nonetheless, was one of the first American poets to broadcast her verse over the radio, and did so in an environment of increasing excitement over possible intersections between literature and broadcasting.

The juxtaposition of Millay's contributions to these very different modes—live and broadcast voicings of poetic texts—illuminates Millay's work, modernism generally, and the movements that succeed modernism. In Millay's performances, aurality and presence become linked poetic attributes, and the meaning of the term "poetry reading" alters significantly.

Millay's Voice on the Page and the Stage

Millay's published poetry is more closely attuned to aural elements than to visual elements. However, it does demonstrate a persistent self-consciousness about both aspects of poetry and how they conspire to create the lyric's signature illusions. Some of her poems depict how voice, sound, and music produce material changes in the world. In the narrative poem "The Ballad of the Harp-Weaver," for instance, a mother's music conjures clothing out of the air for her cold and hungry son, though the mother sacrifices her life in order to accomplish this alchemy. Many other lyrics demonstrate how the voices of the natural world haunt the poet, as in "Northern April," full of pained praise for spring's incessant music of wind, rain, and reawakening life. Both kinds of poems, even in the silent medium of print, signify the transformative potential of sound.

Millay's elegies to Vassar classmate Dorothy Coleman and fellow poet Elinor Wylie further amplify her fascination with the idea of voice. In these extended pieces, Millay represents a double presence, resurrecting the voice of grief's object and responding with the voice of grief's subject. In so doing, she discovers physical voice to be even more ephemeral than the body from which it emanates. In "To Elinor Wylie," further, poetic voice, like physical voice, seems to be a transitory effect. Its second section, a two-stanza poem beginning "For you there is no song," equates poetic production with the resonance of an oral voice, comparing "the shaking / Of the voice that meant to sing" with the "sound of the strong / Voice breaking" (CP 370).[5] These lines also blur the subject and the object of the elegy. Both Wylie's and Millay's voices might be perceived to break, one through death and the other at the difficulty of articulating grief or paying adequate tribute. While this piece emphasizes sound, it also depicts the writing situation, acknowledging the poem not only as an oral but as a textual artifact. The poem's final comparison—"There are ink and tears on the page; only the tears / Have spoken"—links the act of writing even more profoundly to the act of grieving, only to devalue writing's relative efficacy in expression. Both writing and weeping are physical behaviors and both leave residues on the page. However, this poem insists that Millay's body only communicates properly through its tears; this broken little piece, apparently, is a much less powerful manifestation of emotion than her articulate weeping.

Millay's derogation of her art is paradoxically essential to praising her peer: poetry has died with Wylie, Millay implies. However, because of its self-consciousness, the use of the voice trope is particularly interesting in "For you there is no song." Again, Millay emphasizes that life resides in voice and that voice emerges from human bodies. Even while textual voice in "To Elinor Wylie" evokes Millay's own presence and summons the memory of Wylie's, Millay does acknowledge the artifice of poetic voice, its inadequate translation of the physical world, and even of profound feeling.

Millay is drawn to voice as an idea because of how it materializes authorial presence. Her printed poems that experiment most strikingly with voice often ask, therefore, what it means to be present at all. Certainly she depicts the self in terms of performance and investigates the gap between public and private selves, as in the sonnet "[If I should learn, in some quite casual way]," which contrasts a cool appearance with inner turmoil. In a later poem, "The Plaid Dress," even private, secret identities are layered performances, as the speaker wears outfit over outfit, mask over mask. "The Fitting" shows a "secret body" being fussed over by French seamstresses, who lament that body's diminishment; the speaker seems to waste away over a private sorrow alluded to with ellipses, and her conversation with the women workers occurs in untranslated French, emphasizing how distant human beings can be from one another, even when they are apparently intimate (CP 342–43). All this secrecy and reticence, however, have a paradoxical effect. Not only does this irregular sonnet publicize the existence of its romantic secrets, but it expands dramatically with the force of them, some lines containing as many as 28, 29, and 31 syllables. Bodies definitely speak here through sweat, gesture, swelling, and shrinking, even when voices (and poetic forms) are disguised.

In other poems, this multiplicity is internal; for instance, Millay seeks to represent how ambivalence or sexual desire can split a poetic speaker against herself in the alternating parentheses of "Macdougal Street." Sometimes, as in "Menses," Millay protests how thought must be embedded in and shaped by a person's physical life. In the latter case, menstrual cycles cause a woman to damn "this body with its muddy feet in my mind!"—this dramatic poem from the persona of a male husband or lover encompasses dialogue and two kinds of internal monologue, and it centers on blurred identities, "double word[s]," and the powerful intersections of mind and body (CP 345–47). Presence in Millay's work is a complex state, changeable and difficult to verify.

Millay's physical staging of these poems is only partially audible today. She was among the most famous and successful poet-performers in this period; in the United States, Vachel Lindsay, Amy Lowell, Robert Frost, and Carl Sandburg also won particularly large and appreciative audiences.

Poems were commonly read in family and community circles until radio's ascendancy, and sometimes played a role in public lectures, themselves a major part of a fading nineteenth-century "culture of eloquence."[6] American modernists had, as children, recited poems at school and listened to other recitations on a regular basis. However, as I noted in the introduction to this book, the poetry reading as an institution—the practice of poets devoting all or most of their public appearances to reading, reciting, and/or performing their own poetry—was novel in the twenties, although it would become an important source of income and prestige as the century progressed.[7] A shift was occurring in how poetry was sounded as emphasis was changing from recitation skills to the delivery of authorial presence. Millay, both an expert performer with nineteenth-century training and a celebrity with twentieth-century star power, worked right at the edge of this cultural shift, pioneering a new kind of literary spectacle.

Sound and performance were lively elements of this era's literary culture. Poetry's aural pleasures were also becoming increasingly identified with the live presence, and especially the physical voices, of its authors. Presence and voice played a particularly complicated role in the poetries of writers who, like Millay, Lowell, Hughes, and others, presented obvious challenges to the identity of "poet" in their very bodies.[8] Millay exhibited a keen interest in the connections between poetry and the poet's person, especially through her investments in physical and metaphorical voice. As Laura Severin theorizes in *Poetry off the Page*, "the public appearance of a woman's body would seem to guarantee that her work would not be masculinized" (17)—it emphasizes the relevance of gender and personality to the work in a way that counters some of high modernism's mandates. Bringing physical presence to poetry, as Millay did so successfully, foregrounds gender in Millay's poetry and reputation.

Millay's performance skills were instrumental in her early achievements. Millay was trained to recite verse in an educational system strongly influenced by nineteenth-century theories of elocution, and this background shaped her very earliest public successes.[9] Edmund Wilson, in fact, speculates that her transatlantic accent originated in this instruction: "I suppose it was partly the product of the English tradition in New England, and no doubt—since she had acted from childhood—of her having been taught to read Shakespeare by a college or school elocutionist" (749). Her talents attracted the attention of the patron who funded her Vassar education. At the urging of her sister Norma, then working as a waitress at the Whitehall Inn in Camden, Maine, Vincent Millay played piano and sang for the summer guests, then recited "Renascence." According to Milford, one member of the audience, Caroline B. Dow, "was stunned by Millay's poem, but even more by this provincial girl's assured performance" (69). Dow arranged scholarships for Millay to attend Vassar after a year of preparatory coursework at Barnard.

Millay acted at Vassar and, after graduating in 1917, moved to New York City and performed with the Provincetown Players. She soon became truly famous and successful as a performer of her own poetry.[10] Starting in the teens, she recited her poems in a variety of venues, including bohemian parties, clubs, colleges, and large lecture halls. By 1933 she was not only a best-selling poet and a celebrity, but also a veteran of protracted reading tours, which she claimed to dislike but which offered a significant source of income. In her letters, for example, she describes feeling like a prostitute during these events (181). Certainly she sold her physical presence on these evenings, and both poetic convention and stereotypes of proper femininity pressure her to deplore the transaction. However, these readings were a vital part of Millay's art and an avenue for poetic innovations. Millay superseded the actress-reciters of the nineteenth-century by performing poems with similar skill and training but with an added thrill. Onstage, she performed the poetess, but paradoxically she also performed authenticity, as twentieth-century audiences would increasingly require. Descriptions of her readings typically emphasize the paradoxes of her physical presence: a powerful voice issuing from a slim figure in a long, formal gown. Virtually everyone who reports on Millay's recitals in articles, letters, and memoirs describes the fabric, cut, and color of her dresses, and they also indicate that she performed a series of roles as she read, altering her posture, gestures, and inflections to present a range of characters. Sprague, for instance, describes how "the poet's face and figure change in interpretation from princess to slut at a lift of an eyebrow or twist of the lips, the movement of a hand or turn of the head" (137–38).[11] Millay, in fact, did not seem to practice the lecture-recital model of Sandburg, Frost, or even Lindsay or Lowell. Instead her poetry readings were intensely theatrical, using not only props and gesture as Lowell did, but moving through a sequence of personas. Unlike Sitwell performing *Façade* from behind a curtain, Millay did not efface her body; her readings suggested both an insistent physicality and the dramatic surrender of an actor to her script.[12]

Bernstein writes that the poetry reading "materializes the text not the author," but the contrary seems true for Millay (13). Despite her delivery of each poem in the formal tones of her elocutionary training, even given her theatrical adoption of a series of characters, Millay clearly tried to materialize the author as well as the text. Further, although a few felt notably "unmoved" by her performances (Eastman 80), many experienced a connection across large halls with what they perceived to be the author's true self. Some audience members, despite the theatrics, found her poems to be "unobscured by posing and affectation" (Milford 260). As many of Millay's best readers have rightly observed, her persona was intrinsic to her work and its public success.[13] The remainder of this chapter analyzes how she translated the successful spectacles of her poetry readings into two developing aural media: broadcasting and recording. As in her live performance style, her radio work delivers familiar ideas into fresh contexts. Both her live and broadcast readings represent an underappreciated mode of innovation in modern literature.

Millay's 1930s Radio Broadcasts

The startling newness of early radio, the speed at which it transformed American life, resonates with modern literature's parallel investment in change, originality, even revolution. Millay, however, while involved in both enterprises, was hardly an avatar of the new. Although she promoted and embodied women's increasing social and sexual freedoms, in her readings, printed poems, and other publicity she could perform the stereotypes of bohemian femme fatale and poetess with zeal. She was, in many ways, a conventional figure, and not only because she often wrote in forms and imagery that any nineteenth-century reader would recognize as poetic. Nevertheless, Millay was, in a small way, a broadcast pioneer. In 1932 and 1933, Millay became one of the first poets to read her own work over American airwaves. In doing so, she responded to a call issued by many parties to "save" poetry by taking advantage of this innovative technology, this original way of transmitting poetry to a national audience. She also offers an important example of how poets in the modern era used, and were used by, a developing medium.

Millay's broadcasts succeeded in reaching appreciative listeners, yet the surviving evidence indicates that she did not, in fact, treat radio as fundamentally new. For Millay, radio's effects closely parallel the advantages conferred by the much older technology of print. Both broadcast and printed poetry, that is, deliver an illusion of intimacy and presence despite distance (geographical, and in the case of books and recordings, temporal). Even public recitation by the author constitutes a materialization: the poet may be physically present in the lecture hall, and yet the poetic self remains a performance managed much more convincingly by some writers than others. Millay regarded this illusion of presence and intimacy as the battery, the indispensable power source, for the twentieth-century lyric in any medium. Radio delighted her, as the epigraph to this chapter suggests. Nevertheless, Millay's broadcasts question the artistic value of novelty and register skepticism of radio's supposedly radical, utopian possibilities. For Millay, radio is a means, like print, to overcome distance, and a forum, like the live poetry reading, in which poetry's tropes of sound may become briefly literal.

Millay's public reading practices developed, as the previous section shows, from many sources and antecedents. She positioned herself well to serve two different sets of audience desires and expectation: she was both theatrical and authentic, delivering skill as well as presence. Her reputation as well as her hard-won skills nourished her radio success. However, her broadcasts borrow less from the lyceum, the theater, or even the salon than they do from domestic recitation. Radio voiced poetry, as families and other small groups did, right in the living room, and Millay capitalized on that intimacy, scaling her trained voice down for domestic spaces, seeking a tone that mediated between publicity and privacy. Voice and presence link her live and broadcast readings, but she succeeded at both because she approached them differently.

Millay's broadcasts occur at an important juncture in radio history in the United States. Their timing strongly inflects their meaning. Two concerns are prominent, shared by these pieces and magnified by her style of delivery: tropes of sound and presence, and Millay's engagement with the idea of "naturalness."

According to Suzanne Clark, "The reader of Millay is not likely to find writerly pleasures in her text, called so frequently from play back to the spectacle of personality" (*Sentimental Modernism* 95). In fact, Millay's poems manifest her considerable interest in this distinction between writing and sound. Further, Millay's broadcasts magnify the potential tension between print and performance remarked by so many poetry critics: does the real poem exist on the page, the stage, or the airwaves?[14] At stake are Millay's ambivalence towards distancing technologies (including writing itself); her conception of poetry as a dialogic art; and her persistent interest in the idea of poetic voice. Her implicit answer to this question is that no version, no medium, possesses ultimate priority over another. Millay also reveals intimacy as an illusion in any medium. Unlike many modernists and postmodernists, however, she regards this fragile illusion of presence as poetry's (and radio's) *sine qua non*.

Susan Smulyan writes persuasively in *Selling Radio* that "treating radio programs as literature . . . misses the point of broadcasting; the material sent over the airwaves exists primarily to gather and retain an audience for advertising" (6). Millay's broadcasts were, arguably, radio programs in Smulyan's sense: they served her financial interest in self-promotion, and served early radio's desperate need for material as well as cultural legitimacy. However, literature itself is never pure of context, never entirely separate from commercial concerns, although it can secure prestige through a fantasy of autonomy from market forces. Broadcasting is, in fact, one of many economically inflected contexts shaping the meanings of modern poetry. This is particularly true because network radio helped invent a national culture for the United States. Millay, already one of the nation's best-known artists, manipulated and was manipulated by radio to shape that culture. Her work deserves attention on its own account, but it also speaks to the limits and advantages of broadcasting for poetry generally.

The popular poetry of the modern era, including Millay's work, does not correspond well with the stories scholars have told about modernism. The current moment in literary scholarship, however—characterized by a decline in "phonophobia," as Garrett Stewart calls it, and a renewed interest in acoustical technologies—offers an opportunity to revise the poetic history of the twentieth century. Millay's broadcasts suggest a different take on what is interesting, important, and provocative about this period. Her radio experiments suggest that the best insights about modernity do not necessarily emanate from the avant-garde, and that poetry can use new media to deliver on old promises.

In 1932 and 1933, American radio was undergoing a major transition. As Eric Barnouw and others document, the lively chaos of amateur radio in the teens and early twenties yielded, by the end of the latter decade, to the ascendancy of networks and the advent of commercial radio. During the 1930s, radio became a "pervasive influence in American life" (Robert J. Brown 2). Instead of offering haphazard programming of local talent in the evening hours, as had previous small transmitters associated with newspapers and department stores, the networks invented a national mass culture, bringing advice programs, dramas, and famous performers into homes across the country, all in the service of advertisement (Smulyan 6). Shortly after Millay's reading series ended, in fact, in March 1933, Franklin Delano Roosevelt began his "fireside chats," capitalizing politically on this technology of intimacy and sincerity.[15] During national crisis, with millions out of work and Hitler rising to power in Germany, radio seemed to possess utopian potential as "a unifying and culturally uplifting medium" (Hilmes xviii).

Radio's power to build community over geographical distances coexisted uneasily, however, with its increasingly commercial function. This tension sometimes manifested in contests between highbrow and lowbrow culture: "Broadcasting . . . became a key element in the ordering of the American cultural hierarchy. Early regulatory decisions attempted to mark radio out as a controlled and sanctioned apace in which the 'vulgar,' such as black jazz performers or race records, could find only a tenuous and sanitized foothold" (Hilmes 186). Poetry recitation, however, along with symphony, opera, lectures, and some drama, could offer cultural improvement that mitigated radio's infiltration of private spaces by hucksters.[16] Millay's one experience with radio prior to her 1932 reading is a good example. An opera called *The King's Henchmen,* for which Millay had written the libretto, was broadcast live in 1927 by the brand-new Columbia Phonograph Broadcasting System (Barnouw 222). This performance with Metropolitan Opera artists was marred by technical difficulties, but it augured the high-culture ambitions of young American radio networks.

American poetry's relationship to the radio commenced early in the history of broadcasting. News and talk radio began in the 1920s, with poetry readings by the announcers occasionally filling the gaps between programs (Barnouw 134; Kaplan 3). These recitations became popular in the late 1920s, and in 1930 WJZ, New York, broadcast several poetry readings by the authors themselves (Kaplan 4). Harriet Monroe devoted an editorial in *Poetry* magazine to this program, deploring the quality of the verse WJZ aired but insisting that "Poetry is a vocal art; the radio will bring back its audience" (April 1930, 35). Later the same year, César Saerchinger, the first U.S. "foreign radio representative," persuaded Britain's poet laureate John Masefield to broadcast to American audiences. Masefield, who was instrumental in the verse speaking movement and Oxford festivals, as described in this book's introduction, expressed hope that radio in particular could highlight the role of sound in poetry and widen its audience (Saerchinger ix, 34–35).[17] These calls continued well after Millay's first radio venture. Archibald MacLeish, for instance, published a verse radio play called *The Fall of the City* in 1937, prefaced by a passionate argument for this new genre, in which visual elements cannot compete with the "word-excited imagination" (x); radio's provision of large audiences "should deeply move the American poet whose present tragedy is his isolation from any audience vigorous enough to demand his strongest work" (xiii).[18] Similarly, in his 1949 book about poetry on the radio, Milton Kaplan expresses optimism about the future of poetry on the radio, arguing, however, that verse drama is better suited to the medium than lyric poetry.[19]

Millay, then, enters broadcasting at a moment of consolidation, reciting her poetry over one of the relatively new national networks. On Christmas Day in 1932, a Sunday night, Millay read her poems over a nationwide hook-up on the WJZ Blue Network.[20] Audiences responded warmly to her work and she continued the broadcasts over a total of eight Sunday evenings through the winter of 1933. One of these sessions survives in recordings, enabling me to compare the sound of the broadcasts with printed remarks about them.

Millay would make famous and effective use of verse drama over the radio during World War II (Kaplan 14), but in the early thirties she was new to the medium. The full scope and effect of her early transmissions are hard to measure now. Poetic radio broadcasts, like poetry readings generally, are ephemeral events, surviving chiefly through contemporary accounts; recordings were relatively rare in the modernist era. In this case, however, one of the sessions was preserved on two discs now archived in the Brander Matthews Collection at Columbia University with copies at the Library of Congress. In 2001, some of the poems from this recording, minus most of the introductory patter, were issued by Random House as part of an audio anthology.[21]

The archived recording is about twelve minutes long and seems to represent all or most of the program, not including any advertising that may have preceded or followed it.[22] This particular session clearly occurred during the middle of the series. She begins by explaining that she will not read her famous long poem, "Renascence," remarking that "so many of you have requested that" and promising to read it the following Sunday. Instead, she delivers eight shorter poems with brief intervening commentary. She identifies the collection each poem appears in as well as its title, but makes very few additional observations. In particular contrast to contemporary poetry readings, she never comments on the content of any of the poems, much less describes their sources in personal, social, or intellectual contexts. Millay presents these poems not as documents of personal experience or cultural history but as performance pieces.

Acting as a representative of high culture, and deploying her considerable popularity over the airwaves, Millay serves corporate interests, both gathering an audience for advertising and easing fears over radio's bad influence. In this way, her broadcasts function like Penny Readings or school recitations discussed in my introduction, but with the participatory element removed. Audiences must be edified merely by listening, and not by sounding the poems themselves. "Linguistic unity" was one of the utopian projects of early radio. "Not only English, but proper, uninflected English, would become the national standard and norm—not a goal to be taken lightly amid the educational and regional diversity of the 1920s" (Hilmes 18). Millay's broadcasts, shaped by her mastery of the elocutionary arts, served an educational purpose even at the level of pronunciation.

Further, Millay manipulates and advances radio's reputation as a "sincere medium" (Smulyan 78), a reputation that also serves the interests of advertisers. Millay's life and poetry were marked by radical social and political dissent, especially through her celebrations of female sexual freedom and resistance to censorship and discrimination, the latter exercised

most famously through her protests against the Sacco and Vanzetti deci-
sion. The available information concerning her broadcasts, nevertheless,
suggest that she did not select her most subversive poems for the airwaves,
nor did she present herself in a way to challenge middle-class prejudices.

Millay's colorful presence informed her live performances, but, like
other modern era recitals, these were truly ephemeral; even contemporary
poetry readings cannot be fully captured by video, and Millay's, of course,
are only accessible now through print accounts. The poetic selves she presented were entirely vocal, and her presence more illusory, in her broadcasts.[23] The look of broadcasting studios, as well as Millay's appearance,
were familiar to her listeners, so that they could visualize her speaking to
them from a microphone somewhere in New York City.[24] Her listeners on
those Sunday evenings were geographically but not temporally distant from
the performance. In recordings, however, an illusion of presence is further
attenuated. Millay hoped to reach posterity as well as paying contemporaries with her work, but sustaining the sorcery over generations is a tricky
proposition. The recordings no longer convey the qualities her contemporaries recognized as intimacy and naturalness.[25]

The recordings from the Brander Matthews collection indicate how in-
telligently she managed radio's relative limits and opportunities. As in her
reading tours, she creates different voices for various poems by varying her
pitch and timing significantly. Millay reads her sonnets from *Fatal Interview* in relatively deep, melancholy tones, while other lyrics, especially
"City Trees," elicit a high-pitched sweetness. Her slow, formal reading
style also contrasts sharply with the intimate lightness of her commentary;
in between poems, she speaks rapidly and casually. She manipulates two
media so effectively, the broadcast and print lyric, by understanding their
point of intersection. All depend on the illusion of presence created by
voice. The third medium under discussion—audio recording—was more
difficult for Millay to manage, because she did not anticipate how speaking
and reading conventions would change in the second half of the twentieth
century. Below, therefore, I treat the recordings primarily as documents of
her radio practices. However, they also represent a foray into recording as a
medium, and I do discuss its mixed outcome.

Millay's selections for the recorded radio broadcast help define her on-air
persona; they also reveal her understanding of radio's distinctiveness. Her
comments about reader requests and plans for future evenings confirm that
Millay chose a different set of pieces for each broadcast. In this particular
performance, she reads short pieces from four volumes: *Renascence* (1917),
Second April (1921), *The Harp Weaver* (1923), and *Fatal Interview* (1931). She

skips the racier, urban poetry of *First Figs from Thistles* (1928) and the overtly political work collected in *The Buck in the Snow* (1928) in favor of poems concerning romantic love and the nature of beauty. Her playlist exhibits a variety of moods and ignores chronological order, proceeding as follows:

1. "God's World" (CP 32)
2. "Not in a silver casket cool with pearls" (CP 640)
3. "Moon, that against the lintel of the west" (CP 656)
4. "You say: 'Since life is cruel enough at best'" (CP 667)
5. "Oh, sleep forever in the Latmian cave" (CP 681)
6. "City Trees" (CP 54)
7. "Euclid alone has looked on Beauty bare" (CP 605)
8. "Elaine" (CP 96)

Although these choices surely represent a bid to please radio's heterogeneous audiences, they also reflect a particular concern with presence versus absence and the role of sound in poetry. While these themes intersect in many poems, I treat them separately, as far as possible.

In and beyond this broadcast, Millay's poetry urges the importance of sound not only through formal characteristics, such as rhythm and rhyme, but recurrent imagery of music and voice, especially birdsong. Millay chose poems for this program that invoke human voices and/or natural sounds, then turn away from them towards silence. Certainly it would have been difficult not to include these subjects, since such references dominate her work. The context of radio, however, lends new resonance to these allusions. While printed poems engage silence visually through the existence of white space, and a performer standing before a crowd can use pauses strategically, silence over the radio becomes simply dead air. When the voice stops, the illusion of presence dissolves and the thread of connection between broadcaster and listener breaks. Although Millay was new to radio as a performance medium in 1933, her patter between readings demonstrates her desire to avoid aural white space. Before she reads "You say: 'Since life is cruel enough at best,'" for instance, Millay fills the air by remarking, "The next sonnet I'm going to read I'll have to hunt for because I've lost the page in the book. . . . I hope these pages aren't making an awful crackling noise. I know this is creating a pause for you." While Millay's comments create intimacy between listener and poet, they also throw into sharp relief the difference between unscripted speech and poetry reading. Between her firmly delineated performances of individual lyrics, Millay uses relatively casual language full of contractions, speaking more rapidly and in a higher pitch than she does while reciting verse.[26]

The content of the poems further highlights the interdependence of sound and silence. Millay begins the broadcast with an early poem, "God's World," apostrophizing creation with orgasmic passion that cannot be satisfied: "World, I cannot get thee close enough!" Radio affords simultaneous intimacy and distance, so Millay's poem exploits its new medium through that central metaphor. However, the final plea of "God's World" lays emphasis instead on the power of voice. Lest she be overwhelmed by loveliness, the speaker begs, "let no bird call," and Millay delivers these last words with particular slowness, elongating the final syllables of poetic ecstasy. This technique of stretching a poem's last phrase in performance, and following that phrase with a pregnant pause, in fact characterizes Millay's delivery of many of these pieces. The strategy both forestalls silence and invites it into the poem.[27]

Millay also extends the final sounds of "You say: 'Since life is cruel enough at best.'" In this case, however, her strategy destabilizes rather than reinforces the printed poem's meaning. This piece appears in *Fatal Interview*, a book-length sequence of fifty-two Shakespearean sonnets chronicling a failing affair. Sonnet 38 is the only poem in the sequence to stage a dialogue between the pair, and it chiefly offers the male lover's excuses for ending the relationship. The first twelve-and-a-half lines consist entirely of one convoluted sentence from the lover, failing to state a plain case for the relationship's dissolution. His wordy rationalization ends, appropriately enough, with an equivocal dash when the apparently impatient speaker intervenes: "Oh, tortured voice, be still! / Spare me your premise: leave me when you will." Her command to silence in short, direct phrases combines on the page with full rhyme and end-stopped lines to emphasize not only finality, but a tone of scathing disgust. At least in the 1933 broadcast, however, Millay's reading runs counter to the impatience conveyed by the printed poem. Interpreting the last lines, Millay slows and deepens her voice, enacting a *reluctance* to part instead of a will to closure.[28]

Millay delivers "You say: 'Since life is cruel enough at best'" and the other sonnets from *Fatal Interview* in a relatively low pitch, emphasizing their serious tone as well as the maturity of the speaker, whom the book characterizes as older than her gutless lover. When she performs the earlier "City Trees," however, she adopts a higher and lighter tone. Further, while she lends "City Trees" extra significance by remarking that "I thought of naming the book [*Second April*] for this poem," she also characterizes it with diminutive adjectives, referring to it as a "short poem" and a "little poem." While these comments trivialize the piece, littleness is also central to its point. Millay clearly identifies with the misplaced trees, and this contradictory language resembles the paradoxes of the petite, charismatic poet's physical presence. It also suggests the dialectic between sound and silence that characterizes not only this piece but Millay's overall approach to the lyric in print and performance.

Speaking over WJZ, Millay raises her voice to evoke the "thin and sweet" music her speaker attributes to trees. This piece compares the voices of country trees with their urban sisters, who are "dumb / against the shrieking city air," to suggest the young poetess from Maine struggling to be heard against the clamor of Manhattan. The strong iambic rhythm, regular rhyme, and alliteration (especially sibilance) in both versions emphasize the music of poetry itself. The ending of the "City Trees," however, also calls attention to poetry's visual dimensions. It refers to sound as something she can see rather than actually hear: "I watch you when the wind has come,—" she apostrophizes the displaced trees, "I know what sound is there." If poems strive to make music, an art of sound, and yet on the page they can only offer inaudible signs of the will to music, this suggests that print cannot be poetry's primary medium. Reading poems, then, resembles reading sheet music: a skilled person can imagine what the notes would sound like, but the composition cannot achieve full existence until an instrument sounds the script.

"God's World," "You say: 'Since life is cruel enough at best'," and "City Trees" invite Millay's radio audience to consider the centrality of sound and voice to poetry, as well as highlighting the threat of dead air, the cessation of voice and connection. In so doing, they also emphasize the disembodied voices and illusion of presence that animate both printed poetry and radio as media. The issue of presence also haunts the other three poems Millay chooses to read from *Fatal Interview*. "Moon, that against the lintel of the west," for instance, beseeches that celestial body not to set, so that the speaker may prolong her night with her beloved. In performance, Millay emphasizes syntax over line breaks, dramatizing her speaker's refusal of interruption. Future absence haunts the sound of the present.

Millay concludes the program with another piece in this mode, "Elaine," a dramatic monologue addressed to Lancelot by his betrayed wife. Elaine asks her husband to return to Astolat then hypothetically discusses the questions she would not ask him and insists that he would not notice her presence—in fact, he would imagine that she had died and the gardens were empty. "I will not say how dear you are," she promises, and offers her own silence and even the landscape's quietness to please him: "So still the orchard, Lancelot, / So very still the lake shall be." The poem concludes with Elaine's own desire "To see you speak" from a distance, a reference to watching unheard sound that echoes the ending of "City Trees." Millay highlights the oddness of this poem's closure by reading against the iambic meter; instead of stressing the second and fourth syllables in the final phrase, "if you should smile," she places an unlikely accent on "if" and "should." The lilting surprise of Millay's performance focuses on Elaine's desperate self-prostration, on the conditional nature of her plea, and on the very small chance that she could woo him by effacing herself.

This seduction, premised on absence, strongly evokes the paradoxical nature of these radio broadcasts. Audiences listened to Millay's voice on wireless sets in rural living rooms, and like many announcers in that time, Millay cultivated the potential intimacy of this situation. She seems to have understood the irony of a disembodied voice: a radio reading shorn of theatrical spectacle, strangely enough, brings the poet closer to her audience than when she recites work in a crowded hall. This is even more true in a live broadcast than it would be in a recording: no temporal distance exists between speaker and audience, although geography divides them.[29] By linking her position with Elaine's, Millay characterizes herself as an invisible seductress, seeking her audience's attention with exquisitely self-effacing modesty.

Millay's constant troping on sound—hearing rather than seeing Beauty, for instance, in "Euclid alone has looked on Beauty bare"—demonstrates her fascination with the relationship between poetry and performance. Her lyrics both depend on voice and call attention to its illusory nature, at least in poetry's textual incarnations. Further, Millay's first foray into radio demonstrates her grasp of that medium's similar magic. It manufactures intimate proximity despite distance and intervening machinery. Millay performs the same sleight-of-hand with the idea of naturalness. Just as her formal verse strives to convey impulsiveness and lack of artifice, Millay's mannered performance style, in fact, translated to authenticity for her contemporary audiences. Broadcast technology amplifies these effects. Millay's "naturalness" reveals important differences between modernist and recent performance practices: the signifiers of authenticity have radically changed.

Some of the poems Millay chose to perform focus on resistance to natural processes: the speaker wishes to still the passage of time, for instance, in "Moon, that against the lintel of the west" and "Oh, sleep forever in the Latmian cave."[30] However, Sonnet XI from *Fatal Interview* instead celebrates naturalness and derogates artifice. "Not in a silver casket cool with pearls" devotes its octave to descriptions of ornate, ingenious love-gifts. Both the casket and the poison ring are beautiful, valuable receptacles for well-concealed secrets, and therefore apt metaphors for the compact, cleverly wrought form of the sonnet. The sestet, however, compares the speaker's love to a series of unpretentious gifts offered openly: "cowslips in a hat," "apples in her skirt." The flowers and fruit are "natural" in that they arise directly from nature, unlike the casket and the ring, but they are also presented in a casual way as if by an uncalculating giver. Millay ends the poem by attributing a child's innocence to her speaker's closing remark: "'Look what I have!—And these are all for you.'"

Several contextual details draw attention to these images. First, Millay may have been particularly mindful of the boundaries of the natural as she delivered her poetry through the relatively new technology of radio. Generally, Millay resisted technological interventions between poet and audience—for example, there is a wonderful anecdote from one audience member, quoted in the recent biography, *Savage Beauty*, about Millay's refusal of amplification in the Los Angeles Philharmonic:

> She was to give a reading at the Los Angeles Philharmonic—a big place, packed to the top gallery. Bare stage, except for a standing mike. She came out, alone, wearing the usual loose something, green, I think. Standing well away from the mike, she began. Almost at once came cries of "Louder!" "Can't hear!," &, insistently,—"Use the mike!" A crescendo that drowned her out. She stood there, waited till it sank to grumbling, then gestured at the mike & said something like—"I will not tell my poems through this mechanical contraption. They come from me to you, direct. Please be entirely silent & I will make you hear me." Oh no! It started up again, and she resumed. Twice. My seat was very near the front, & I never felt such tension. Growing, too. There was resentment in it, then anger, finally real antagonism. I suppose it took 5 minutes, while she stood still & fought them. Scary minutes, for there was a sort of peak when she almost lost them. But she didn't. Somehow they did settle & listen. She said every poem she'd chosen, just with her voice, an hour or so of speaking. Then she turned to go off—& then the house came down. Cheers. People stood up. Some cried. It was a show of guts & stubbornness & pride. And foolishness, I suppose. (422–23)

Millay's training in theater enabled her to project her voice and communicate character in a large hall without amplification; this tale from the late 1930s reflects her confidence and experience. However, her quoted remarks also imply an aesthetic of intimacy and immediacy that visible technology could interfere with. Radio's difference, for Millay, resided in its resemblance to nineteenth-century domestic reading practices: a voice delivering words at a normal volume in the family parlor, to a small group. As Barnouw observes, performers began to approach radio differently in the mid-twenties, when crystal sets in garages became cabinet-housed wireless sets in living rooms. "In 1922 performers still imagined themselves in a vast auditorium . . . but by 1925 a cozier image was established. Many artists liked to imagine the audience as 'a single person.' Letters encouraged this; no other medium had ever afforded an audience this illusion of intimacy shielded by privacy" (164).

A second reason for thinking about naturalness lies in the very sound of Millay's performance. To current listeners her pronunciation sounds comically artificial. When I play recordings of Millay to my undergraduates at Washington and Lee University, they exclaim, "She sounds like Glinda the Good Witch!"[31] However, this elocutionary manner seemed like the height of naturalness to many of Millay's own contemporaries. Perhaps responding to this very broadcast, one audience member wrote: "Don't ever change, and become stiff or formal or eloquent. . . . You sound so real, so natural, so—so very much alive" (quoted in Milford 368).[32] This quote—and it's not an isolated remark—illustrates how profoundly conventions of naturalness have changed in just eighty years. It also helps to ground the American poetry reading in history, demonstrating some of the profound changes that have occurred in an under-examined poetic institution.

Throughout the latter part of the twentieth century, the sound of poetic authenticity has been free verse presented in the manner Peter Middleton describes: "A person stands alone in front of an audience, holding a text and speaking in an odd voice, too regular to be conversation, too intimate and too lacking in orotundity to be a speech or a lecture, too rough and personal to be theater" (262). Other performance aesthetics have coexisted with this one, from Beat-era chanting to hip-hop influenced poetry jams, and perhaps the sound of authenticity in American poetry has shifted again—some of my current students claim a preference for formal verse, their tastes influenced by rap's accentual rhythms and intricate rhymes. However, in the thirties, what sounded artificial were the deliberate jolts and disharmonies of modernist *vers libre*. Millay, to the contrary, transmitted the sounds her audience had grown up with: metrical poetry recited in parlors, recitation clubs, school auditoriums.

Millay's aims, in this respect, again resonate with the network interests, and not only because she tries to please a wide audience. Advertisers promoting radio sales in the 1920s pitched broadcasting as a "sincere" medium, as "incorruptible" as photography was understood to be. "The imposition of a machine was perceived to give the information an additional veracity. Radio, in the argument of the promoters, could protect the listener/consumer by automatically exposing lies" (Smulyan 78). The more radio is perceived as a trustworthy medium, the more advertisers are attracted to it, and the more profits networks stand to realize. Millay's poetic broadcasts capitalize on the increasing association of radio voices with sincerity, but also help to bolster that association.

Millay's investment in "naturalness," on forging connections with her middlebrow audience, has contributed to her exclusion from the canon of modernism, as Clark argues so convincingly. However, her manipulation of poetry's many media also signals how aware she was that authenticity constitutes a pose conditioned by context. Millay's work may evidence more delight in art's illusions than some of her contemporaries. However, whether the definition of modernism requires expansion or whether modernism's very curricular and scholarly dominance needs to be challenged, Millay should not be relegated to that movement's margins. Her radio broadcasts, other performances, and the published texts all demonstrate a radically open approach to the lyric as a multimedia creation. For this reason, as well as for the challenges her poems and performance pose about gender roles, Millay's complex and entertaining work still merits the prominence it earned in her own time.

Presence and Absence in Aural Media

The dream of intense, directly personal contact is an essential part of the experience of reading literature. It is what drew us in the first place towards the books we chose to read, the subjects we chose to study, the work we chose to pursue, the lives we chose to live. Somewhere in the midst of all the frenzied activity that occupies us . . . is a silent moment, constantly renewed, in which we feel that someone—often someone long vanished into dust, someone who could not conceivably have known our names or conjured our existence or spoken our language—is sending us a message.
    Stephen Greenblatt, "MLA Presidential Address 2002"

Millay's readings and broadcasts offer important insights into the intersections between performed and printed poetry as well as how acoustical technologies complicate the dynamic. Her approach to live performance bridged cultures of elocution and authenticity, skill and presence. In a break from nineteenth-century convention, poets became interesting as public performers; Millay both influenced and capitalized upon this shift. Her sold-out reading tours offered a physical, as opposed to a textual, realization of the "dream of intense, directly personal contact" between poet and audience.

Her performance practices, however, do not signify a preference for stage over page; instead, they demonstrate her commitment to the lyric genre through multiple media. Millay experiments with the "acoustical technologies that grew up with modernism," as Morris puts it ("Introduction" 8), but for her it does not inspire Joycean cacophonies (as James A. Connor argues) or a renewed interest in national poetic forms such as epic (as Adalaide Morris finds in "Sound Technologies").

Michael Davidson, writing insightfully about postmodern poets Allen Ginsberg, David Antin, and others, finds that some artists use the newly cheap and available technology of tape recording to produce a "poetics of presence." Tape recording, he writes, "transformed the notion of voice from something heard to something overheard" ("Technologies of Presence" 117, 99). Davidson's implicit allusion to John Stuart Mill's definition of lyric as "overheard utterance," however, actually undermines his point. The paradox of disembodied presence was, in fact, a central trope and strategy of the printed lyric long before recording technology became available, or radio pioneer Reginald Fessenden managed to transmit the human voice. Print itself is a distancing technology; Millay's poetry demonstrates this. Radio's heterogeneous voices changed the sound of the world and infiltrated modern literature in the ways James A. Connor and Morris suggests, but broadcasting poetry does not necessarily transform it, or dismantle the lyric I, or force modern alienation upon texts or their audiences. Nor have broadcast or recording ever become especially prevalent media for poetry, although poetry readings remain ubiquitous.[33] Advances in acoustical technologies may have fostered or inspired some kinds of poetry that are intensely sound-saturated, but they need not revolutionize definitions of the lyric.

Millay encodes performance insistently within printed poetry and dramatically performs poems that represent sound in visual terms. She conveys presence through voice but links their power to their evanescence. Through these strategies, Millay interrogates the status of the lyric poem. Her testing of lyric boundaries, however, has been less visible because she mounts this challenge from a different direction than many of her contemporaries and because most of her actual performances were utterly ephemeral.

Millay explores the limits and advantages of the modern lyric in various media. Her experimentation may not be recognizably modernist, and yet it plays a significant role in the technological and cultural changes that transformed American life in this period. She was not only a fan of radio magic but also an important participant in it, just as her successful tours helped alter audience expectations concerning what happens during a poetry reading. Her broadcasts represent an important example of how twentieth-century technology shapes poetic practice, and of how poetry can interpret modernity.

VOICE AND THE VISUAL POETRY
OF LANGSTON HUGHES

Although of course lyrics in all ages are addressed to the ear, the rise of fiction and the printing press develops an increasing tendency to address the ear through the eye.
　—Northrop Frye, *Anatomy of Criticism*

The African American poet uses scriptings as a way to communicate voicings. Writing is an extension of speaking or singing.
　—Fahamisha Brown, *Performing the Word*

Many poets deploy their physical voices brilliantly by reciting their work, broadcasting it, and recording it. Accordingly, the phrase poetic voice can designate the actual rhythms, pitches, and timbres of such delivery, or express how the memory of a poet's performance inflects the experience of silent reading. T. S. Eliot, for instance, died before I was born, but his slow, nasal, oddly accented recording of *The Waste Land* has permanently shaped my response to the poem—not only how I might read a passage aloud to a class, but my perception of its pace, tone, and ultimately its meaning. Further, because I have heard a recording of the poem uttered by its author, it possesses more unity for me than it might if I had only encountered the printed version. Even when a writer varies her performance style to suggest different speakers, and even when, as in the case of *The Waste Land*, a poem quotes many sources and emerges from a collaborative process, performance by a single individual lends coherence to the work. The spoken poem emanates from one body.

Poetic voice, in this and other cases, can therefore designate a side-effect of performance, perhaps accidental but potentially powerful. Nevertheless, while Eliot's recording is well-circulated, print versions of *The Waste Land* retain primacy by almost any measure: the printed poem has reached more people, influenced more writers, and received more critical attention than the audio-text. In what sense, then, can a poem regarded only in its textual incarnation possess a voice? Certainly Edna St. Vincent Millay, Langston Hughes, and many others refer to sound constantly (as does *The Waste Land*). But if voice exists beyond tropes in a printed text, it must be an illusion created by syntax, diction, repetition, rhyme, other sonic echoes, and/or a variety of graphic elements. The latter include lineation, margins, orthography, typography, and a range of less common strategies. Voice, in other words, must be represented or created by visual means.

This chapter, therefore, addresses the graphic techniques poets use to notate and sometimes to obliterate physical voice. Twentieth-century works depending on such strategies are sometimes referred to as visual poetry, though related terms include shaped poetry, pattern poetry, concrete poetry, and carmina figurata.[1] Willard Bohn defines visual poetry as follows:

> In one sense, to be sure, every poem is designed to be seen, since the eye must process the words before the mind can interpret them. At least this is true of written poetry which, no matter how hard it seeks to transcend its condition, can never escape its material origins. . . . Where visual poetry differs from ordinary poetry is in the extent of its iconic dimension, which is much more pronounced, and in its degree of self-awareness. Visual poems are immediately recognizable by their refusal to adhere to a rectilinear grid and by their tendency to flout their plasticity. In contrast to traditional poetry, they are conceived not only as literary works but as works of art. (15)

One problem with Bohn's definition is the imprecision of its antithesis. He refers too vaguely to "ordinary" or "traditional" poetry as pieces that seek transparency through adherence to rectilinear conventions. This category of work does not, however, exist in any unified way. Rather, all written, printed, projected, or web-disseminated poetry exists on a continuum, ranging from works that deemphasize visual elements to works distinguished by prominent graphic play.

By Bohn's usefully narrow standard, Langston Hughes does not produce a great deal of visual poetry. For the most part, his poems either proceed in familiar-looking left-justified columns or rely on the "relatively modest" visual effects that characterize modernist work in English: "irregular line-lengths, multiple indentations," the use of capital letters and italics

(Bohn 31). Nevertheless, because Hughes has been received as a poet of voice, and because he did experiment with visual poetry during some key phases of his career, his work serves as my chief example. Vernacular speech and African American music epitomized authentic communication for Hughes—and this was all the more reason to represent a fragmented, mechanized, and forcefully silenced world through a variety of typographical devices. On some occasions, too, the visual world clearly inspired Hughes, and therefore he sought poetic analogs for its vibrancy, as in "Neon Signs."

According to poet and critic Harryette Mullen, "Any theory of African American literature that privileges a speech based poetics, or the trope of orality, to the exclusion of more writerly texts will cost us some impoverishment of the tradition" (624). Mullen is concerned here with the persistence of African script and visual culture in nineteenth-century American visual art and literature, arguing that for African Americans in this period, "graphic systems have been associated not with instrumental human communication, but with techniques of spiritual power" (625). Her focus, therefore, predates the Harlem Renaissance and/or modernist art of Hughes, although her observations resonate powerfully with Hughes's concerns. Other critics, including Meta DuEwa Jones and Aldon Nielsen, highlight contemporary African American poetry, urging readers to attend more closely to its graphic elements.[2] Their admonitions, similarly, are relevant to the study of earlier African American writers. In fact, although Hughes has probably attracted more scholarly attention than any other African American poet, his visual poetry has received relatively little notice.[3]

From the beginning of his career, Langston Hughes sought ways to deliver voice and music into the visual medium of print. Even his famous musically based ventures—the development of poetic correlatives to blues and jazz—form part of his visual poetics, since in them he attempts to make sound visible. To evoke the blues in a poem is to provoke a series of questions about both art forms: in what senses can a poem be musical? Is a blues poem analogous to a performed blues song, sheet music for a blues song, or only the lyrics to a blues song? These problems, of course, depend in the first place on how one defines lyric poetry. Is a poem a set of sounds sometimes transmitted via print, or a textual creation that is sometimes transmitted via voice? Hughes's use of dialect and slang in poetry raises analogous issues, as do his poems that script multiple voices, and others based on letters, drama, broadcasts, advertisement, propaganda, and myriad other models of human communication. That is, in what sense can a poem have a voice? How does textual poetry resemble speech, or even other forms of writing, and in what respects does it differ? By engaging such models in his poetic labors, Hughes demonstrates his vital interest in what a poem is as well as what it can do. The potential social power of literature is always vivid to this revolution-minded African American. His goal as an artist is not only to reflect and celebrate African American vernacular culture but to transform this array of voices into a comparably rich array of visible texts. Print, he knows, offers unique permanence and power; although Hughes was a successful public speaker, his art, his income, and his activism were often realized best through books and periodicals.

The examples of Hughes's visual poetics as discussed below demonstrate his concern with poetry's graphic potential. These pieces use visual elements in particularly striking ways. Their strategies do not pervade all of Hughes's work, but they do signal the author's persistent consciousness of poetry's spatial dimensions. Within the larger scope of this book, Hughes's poetry also exemplifies a common complication of poetic voice as an interpretive category: voice or sound can intersect with script in many ways, but the two media also remain essentially different. That is, a poem can exist as sound, but the voice of a printed poem is usually a metaphor, and metaphors obtain their very force through the distances they contain. The gap between physical sound and tropes of sound constitutes one of the most deeply interesting problems of lyric poetry, especially as Hughes practiced it. Voice as a figure is highly relevant to Hughes's work in many senses—he seeks to give a voice to African American culture, for example—but his transformation of sound culture into print form is particularly ingenious.

Hughes's relationship to visual poetry evolved over time, as the next portion of this chapter illustrates, but two periods of his work are key. Three poems from the early- to mid-1930s show the range of Hughes's models and techniques, drawn from both avant-garde and mass culture. "Advertisement for the Waldorf-Astoria," "Cubes," and "Elderly Leaders" make resourceful use of illustration, typography, and iconic symbols to place the trope of voice, so prominent in his work, under productive pressure. Hughes's jazz-inspired long poem about Harlem, *Montage of a Dream Deferred*, also concerns the idea of a visual voice, especially in "Dream Boogie" and "Neon Signs." Where possible, I have examined various printings of these poems and their evolution through manuscript and typescript. Hughes's drafts, insofar as they survive, are archived in the James Weldon Johnson collection at the Beinecke Library in New Haven; I refer to these papers throughout.

The Paradox of Visual Voice

As scholars such as Claire Badaracco, Johanna Drucker, Willard Bohn, and others have noted, the early twentieth century was characterized by tremendous invention and a vibrant visual culture. Modern print technology enabled fresh looks not only for book composition but for a range of advertisements, including posters, billboards, handbills, and so on. Avant-garde aesthetic movements both influenced print design and appropriated its new technologies. Cubism, Futurism, Dadaism, Constructivism, Imagism, and many other influential groups respond to the inventions and extend the idiom of advertising.[4] Langston Hughes's own interest in poetry's graphic possibilities may have been jolted by exposure to avant-garde experiments. Scholars have not documented many encounters between Hughes and these strands of modernism, but his years in Paris and New York, his voracious reading habits, and references in the poems themselves suggest that he was aware of them. Just as importantly, like the Cubists, Hughes was affected by mass culture itself; his reading materials and even his passage through the streets were littered with print promotions. Like other artists who sought to earn a living by their work, Hughes also had an economic interest in such techniques. Visual design is a key element in appealing to audiences, and Hughes was incredibly resourceful in his effort to create a responsive public for his work.

Hughes considered many models for poetic dissemination. Hughes performed poetry in clubs, churches, schools, and many other venues, seeking to reach and build audiences that were highly various in terms of race, class, politics, and educational level. Hughes also co-founded a small press, participated in the design of his books and individual poems, and collaborated eagerly with artists in other media, including illustrators, allying his poetry with the visual arts.[5] His forays into visual poetry are often genre-blurring in other ways; for instance, Hughes publishes poems that are also recitation pieces for one or more speakers and hence mimic plays in their format. A few poems use typographical elements more uniquely—in ways that might be performable, but are not strictly pronounceable. One example is his occasional use of *paraggonage*, or the employment of different typefaces and/or sizes within a single line (Bohn 20), as when an oversized numeral eight begins and ends "Scottsboro" (142–43). The eight unjustly imprisoned young men are separated from ordinary text and united in one bold icon, difficult to ignore. The symbol's resemblance to the sign for infinity amplifies the historical importance of their cause and highlights the steadfastness of their supporters. Through one minor font change, Hughes adds another dimension of meaning to "Scottsboro."

In "Scottsboro" and elsewhere, Hughes's poetry is "speech based" and "writerly" simultaneously, to use Mullen's terms. The latter poem communicates meaning through *paraggonage*, but it also rhymes in couplets, gaining force through sound; its dependence on catalog is simultaneously a graphic and an aural strategy. Much of Hughes's other work likewise investigates the paradox of a written voice, a central problem for poetry during the cultural changes of the modernist period. Lyric poetry by definition is rooted in sound and song, even when it circulates primarily through print. Even as the nineteenth-century culture of eloquence receded and poetic audiences fragmented, as technology changed both print culture and the sounds of American life, this traditional association between poetry and song still inspired many writers. Hughes was prominent among them, as the many critics focusing on Hughes's jazz and blues poetry have documented.

The negotiation between sound and script is especially urgent for Hughes, because so much African American poetry declares its roots in oral culture, with important political implications, as Hughes makes very clear in his early manifesto celebrating black folk traditions, "The Negro Artist and the Racial Mountain." Scholars, therefore, have dwelled on the music of Hughes's writing for excellent reasons: his poetry depends crucially on sound, most obviously in his pioneering adaptations of blues and jazz forms but also through pervasive strategies such as anaphora, rhyme, alliteration, and repetition. Further, Hughes sought to celebrate African American speech in all its variety; he wrote frequently in persona, using visual and aural devices to delineate a range of characters. These efforts are particularly striking in his later poetry, from the thirties through his major long poems, *Montage of a Dream Deferred* and *Ask Your Mama*.

An impressive range of studies treat sound and presence in African American literature generally (see Gates and Benston for book-length studies on "speakerly texts" and "performing blackness," respectively), and African American poetry more specifically (see Fahamisha Brown). The most insightful critics of Langston Hughes's poetry have likewise emphasized its aurality. Richard K. Barksdale finds "the distinctive marks of orature" in Hughes's folk poems (139), while George E. Kent and others stress his commitment to folk sources; James Smethurst analyzes Hughes's "folk voice" (7, 11, 93–115); Steven C. Tracy and David Chinitz offer particularly valuable and specific readings of the role of music in Hughes's work. For many readers, Hughes's references to music in *Montage* reinforce his representative vision and the social function he envisioned for poetry. Peter Brooker and Robert Hokanson stress the significance of jazz's dialogism, its conversational aspect, to Hughes; John Lowney explores the cultural meanings of be-bop to show the poem's "conflicted sense of audience" (358).[6] Jones challenges "Hughes' literary stature as a folk poet," emphasizing "the genre-breaking and technically innovative features of Hughes' later writings and recordings" ("Listening to What the Ear Demands" 1146).

In order to represent and create sound, voice, and music on his pages,
Hughes built poems around visual devices from the very beginning of his
career. Even in the twenties Hughes often drew on graphic as well as phonic techniques to shape his poems. In his first volume, *The Weary Blues*, for
example, Hughes uses typography to represent cacophony in "The Cat and
the Saxophone (2 a.m.)." The capitalized lyrics to a song by Jack Palmer and
Spencer Williams, "Everybody Loves My Baby, But My Baby Don't Love
Nobody but Me," alternate with scraps of a bar conversation—drink
orders, flirtation, and an invitation to dance the Charleston. Capital letters
suggest the loudness of the music compared to snatches of lower-case talk,
evoking the context vividly. The soundscape of a Harlem cabaret, in fact,
holds this fragmentary poem together. The conversation's content also
resonates with the song lyrics, although the capitals help to designate different voices. The placement of an exclamation point by itself in the final
line carries the graphic play one step further, attempting to convey excitement without semantic content. This may not be a "visual poem" by Willard Bohn's definition, but "The Cat and the Saxophone (2 a.m.)" is an early
example of how Hughes represents a complex array of sounds in print.

Appropriately, experts on Hughes's blues poetry—a mode he invented
in the twenties and revisited often over the years—highlight the visual
elements of these musically inspired poems. Tracy's important book-length
study, for instance, focuses considerable attention on graphic strategies
that imitate blues performance, especially lineation. Hughes had an economic interest in doubling the lengths of his poems by using half-lines, as
Tracy points out, but Hughes thereby evokes the sound of blues more
clearly (154–56). Chinitz, analyzing the tensions between literary elements and folk authenticity in Hughes's blues poems, finds that the poet
"used typography—particularly indentation and italics—to indicate
changes of tempo or voice" ("Literacy and Authenticity" 185). Both Tracy
and Chinitz, however, treat Hughes's blues poems primarily as transcribed blues lyrics; they do not argue for the poems as performances in
themselves.[7] Tony Bolden, while finding analogues to blues musical techniques in various literary blues, also stresses that "most blues poets write
poems that should be read aloud" (53). These poems therefore seem to
extend folk materials, even preserve them, but simultaneously doom themselves to relative failure; if Hughes's blues poems yearn always after an
aural medium, their print existence must always seem secondary. Indeed,
this sense of belatedness magnifies the melancholy tone of some of Hughes's
blues.

Some Hughes critics, however, emphasize the difference between song
and poem, and some of the poems themselves encode it.[8] Hughes himself

separated "Poems" from "Song Lyrics" when he assembled *The Langston Hughes Reader;* while his prefatory notes do not explain the difference between blues song and blues poetry, his organizational strategy establishes it firmly. Hughes's blues poems are complete in textual form, as visual evocations of sound that can be, but need not be, performed.

Hughes's political poems of the thirties, while they retain a commitment to black speech and music, engage poetry's visual aspects with particular inventiveness. Works including "Scottsboro," "Advertisement for the Waldorf-Astoria," "Wait," "Cubes," "Elderly Leaders," and many others take brilliant advantage of print's possibilities. For instance, these poems capitalize key phrases in order to borrow the urgency of newspaper headlines; juxtapose text in simultaneous vertical columns; and use fluctuating margins, italics, font sizes, and boldface type to suggest the interplay of multiple voices. In fact, in this decade, as James Smethurst argues, Hughes's poetry became more insistently polyvocal as he tried to reach different audiences with different agendas (94–95).[9] He represents these various and sometimes competing voices through a range of graphic strategies.

Some fifteen years later, in *Montage of a Dream Deferred*, Hughes manipulates many of these graphic elements in concert with his strong emphasis on music, speech, and the background noise of Harlem just after World War II. The latter collection, which Hughes began writing in 1948 and initially published in 1951, possesses the coherence of a poetic sequence or long poem, although individual lyrics are often anthologized without reference to this crucial context (especially "Harlem" and "Theme for English B"). In fact, movements between visual experiment and sound play are central to its overall meaning. *Montage* deliberately teases out the relative roles of music and visual design in lyric poetry, what Northrop Frye, writing about lyric a few years later, calls "babble" and "doodle" (275), and what Garrett Stewart refers to decades later as the "phonotext" and the "graphotext." The figure of voice becomes paramount in these negotiations.

The paradox of a written voice, of sound represented in a visual medium, is at the heart of *Montage*. As others have discussed with thoroughness and insight, Hughes's references to music and speech are abundant. Elements of the sequence, however, resist orality by emphasizing the poem as a visual creation, as in "Neon Signs." Finally, printed and recorded versions of "Dream Boogie," the first poem in *Montage*, reveal how typographical elements relate to oral performance. *Montage* not only engages the idea of poetic voice with sustained intelligence, but it tests lyric poetry as a genre in a way that poetry criticism has not yet fully recognized and celebrated.

Eloquent Silences in the 1930s

Excellent biographical and scholarly work exists concerning Langston Hughes's rejection of Charlotte Mason's patronage at the end of the 1920s; his increasing sympathy with the American communist movement in the early 1930s; and his renewed commitment in the same period to reach African American audiences, despite the Great Depression. Public speaking became an increasingly important strategy, especially in terms of the latter goal. Hughes was a charismatic performer. His lecture notes and later recordings document his ability to make challenging poetry accessible. Oral performance was, for Hughes, not only a good medium for winning audiences, but the very ground of his own aesthetic project, which was largely inspired by the accents, vocabulary, stories, songs, sermons, and humor of black Americans.

Hughes's interest in oral culture and his professional activities as a touring speaker might seem to compete with his writerly talents. In fact, the gap between oral and textual performances did interest and even inspire Hughes, as the poems themselves demonstrate. His response to this "problem," really a source of energy in so much of the work, was manifold. In the thirties, Hughes experimented with material aspects of publishing, founding the Golden Stair Press with Prentiss Taylor.[10] Their first production, a pamphlet of recitation pieces called *The Negro Mother*, enabled Hughes to carry inexpensive pamphlets with him to sell at each booking, as well as still cheaper broadsides. (Their second and last major venture, *Scottsboro Limited*, was less successful for several reasons.[11]) Hughes also became increasingly interested in the persuasive appeals of visual advertising as a means to advance his career and promote his politics.[12]

"Advertisement for the Waldorf-Astoria," which ingeniously turns the strategies of capitalism against itself, is an ideal starting point for considering the relative roles of visual and aural elements in Hughes's work. Two other poems of the thirties also convert voice into print with particular dexterity: "Cubes" and "Elderly Leaders." These poems illustrate how art becomes complicit in oppression and how money silences democracy. Visible language, these works imply, is full of perils equal to its power. Further, when visual design becomes the language of commerce, music and voice become even more important as media for authentic communication.

In October of 1931, amid advertisements for Tiffany, Chrysler, and various purebred dogs, *Vanity Fair* promoted the reopening of the Waldorf-Astoria. The Empire State Building had just been built on the former site of this posh New York hotel and the Waldorf-Astoria had been recreated Art

Deco-style at a new location on Park Avenue. The full *Vanity Fair* spread, several pages long, begins with a short essay on the hotel's history, called "New York's Unofficial Palace" (17); this piece is formatted to resemble journalism, although it is not listed in the table of contents. A two-page illustration and list of features follows (18–19), succeeded in turn by three pages of linked advertisements from the Waldorf-Astoria's interior decorators and hardware suppliers. The entire advertising spread emphasizes opulence and privilege, ignoring the worsening economic depression, and elides the difference between news and commerce. In these attributes, not surprisingly, these pages are typical of *Vanity Fair*, generally, which then and now concerns itself with the consumption of expensive products and services, including the arts.

Hughes's response to the *Vanity Fair* spread was rapid and scathing. Within two months, his counter "advertisement" appeared in his "major outlet" of this period, *New Masses* (Rampersad 215; the masthead of the latter publication lists Hughes as a contributing editor). His poetic salvo evoked many different responses from readers. Perhaps for this reason, Hughes showed little commitment to the poem in future years, choosing not to reprint it in any poetry collections, although he cited it in his memoir *The Big Sea*.[13] One of Hughes's most constant supporters, Carl Van Vechten, called it "bad politics and bad poetry" (quoted in Rampersad 1:376); both writers, in fact, had some reason for allegiance to *Vanity Fair*, which had been the first periodical to print Hughes's poetry.[14]

Certainly, this piece's polemic is fierce and its poetic markers are few. "Advertisement" is not lineated, uses little figurative language, and its repetitive vocabulary depends not on familiar poetic tropes but on slang ("swell") and colloquialisms ("cold as hell") (quoted from *CP* 143–46). This anti-literariness, however, is carefully grounded in the poetics of advertisement and serves interlocking aesthetic and political aims. Further, the poem is far richer in its original contexts—carefully laid-out and provocatively illustrated—than in the stripped-down versions offered by its later reprintings. Using visual and rhetorical elements to create and appeal to its constituency, "Advertisement" turns Madison Avenue against itself and offers a potent example of the interplay between sound and vision in Hughes's work.

The contexts of the original advertisement and Hughes's answer to it could hardly differ more radically. Materially, *Vanity Fair* was and is an attractive, glossy magazine, while *New Masses*, costing fifteen cents, appeared in cheap newsprint. As Michael Thurston observes about the latter periodical as it existed in the twenties, its quality seems "almost disposable" and it concerns contemporary events of political moment; however, bold covers and other elements ally it with artistic innovation (24). Further, the radical periodical made a practice of printing what Cary Nelson has called "poster-poems" (216): "*New Masses* regularly devoted one of its large pages to a single long poem or five or six short poems by one author, thereby simultaneously drawing on the long history of the broadside in England and America and making an early magazine version of the large poetry broadsides that would become especially popular in the 1960s" (Nelson 209). Nelson reprints the *New Masses* version of Hughes's poem in his own book *Repression and Recovery* (212–13), arguing for it as a "complex example of the interaction between text and illustration," although he compares it to a "fancy hotel menu" rather than to the original advertisement, which, in fact, it closely resembles (219).

The surrounding content of *New Masses* also helps to shape the meaning of "Advertisement for the Waldorf-Astoria." The December 1931 issue, in which Hughes's prose poem appears, features an ominous cover illustration of an angel in a gas mask floating over a field of dying soldiers. Its real advertisements are relatively few and ideologically coherent with the literary left, including notices for lectures, debates, and a ball sponsored by the League of Struggle for Negro Rights. The first article in the December 1931 number concerns the poverty and struggle of coal miners in Harlan County, Kentucky; this issue also includes an essay by John Dos Passos and poems in a variety of styles.

Hughes's "Advertisement for the Waldorf-Astoria" is the centerfold, a two-page spread imitating pages 18 and 19 of the *Vanity Fair* sequence (immediately after the faux article). His poem echoes phrases and strategies from the advertisement that inspired it and alludes to *Vanity Fair* twice by name; it starts exactly as the real advertisement does with a seductive heading in a large font ("Fine living, à la carte. . . . Come to the Waldorf-Astoria!"); Hughes concludes his poem with the hotel's actual phone number. The visual elements of the *New Masses* printing, further, mimic the original even more closely than the words do. Both the text of the advertisement and Hughes's poem are printed in columns with bold subtitles flush right (not capitalized and centered as in the *Collected Poems*). Further, the *New Masses* illustration by Walter Steinhilber both quotes *Vanity Fair* and contributes substantially to the poem's meaning. The glossy magazine contains a black and white drawing of the rebuilt hotel that emphasizes its grand façade, particularly the tall reflective windows, while sleek automobiles and tiny, slim figures appear dwarfed at the bottom. Steinhilber depicts the hotel from the same angle. This time, however, the grand windows reveal the Waldorf-Astoria's occupants, all fat old white men in various acts of debauchery with liquor bottles, playing cards, and scantily clad flappers. In a panel across the bottom of the page, Steinhilber has drawn the suffering faces of poor men and women, black and white. Interestingly, this artwork gives most of its attention to the elite residents, while in his poem Hughes barely gestures toward them, instead imagining and addressing the people who haunt the understory of Steinhilber's representation. The visual elements critique and parody the status quo, laying a kind of groundwork for the poem's revolutionary agenda. Because Steinhilber has represented how the ruling class abuses its power, Hughes is better able to advocate seizing the hotel's amenities for more urgent uses. Hughes's poem not only satirizes advertisement, but it is an advertisement, urging its audience not to consume, but to rebel.

With publication, poetry almost always becomes collaborative, since at various stages editors and publishers help to shape the work, whether or not they alter a word. This is especially true when another artist, such as an illustrator or composer, becomes involved in the poem's presentation. Hughes tended to welcome such collaboration in various publishing and performance ventures, from his illustrated pamphlets of the same period to the musical settings his poetry often received, and Steinhilber's artwork is likewise a substantial contribution to the poem.[15] In this case, however, the visual elements of "Advertisement" are not only, or even chiefly, attributable to Steinhilber and the editorial team. Drafts reveal that Hughes conceived of "Advertisement" as a visual poem before he submitted it to *New Masses*. The poem was born in longhand penciled on scraps of paper, giving an impression of swift inspiration; occasional substitutions and rearrangements are marked in with carets or scrawled on the versos. The first typescript, now brown and crumbling, shows Hughes's desire to parody not only the content but the layout of the offending advertisement. Hughes's subsections in this draft closely follow the format of the original. He even sets his subtitles flush right, as they are in *Vanity Fair*, although their content shifts in later versions ("LISTEN, BUMS!," for example, becomes "Listen, hungry ones!"). At the top of the next version, submitted to *New Masses*, Hughes typed, "(For ad form: See October VANITY FAIR, page 19.)." Whether or not Hughes discussed the layout further with Steinhilber, he clearly meant his poem to evoke the original ad in its appearance as well as its language.

Through visual design, through direct quotation, and through allusions, Hughes forges a clear and highly specific link between his poem and an actual advertisement that had appeared just two months before. That specificity is important. It signifies that Hughes indicts not just capitalist excess generally but this particular magazine, this promotion, this building. In *New Masses*, "Advertisement," in fact, urges a course of action. Come to, call the Waldorf, Hughes repeats in a series of imperatives whose tone seems simultaneously satirical and sincere. The colloquial looseness of the language is not a side-effect of quick composition or a failure of art, but a strategy for conveying authenticity within the false medium of advertisement. Hughes promotes revolution, highlighting gross excess to convey urgency; he both parodies a sales pitch and, in a gesture of interdependent cynicism and idealism, offers one of his own.

Thurston calls "Advertisement for the Waldorf-Astoria" Hughes's "most effective explicit attempt to invite readers of various types into his revolutionary collective" (92), noting how nearly all its subheadings identify disenfranchised groups with common interests:

> Hailed by the appropriate "advertisement," all of the oppressed communities come into place. As in the earlier sections, Hughes structures this one around antithesis. The "Everybody" addressed consists of those left out. Their identity derives from the "n't" in Hughes's verbs; it depends on their negative relation to those on the inside. (93)

The status of "Advertisement" as an advertisement bolsters this claim. Hughes's community-building gestures bear more than a superficial resemblance to real advertising strategies. For instance, the mock-journalistic history of the Waldorf-Astoria offered by *Vanity Fair* describes a community that lacks common space—the wealthy elite of New York, "homeless" in their own tragic way. George S. Chappell writes that

> forty years ago the dominant citizens of New York recognized that their city had no adequate background against which the progress of its fashionable life could be displayed; no setting in which its society could, as it were, hold court. . . . And, with the opening of its doors, the World of Fashion, no longer alarmed, may lean back and say, "Well, *now* we know where we can go!" (17)

Chappell names a need, and the full spread identifies in detail how that need might be satisfied. Subsections in the advertisement's text indicate the services that qualify the Waldorf-Astoria to fill this need, emphasizing luxury, privacy, and newness: "The New Waldorf," "The Residence Apartments," "Privacy," "Freedom from Responsibility," "Modern Conveniences," "Private Entertaining," "Public Functions," "Commendatore Giulio Gelardi," "Oscar of the Waldorf," "Alexandre Gastaud," "Domestics," and "Now Renting." Hughes's subsections are very different in substance but go even further than the original by naming the right consumers for his alternative venture, social change: "Listen, hungry ones!," "Roomers," "Evicted Families," "Negroes," and "Everybody." His subtitles are more direct and plain than the original's, just as the text is more conversational, more aggressively persuasive.

Hughes's subtitles indicate that while race is an important element of exclusion, it is not the only one; economics are primary. Nevertheless, he highlights race, as James Smethurst suggests elsewhere, by employing traditional poetic strategies with particular frequency in the "Negroes" subsection, including the poem's only metaphor as well as alliteration, rhyme, and other sound effects (111). This is the only section, further, to encode not only a call but a response. Hughes sets these textual "voices" apart from his own not by quotation marks, as he does when citing the *Vanity Fair* ad ("'A lease, if you prefer, or an arrangement terminable at will'"), or by centered capital letters, as he does in mimicking a lavish Waldorf-Astoria menu, but through italics (in the typescript Hughes uses underlining). Dialect spellings indicate not only the distance traveled from Park Avenue but the oral nature of the exchange. Because visual design is crucial to advertisement's persuasions, authentic relations between people must occur through voice. References to oral culture encode capitalism's alternative.

In the same section, the poem's moral imperatives begin to assume religious overtones. The dialog in "Negroes" explicitly refers to the call and response patterns of church services through form and diction. The italicized voice begins: *"Hallelujah! Undercover driveways! / Ma soul's a witness for de Waldorf-Astoria!"* After several exchanges, it concludes, *"Glory be to God—/ De Waldorf-Astoria's open!"* The very act of putting praise for the Waldorf's amenities in the dialect of a black churchgoer contributes to the biting satire by emphasizing the distance between the two discourses: white and black, worldly and pious, smug and humble. The penultimate section, "Everybody," drops the Christian allusions until its very last line, which begins with an apparent epithet: "Jesus, ain't you tired yet?" The irreverent ejaculation, however, is immediately followed by an invocation in the poem's last section, which begins, "Hail Mary, Mother of God!" Context is everything, Hughes reminds us; the same words can constitute a curse or a prayer.

Hughes titles the last part of his poem "Christmas Card," drawing attention to its publishing context (the December issue of *New Masses*) and borrowing force for his own appeal from the Christian gospels. This verse paragraph reads Christianity as a potentially radical religion—its radicalism lacquered over by convention and familiarity, but still at its core incompatible with oppression.[16] He compares Mary to a little girl "turned whore because her belly was too hungry to stand it anymore" and begs a room for her at the Waldorf-Astoria, "the best manger we've got." Poverty and homelessness, Hughes suggests, mark Christian legend as well as the American present. He preaches harshly on the parallels, implying a deep inherent conflict between capitalism and Christianity. The solution to contemporary suffering, according to Hughes, however, is not religious but political. He prophesies the birth of "the new Christ child of the Revolution" and apostrophizes him in parentheses, urging him to "(Kick hard, red baby, in the bitter womb of the mob)." The infant enclosed in womb-like parentheses is neither black nor white but Communist, and while the poem does not urge violent upheaval, it teeters on that brink. Although "Christmas Card" contains advertising references—such as the mock-imperative "Somebody put an ad in *Vanity Fair* quick!"—this is the section of "Advertisement for the Waldorf-Astoria" that departs most from the tone of the original. With the title "Christmas Card," however, Hughes again emphasizes the poem's visual elements. Christmas cards depend strongly on image rather than text, as magazine advertisements do. They also work, as promotion does, to build or reinforce networks of connection, to establish communities of like interests over distance. Poems can operate the same way, especially when they are as carefully targeted as this one. Hughes uses the visual strategies of advertising even as he critiques advertising's aims, demonstrating his eager interest in how all facets of the poem convey meaning and appeal to audiences.

"Cubes," another poem which appeared only in *New Masses* (1934), explores the graphic potential of poetry using a very different set of allusions and tactics, but with the similar goal of exploding silence about suffering and oppression. Here Hughes develops a poetics of the fragment that responds to Picasso's version of Cubism. He patterns "Cubes" through repetition, fluctuating margins, and the typographical breakdown of language into its component characters. The visual analog that "Cubes" invokes, however, is not magazine advertising but modern painting. Another important difference between "Advertisement for the Waldorf-Astoria" and "Cubes" is that the latter piece makes use of lineation, perhaps signaling its allegiance to art over propaganda. It is far briefer and less discursive than the earlier poem and not aimed at a particular audience. It uses visual design to deliver a critique, but not to inspire social change. "Cubes" represents another experiment with the graphic elements of poetry, and in conjunction with "Advertisement," it illustrates the great breadth of resources Hughes considered in bringing poetry to the page.

As is typical with Hughes's most writerly poems, "Cubes" has received little scholarly attention until recently. Schulman (2000) in a book on the literary left (279–281) offers a brief discussion of the poem's language games, particularly the transformation of Picasso's cubes into dice. Two years later in *Callaloo*, Seth Moglen produces an extended treatment of the poem as a "manifesto of black modernism" (1190). Both emphasize the link that "Cubes" draws between race and fragmentation. While Hughes begins and ends the poem with references to an era (the twenties), a city (Paris), and the "broken cubes of Picasso" (CP 175–76), most of the poem focuses on the effects of French imperialism on the black residents of its colonies. The white French, according to this poem, "amuse" themselves with exercises of power, and as a result the "young African from Senegal" whom Hughes meets on the boulevards brings the "gift" of disease back to his home. The "disease" this poem refers to is both a set of ideas—the psychological and social effects of colonization—and, by the end of the poem, a venereal disease the Senegalese man has contracted from "the three old prostitutes of France—/ Liberty, Equality, Fraternity" (176). Even apparently noble products of Europe, democracy and art, are pernicious because they are insincere games, both of them "broken" and exploited for economic gain.[17] Certainly, as Moglen makes clear, this poem "is at once an innovative modernist experiment and a powerful critique of modernism from a black diasporic perspective" (1189).

"Cubes'"s graphic play is one of its most salient characteristics. The poem itself supplies a ready explanation for its unusual appearance through the framing allusions to Picasso. Picasso's cubist paintings break down or analyze the components of visual form. Hughes mimics his strategies by breaking down and analyzing verbal image and language itself. Specifically, Hughes uses two strategies: repetition and visual patterning. The latter is especially clear in the typesetting of the poem's final word:

d

i

s

e

a

s

e

The Cubist style, originated in Paris by Pablo Picasso and Georges Braques, dismantles the illusions wrought by representational painting—the depiction of three-dimensional people, landscapes, and objects on the two-dimensional plane of the canvas. Some Cubist works also address temporality: How can a spatial medium represent time and movement? The

conundrum of poetry is parallel though not identical: How can one transform voice into script, body and experience into the two-dimensional plane
of the printed leaf? Further, in what senses is poetry temporal or linear,
and in what senses spatial or static?[18] Clearly Hughes considered Cubism as
a model. Indeed, Hughes may have come to Cubism as a poetic strategy
through reading Guillaume Apollinaire's calligrammes, poems that involve
a radical and painterly use of the page. Picasso's Cubism, however, owed a
great deal to African masks and sculpture, which Hughes may have seen as
artistic imperialism—certainly this poem connects aesthetic and economic
exchange between the continents in a way that indicts Europe severely.[19]
Although the dramatic graphic strategies employed by "Cubes" are not
prevalent in Hughes's work, they effectively render the mental and physical
dislocation and sickness of European imperialism.

The relation between Africa and Europe, "black and white," is at the
heart of this piece. The repetition of this color binary also suggests a series
of less deadly contests, also in black and white. The game of craps is one; it
parallels the games of avant-garde art, the production of alienating mono-
chromatic canvases. Another is the transformation of voice into print. Little draft record exists of how Hughes embarked on the game of composing
"Cubes." The Beinecke contains one typescript that looks very like the version appearing in *New Masses* and reprinted in the *Collected Poems*. Hughes
penciled in two possible variations: identifying the "African" of the seventh
line as a "soldier," which would highlight war as another human "game,"
and changing "prostitutes" to "harlots" (Langston Hughes Papers, JWJ
MS 26 376.6285). The sinuous margins, however, that put repeated phrases
into visual motion like the layered shapes of "Nude Descending a Stair-
case" are already present. In this typescript, too, the broken final word follows the same curve it will in publication. This shaping of the word "disease"
scatters individual letters, but not randomly, as a fistful of dice would fall
onto a flat surface. Nor is there a score for pronunciation here, although
elsewhere in the poem, especially in the third verse paragraph, lineation
does correspond with syntax and suggest which words might, in oral delivery, receive particular emphasis (particularly the ones that stand alone,
such as "God" and "amused / and / amusing"). Instead, the pattern Hughes
gives to the characters of "disease" suggests oscillation and predictability.
This poem is far less optimistic than "Advertisement" with its hopes for
revolution; instead, this poem gestures to a world in which oppression, disease, and even language itself circulate in constant exchange.

"Cubes" cynically implies that the esthetic revolutions of modernism
are merely amusing, while human suffering quietly expands. The context
of the original *New Masses* printing also emphasizes skepticism of high cul-

ture, although the juxtapositions are editorial and in most ways extrinsic to the poem. "Cubes" is printed in two columns in a box at the bottom of a three-column page; as in the *Collected Poems*, which runs this and many other poems over a page break, the printing de-emphasizes the art of poetic layout. Further, other elements of the issue position themselves against academia and intellectual elitism. The cover illustration, a cartoon by Boris Gorelick, shows an obese giant in academic dress sitting on a large book, which in turn squashes hordes of tiny people. The immediate context of "Cubes" is also telling. It appears at the end of an article called "The Golden Key to Snobbery" by Carl Haessler, comparing Phi Beta Kappa to fascist organizations. Hughes identified with the American communist left in the early 1930s more strongly and more openly than at any other point in his career, and he shared its populist orientation. "Cubes" demonstrates Hughes's attention to Apollinaire and other artists who tested poetry's graphic elements with exhilarating boldness. However, to him, avant-gardism in the face of imperialism was at best unproductive, at worst complicit in the alienations of modern life.

The piece that appears in the *Collected Poems* as "Elderly Leaders" (193–94) has a more complicated publication history than "Advertisement" or "Cubes." It appeared first in two magazines that are now fairly difficult to access: *Race* in the summer of 1936, as "Elderly Race Leaders"; and *Unquote* in 1940, as "Public Dignitaries." Decades later, Hughes reprinted "Elderly Leaders" in the *Langston Hughes Reader* (1958) and *The Panther and the Lash* (1967). Like the previously discussed poems, "Elderly Leaders" deploys typographical elements in a crucial way, so that visual design is inextricable from overall meaning. "Elderly Leaders," however, is more radically a visual creation, relying heavily on unpronounceable elements: a cascade of typographical symbols closes the poem. They could not be read aloud without ridiculously cumbersome repetition ("dollar sign," "dollar sign," "dollar sign," "dollar sign," "dollar sign," etc.). In building this and a few other poems partly with icons, Hughes bridges poetry and the visual arts and departs from voice as a governing trope.[20]

Formally, although "Elderly Leaders" does not involve blank lines or designated subsections, it falls into three parts that gradually shift from an aural emphasis to a visual one. The first section is conventionally poetic; in fact, the poem's initial quatrain is highly dependent on sound as a structural element. It progresses in a variable triple meter (loosely dactylic), about four beats per line, rhymed ABAB. The poem as a whole indicts those venerable authorities who resist radical change, because such upheaval would threaten their personal prosperity. In this quatrain, Hughes

rhymes "over-wise" with "lies," equating informed seniority with decep-
tion, as if the two qualities are barely distinct or rarely divorced. The
three-syllable rhyme of "equation" and "evasion" drives home a related
point: the mathematics of wealth produces dishonesty.

The subsequent passage plays these sound qualities against a contrasting
visual design. The fifth, sixth, and seventh lines share the first quatrain's
tendency toward a dactylic meter (emphasis mine):

> *El*derly,
> *Fa*mous,
> *Ve*ry well paid.

This rhythmical pattern, in fact, encourages extra emphasis on the word
"very," highlighting the amount of money at stake. In other words, the
middle portion of the poem echoes the cadence of the first quatrain even
though it looks quite different. Its six short lines could be reassembled into
a couplet with the same triple meter, four-beat length, and full rhyme the
quatrain offers. By indenting and by breaking up long lines into shorter
ones, Hughes slows down this brief piece and provides additional emphasis
to elements of the description; he also dramatizes the tension between poetry's sound and its appearance on the page.

In the final portion of the poem, Hughes switches entirely to a visual
poetics. Shrinking rows of dollar signs culminate in a final ornament, suggesting a period but larger and centered on the line:

> $$$$$
> $$$$
> $$$
> $$
> $
> •

Interestingly, according to the undated typescripts preserved at the Beinecke, Hughes worked hard at perfecting the design of this section—only the
title and the rows of dollar signs alter from version to version (377.6381; the
first title is "Elderly Politicians").[21] In one typescript, Hughes constructs a
similar wedge shape, only much larger; it begins with twelve dollar signs,
whittled icon by icon over twelve lines to the final one. Hughes played with
this in pencil, shortening lines by scribbling over the last two dollar signs
in each one. He also sketched a symmetrical triangle like an inverted pyra-
mid on the page, as if planning a new layout for the next typescript. The

other two typescripts, however, repeat the wedge shape, one beginning with a line of ten dollar signs, the other matching the *Collected Poems* version. The magazine publications are different again: *Race* prints the poem with rows of nine, seven, five, three, and one dollar signs; *Unquote* prints only two rows, one of ten, the second of eight. The latter, however, was a particularly fleeting and amateur publication; one wonders whether the editorial choices really reflect Hughes's design ideas.[22]

Hughes's abundant concern with the shapeliness of the third part of this poem proves how central visual design is to the meaning of the piece. This stream of icons enacts how money silences a leader. Financial considerations can open a gap between a leader's words and his motives, until all utterances can be translated into economics, a precarious pile of dollars. The typographical symbols do not dwindle and come to nothing as much as they focus, finally and inevitably, on a simple point: the meaninglessness of political rhetoric when the speakers are beholden to wealth. More remotely, the wedge shape suggests how money, when inserted between leaders and the constituencies they purport to represent, creates an increasingly wide gulf between them.

Calling the poem "Elderly Race Leaders" might seem primarily an expedient gesture—Hughes originally published this in *Race* (1.2.87, Summer 1936) and just inserts the name of the magazine into one of his working titles (the other was "Elderly Politicians," a narrower indictment than "Leaders"). However, race was already embedded in this poem at an interesting juncture. The middle section of the poem alludes to Aesop's fable of the goose that laid the golden egg, an ancient indictment of greed as a common human flaw. Hughes alters a detail of the story. Whereas, in the original, a countryman discovers the golden egg under his own goose, in "Elderly Leaders" the egg comes from "their master's / goose." The word "master" is far more racially loaded than "boss" or "employer," too, and implies these leaders' continuing enslavement. The problem at hand is not merely wealth, but white wealth, which these leaders serve and covet. Hughes may or may not have known the histories claiming that Aesop was a real historical figure and a slave; in any case, slavery is a subtext of the poem, no matter the title.

Ain't You Heard?

One of the first readers of *Montage of a Dream Deferred*, Carl Van Vechten, responded to an early draft with particular delight about its visual structure. "Dear Langston, Last night I read Montage of a Dream Deferred with mounting excitement and interest. It is one of your best and offers magnificent opportunities to the typographer: I long to see it in print" (11 October 1948, cited in Bernard 255). Van Vechten's letter is particularly fascinating, since this long poem, or sequence of poems, is associated foremost with a setting and its distinctive music—postwar Harlem and be-bop. Readers agree that *Montage* is above all an evocation of sound, and yet Van Vechten's first specific compliment admires its graphic complexity.

This is not a misreading on Van Vechten's part. *Montage* innovates through both graphic and phonic elements. Hughes needs an array of visual strategies to convey the sounds of Harlem, certainly, but *Montage* does not simply use "doodle" to represent "babble." In fact, Hughes does not hierarchize these poetic elements, but tests the limits of both just as jazz musicians extend the boundaries of a song—for the revolutionary, intellectual, destructive, productive joy of it. *Montage of a Dream Deferred* explores a range of problems that complicate the lyric. These include not only the relationship between sound and script, but also the question of how a poem can express or construct a self, how a mass of printed words can seem haunted by its absent author. It engages poetic voice in its various senses simultaneously—as a term that designates tone, serves as a shorthand for originality, emphasizes the illusion of authorial presence, highlights the role of sound, and implies social power, particularly for writers who seek to represent a disenfranchised community through their work.

Later admirers of Hughes often note this book's preoccupation with voice. Onwuchekwa Jemie characterizes *Montage* as a sort of "ritual drama" in which "a community of voices is orchestrated from a multi-set or multi-level stage, the speakers meanwhile engaged in their normal chores or pleasures" (64). R. Baxter Miller comments more generally of Hughes's lyric poems that "in the display of the solo self, they reveal a concern for the choral one as well" (156). These scholars can ground their approach not only in Hughes's multi-voiced poems but in various essays in which Hughes locates his poetic material and mission in African American culture, and describes his duty to articulate racial injustice. Hokanson, discussing the "speakerly play of a variety of voices in a communal context," locates an "authorial or 'poetic' voice" in the long poem, noting that "the poet's voice is distinct from the multitude of other voices in the poem but not divorced from or condescending toward them" (72–75).

Although this tightly unified collection only uses the word "voice" once (32, 406), its vocabulary is dominated by references to music and speech. Some of the most common verbs in the book are variations on "say" and "hear," and *Montage* includes many different kinds of talk: banter, argument, pleading, warning, children's rhymes, echo, oratory, preaching, prayer, and the ubiquitous "comment on curb," as well as scat and references to song lyrics. *Montage* seeks to represent the diversity of postwar Harlem by including an array of speakers: rich and poor, male and female, native New Yorkers and displaced southerners articulating a range of dreams, fears, and pleasures.

The organizing perspective, which begins and ends the volume and comments at frequent intervals in between, traverses Harlem at ground level, uses its slang, and describes its diverse residents knowledgeably and sympathetically.[23] It is impossible, however, to separate this recurring character from the others with absolute clarity, and its most obvious interventions consist of hieroglyphic scat phrases, interrogatives, and imperatives. By shifting register, leaving character, and apostrophizing his audience, Hughes invites us to understand such moments in the poem as soundings of the poet's own voice.[24] Paradoxically, though, these strategies convey not only presence but a sense of authorial inaccessibility: Hughes both addresses his readers and simultaneously holds them at arm's length.

This omniscient perspective moves in and out of the sequence particularly with the recurring salutation: "Good morning, daddy! / Ain't you heard?" Although these moments sound at first like the poet's own voice, articulating Hughes's own controlling vision and warning about the potential consequences of endlessly deferred dreams, such passages pose a gender problem. Tracy asserts that "this address, along with 'Papa,' is common in the blues songs of females and in black culture in general, but the term of address would not be used by a male; 'Daddy-O' would be used, but not simply Daddy" (231). If Tracy is correct, these clearest moments of omniscient poetic voice cross gender lines and complicate the poet's place in the sequence.[25]

Although these ambiguities unsettle his role as spokesperson, Hughes's references to music in *Montage* reinforce his representative ambitions and the social function he envisioned for poetry. Certainly *Montage* invokes the sounds of postwar Harlem and puts its readers on alert about the sufferings of Harlem's inhabitants. However, as Gates observes, African American literature gives sound a complex role, privileging neither speaking nor writing but figuring each in terms of the other (40).[26] Striking visual elements, further, highlight the paradox of a written voice: all this poetic music, after all, exists chiefly in textual transcription.

References to the sense of sight begin in the title, which garnered negative attention from the very first reviews. The first readers of *Montage* judged the book sometimes as a failure and sometimes as a great accomplishment. Nonetheless, themes recur in their conflicting evaluations. Whether critics applaud or attack Hughes's strategies, many of them ally his long poem with "folk art" and all of them highlight the role of be-bop in structuring the verse.[27] A few of the reviews, collected in Tish Dace's valuable anthology, also single out the title for attention, calling it "somewhat high-flown" (*Opera and Concert* 384), or "an unfortunate selection" in this collection "for the people" (*Appeal for Peace and Unity* 398). These readers do not object to the phrase "a dream deferred," which takes up the issue of the working class struggle that readers expected from Hughes after his political poetry of the thirties and forties. Instead, reviewers were troubled by the word "montage," a term imported into English from French in 1929 to describe experimental editing techniques in film (OED), only sliding over later to describe mixtures in other media, including music. Neither reviewer remarks what is most odd about the name: its source lies not only in song but also in the visual medium of film.[28]

Montage, like "be-bop," creates a "diverse unity" out of fragments (Rampersad 151), so the governing tropes of film and jazz do overlap significantly. Hughes's prefatory note to the volume suggests these correspondences, while its emphasis on music has shaped response to the work ever since.

> In terms of current Afro-American popular music and the sources from which it has progressed—jazz, ragtime, swing, blues, boogie-woogie, and be-bop—this poem on contemporary Harlem, like be-bop, is marked by conflicting changes, sudden nuances, sharp and impudent interjections, broken rhythms, and passages sometimes in the manner of the jam session, sometimes the popular song, punctuated by riffs, runs, breaks, and disc-tortions of the music of a community in transition. (xi, 387)

Through this epigraph, Hughes prioritizes jazz as a structural inspiration and emphasizes place and race as his material. However, the title celebrates the experiments of be-bop by paralleling them to the discontinuities of experimental film. It also cues us to watch as well as listen to the poetry. This is especially true in the 1959 version, in which the subtitles and section breaks are removed and the poems play in a continuous reel.

Beyond the title, references to film are relatively scarce, occurring chiefly in the paired poems "Movie" and "Not a Movie," in which Hughes criticizes the falseness of Hollywood productions. However, other allusions to visual culture contribute significantly to Hughes's portrait of Harlem: parades, fashion, television, dreams, the cycles of nightlife and daylight, and most importantly, shades of racial color.[29] In addition to saying and hearing, Hughes's characters do a great deal of looking, in literal and metaphorical ways. Neighbors watch and judge each other, and the police place residents under surveillance. Allusions to writing—essays, letters, and signs—also emphasize *Montage*'s status as a visual creation.[30]

Further, in both the 1951 and the 1959 versions of *Montage*, typography contributes significantly to meaning. Hughes arranges the poems to follow each other closely on the page, emphasizing connection rather than separateness, and makes liberal use of italics, capitals, and indented margins to signal shifting perspectives and registers. In the remainder of this chapter, I examine two poems from this sequence that manipulate graphic and phonic elements: "Neon Signs" and "Dream Boogie."

The most arresting example of visual experiment is the list poem "Neon Signs" (17, 397). Immediately following "Not a Movie" in both printings of *Montage*, this piece enacts a tour of Harlem jazz clubs from an insider's point of view.[31] Hughes places each club's name on its own line, using capitals to mimic the visual loudness of the glowing advertisements. Brief interjections describe the venues of jazz, first as a site of religious experience ("altar of Thelonius"), then as democratic meeting grounds for different classes, and finally in an ecstatic way that suggests intoxication and transformation. The rearranged ellipses Hughes inserts between the names of each capitalized sign might represent elapsed time, the flashing of the neon signs, or even the interval of travel between nightspots for the club-hopper.

The James Weldon Johnson collection at the Beinecke holds early drafts of this poem that vividly illustrate how Hughes transforms a catalog into a vivid visual poem. The first typescript (according to Hughes's pencil notation) adheres to the left hand margin (Langston Hughes Papers 316.5155). While it consists of sentence fragments, it does use punctuation in conventional ways.

> The Wonder Bar,
> The Wishing Well,
> The Wonterey,
> Minton's Altar of Thelonius,
> The mandalay:
> Spots where the booted
> and unbooted play.
>
> Lenox,
> Seventh,
> Eighth,
> Uptown, and down,
> Laced, unlaced,

> Hip, unhip,
>
> Mirror-go-round
>
> Broken glasses
> Smear bop
> Sound.

Some words are crossed out or added in pencil in Hughes's handwriting: "St. Nich" for "Seventh," "In the early bright" added after "Broken glasses," "be-" before "bop." Subsequent versions of "Neon Signs" remain true to this original concept of the poem as a lean list of places, a verbal tour of Harlem's nightclubs ending in an indistinct "smear" of sound.

By the third typescript, Hughes incorporates capital letters and drops the punctuation, crossing out a period that he had typed after the seventh line ("and unbooted play"). He also tries an exclamation point on its own line at the end of the piece—the same strategy he had used in "The Cat and the Saxophone (2 a.m.)" many years earlier.

> The WONDER BAR
> The WISHING WELL
> The MONTEREY
> minton's ALTAR OF THELONIUS
> The MANDALAY
> Spots where the booted
> and unbooted play
> The LENOX
> ST. NICH
> BLUE HEAVEN
> Mirror-go-round
> A broken glass
> in the early bright
> smears a re-bop
> sound
> !

Additional pencil marks delete many of the articles. In this version Hughes is stripping down the poem, reducing its adherence to the rules of grammar and punctuation, and establishing rhythm solely through lineation. Capital letters also prioritize the blazing place-names and deemphasize their human witnesses.

A typescript of *Montage* marked "2nd drafts corrected September 26th, 1948" uses spacing, margins, capital letters, and underlining/italics in a way that more closely resembles the appearance of the published version (5156). In this version, Hughes has typed the poems continuously rather than on separate sheets, and a scratched-out subtitle reveals "Five Movements" structuring the contents. On page 14, Hughes revises "Neon Signs," continuing to place the article "the" before each club name. He also adds asterisks between the list items in red pencil. These asterisks appear in the fair copy he sends to Van Vechten at the end of the month.

Further changes happen in 1949 and 1950, when Hughes prepares the manuscript for Holt. These later versions begin centering the club names, although the uncapitalized explanatory text remains flush left, as it is in the 1951 book. The transformation of Hughes's asterisks into little pyramids of three plain points, however, happened at the instigation of the typesetter, Bill Raney. On the setting typescript, a note appears in pink pencil in Raney's handwriting, next to a drawing of three points in a triangle: "perhaps not an asterisk but a similar ornament than can be set thus" (5164). Hughes appears to reply, asking for "alternative sample signs," and then "OK"ing the result. While all these drafts indicate much testing and revision of the poem's sound and appearance, Raney clearly played a significant role in the appearance of its original book publication—as typesetters often do, although uncredited.

Hughes rearranges the poem slightly in 1959 in ways that shift its meaning. He changes the content slightly by substituting the names of two clubs and adding the word "ancient" to "altar." The graphic alterations, however, are more striking. Hughes centers the poem so that the repeating frames resemble a strip of film. The pyramids of periods that separate the club names become diamonds. They also appear this way in the 1958 setting copy from Knopf, with a note in red pencil at bottom right corner: "Note to Editor: Please center all lines. Set to get effect of bar signs. L.H." (5512). With this four-pointed shape, Hughes has almost effaced the ellipses that originally divided lines in the poem.[32] In revision, the visual beauty of the poem has assumed primacy.

Interestingly, "Neon Signs" conjures a set of sensory experiences without projecting character: this extremely spare poem barely evokes a situation and refuses to construct a controlling speaker. Hughes focuses our attention instead on the blending of visual and aural experience climaxing in an instance of synesthesia, sound and vision blended:

> where a broken glass
> in the early bright
> smears re-bop
> sound

The verb "smear" is especially crucial, since it evokes both jazz techniques and the visual mess of the morning after a long night of carousing. This optic display of a poem also, surprisingly, ends with perfect rhyme, a strong aural signal of closure. By so nearly eliminating stock elements of the lyric, such as speaker, situation, and the process of thought or feeling that poems often strive to convey, Hughes has pared the genre right down to babble and doodle, sound and vision.

The graphic elements of "Neon Signs" might suggest a score for oral performance—cuing different speeds, pitches, and volumes. However, whether or not Langston Hughes performed "Neon Signs," no recording seems to survive. Hughes did record some poems from *Montage* at the Library of Congress in 1959, including the very first poem in all drafts and both book versions: "Dream Boogie" (3, 388). Comparing that performance with the poem's textual version (the 1951 and 1959 printings are identical here) emphasizes the substantial gap between voice on the page and voice on the stage.

"Dream Boogie," in print, delivers promptly on the claims of the volume's epigraph: it is "marked by conflicting changes . . . impudent interjections, broken rhythms." Although the first lines set up a knowledgeable speaker admonishing an ignorant addressee to listen carefully, the italicized interjections seem to represent not another voice, but instead the original speaker's reply to interruptions the reader cannot see or hear. In other words, the speaker incorporates the alternate point of view, articulating it first through rebuttal and then through apparent acquiescence. "Sure, / I'm happy!" might signal sarcastic resignation (since you can't understand, I'll just play along), confusion, or even amnesia. Conflicting opinions about Harlem, marked through shifts in margins and typeface, coalesce finally in a sequence of scat phrases that resists interpretation.

This ambiguity is crucial to Hughes's implicit argument about Harlem's speech and music. According to "Dream Boogie," the vocal and instrumental sounds of Harlem both express the frustration of its residents and conceal it, or deflect attention away from it. Anita Patterson suggests that "Dream Boogie" critiques European-American jazz fans who don't understand that the music is about racial struggle (680).[33] Harryette Mullen's point about African spirit-writing—that, influenced by Kongo religious practice, African Americans have used writing for "ritual protection" and "to enclose and confine evil presences" (625)—also sheds light on the scat deflections. These mystifying transcriptions shelter the artist's social or political dissent from hostile readers.[34]

Scat, however, wasn't part of the original draft (316.5155). Even the very first "Notes & Drafts" dated "September 1–10, 1948" begin with a fragment of "Dream Boogie." The potent question, perhaps rhetorical, of "Ain't you heard?" was originally a statement, "I know you've heard." This draft also contains stanzas that were later dispersed into other poems. The phrase "the tingle of a tear" in "Lady's Boogie" (412), for example, was first in "Dream Boogie" as "the tinkle of a tear" or "the rhinestone of a tear." Likewise, another early description was also moved:

> Tinkling treble
> and rolling bass
> maraca teeth
> In a baseball face.

This became the opening of "Dream Boogie: Variation":

> Tinkling treble,
> Rolling bass,
> High noon teeth
> In a midnight face . . .
>
> (425)

"Dream Boogie" did evolve quickly, however; the next typescript contains scat words, with "yeah!" handwritten at the end of the poem.

The complexity of this poem's voice is much more prominent typographically than in the recorded version of "Dream Boogie."[35] While the printed poem conveys an urgent warning, in performance Hughes sounds "Dream Boogie" with a lightness and coolness that defuses this energy. His accent, as always, owes much more to the Midwest than to the New York or Southern speech patterns his poems typically represent. Nor does he vocally create two speakers, to the limited extent that this is possible, or otherwise sound the switch to italic type. While audience may be a relevant factor here (perhaps Hughes read differently at the Library of Congress than he did for predominantly black crowds), the audiotext is less forceful and less shifty than the print version of the poem. Hughes's elongations of long "e" sounds in "dream" and "beat" conjure rhythm's enchantments, whereas, in a different sounding of the same printed text, stresses on "happy" and "something" could have conveyed anger and disbelief. This recording of "Dream Boogie" even ends with the satisfying closure of full rhyme, not visible until Hughes pronounces "Y-e-a-h!" to rhyme with "away." Complexity of printed voice yields, in recording, to lyric smoothness.

The 1959 performance illustrates a gap between voice on the page and Hughes's own genial public persona. Certainly, Hughes reminds us that the poetic self is an artful construction. His deliberate estranging of the lyric genre from personal expression, here and elsewhere, is deeply significant to Hughes's canon and to modernism generally. Secondly, the contrast confirms what Charles Bernstein argues in *Close Listening*, that "performances constitute and reconstitute the work" (8) and that poems have "a fundamentally plural existence" (9). The recorded "Dream Boogie" is in some real ways different than the printed "Dream Boogie." Prioritizing one over the other has large implications for the interpretation of *Montage* and Hughes's work as a whole. Visual elements create complexity and ambiguity that Hughes chooses not to perform, at least in one context. Between composing *Montage of a Dream Deferred* in 1948 and revising and performing it a decade later, Hughes was subpoenaed by Senator Joseph McCarthy. The literary and political climate shifted. It had always been crucial, perhaps, for Hughes to speak to different audiences in different "voices," but such strategies assumed new urgency in the fifties.

The evocations of jazz and Harlem slang in *Montage* extend Hughes's career-long preoccupation with African American life and art. However, throughout this volume Hughes also exploits poetry's graphic possibilities in order to suggest a conflicting array of tones and perspectives. His visual arrangements do not script vocal performance, or at least not primarily. Instead, they underscore the dual identity of the twentieth-century lyric: rooted in sound but speaking to the eye just as powerfully. In invoking and challenging the trope of voice that is so central to African American poetry and the post-Romantic lyric generally, Hughes both speaks to the mainstream and inscribes himself into innovative poetics.

LYRIC COLLABORATIONS

JAMES MERRILL, DAVID JACKSON, DENISE DUHAMEL, AND MAUREEN SEATON

> The work we produce separately is different in content and tone from the work we do together. The work we do together has a different voice.
> —Leonardi and Pope, "Screaming Divas"

> No voice is as individual as the poet would like to think.
> —James Merrill, *Recitative*

> Collaboration can be addictive—it's squared pleasure, after all. I think some are afraid it will consume the individual voice. I say it's worth the risk.
> —Maureen Seaton, "The Singular and Plural of *Poet*"

In its March and May issues of 2001, *Publications of the Modern Language Association* devoted its "Theories and Methodologies" sections to an array of articles concerning collaboration. The *PMLA* feature is not the first attempt to inaugurate collaboration studies as a field, given that books on literary collaboration began appearing in the late 1980s. *Tulsa Studies in Women's Literature* ran a two-issue symposium on collaboration in 1994 and 1995, and the subject has had a lively history in composition theory.[1] The *PMLA* issues offer a good starting point, however, because they are recent and because the editors recruited work from several of the most prominent theorists and literary critics specializing in this area. The

PMLA's coverage may signal, too, that attention to literary collaboration is entering the professional mainstream.

Within this feature, M. Thomas Inge begins his essay, "Collaboration and Concepts of Authorship," with the observation:

> It is commonplace now to understand that all texts produced by authors are not the product of individual creators. Rather, they are the result of any number of discourses that take place among the writer, the political and social environments in which the writing occurs, the aesthetic and economic pressures that encourage the process, the psychological and emotional state of the writer, and the reader who is expected to receive or consume the end product when it reaches print. Even if not intended for an audience or the publishing marketplace, a piece of writing cannot escape the influences that produce it. (623)

The writers collected in this symposium, however, agree that despite such commonplaces, English as a discipline has lagged in accepting the full implications of dispersed authorship. Title pages rarely acknowledge major collaborators or influential editors; cataloguers struggle with dual signatures; an author's reputation slips at signs of "compromise with the pragmatic and economic forces of time and place" (Inge 630). Further, the attribution of literary texts is not the only author-problem for the humanities. Jointly signed criticism may also meet suspicion from readers, editors, and tenure and promotion committees, no matter how common such endeavor remains in other fields. Academic credentials, as Susan J. Leonardi and Rebecca A. Pope describe, depend on the fiction of "original" research ("(Co)Labored Li(v)es" 631); Lisa Ede and Andrea A. Lunsford address at greater length how academic institutions militate against collaboration ("Collaboration" 356–59). Clearly, collaboration permeates literary study in several ways that trouble English as an academic field. As Holly Laird puts it in her overview of these issues, "If creative collaboration lies behind not just plays and films but novels, poems, and autobiographies, we need a general adjustment of attitudes to make it visible" ("'A Hand Spills'" 346).

Collaborative writing is a fundamental skill for many professions, despite its low status in humanities research and composition classrooms. It is also a crucial element of many artistic endeavors, particularly in film and the performing arts, whether or not a star playwright, screenwriter, or auteur receives top billing. Many of the conventions associated with lyric poetry and poetry criticism, however, offer special resistance to collaborative studies. That is, in all of a poem's potential life stages—composition, revision, publication, critical reception, influence—the contributions of other discourses, as well as those of other human beings, tend to be subordinated to the idea of "original expression." This chapter addresses these problems by examining collaboration and its implications for poetic voice through a generic lens. An unrelated pair of poetic sequences serve as examples: "The Book of Ephraim" by James Merrill and *Oyl* by Denise Duhamel and Maureen Seaton.[2] *Oyl* is cosigned, but "The Book of Ephraim" is not. My very selections set in motion an important question that every book or essay on collaboration must address: What constitutes collaborative writing?

While Holly Laird's *PMLA* essay chiefly focuses on "literary, print-culture coauthorship" (346), a limited area of study, Laird also surveys the "broad and shape-shifting" nature of literary collaboration: "*Collaboration* ranges in meaning from any work in which more than one person has a hand (which makes it a huge academic topic) to full or overt coauthorship (which makes it considerably smaller)" ("'A Hand Spills'" 345). Some theorists of literary collaboration argue that writing is inherently collaborative, extending the definition to editorial relationships, mentoring, influence, inspiration, allusion, quotation, and other situations and strategies.[3] Works of literature tend to be haunted by multiple voices even when authorship is not in question. Nevertheless, despite the familiarity of multi-authored textbooks, scientific articles, and pop songs, regardless of the ubiquity of ghostwriting in celebrity memoirs and other successful genres, cosigned literary works are published relatively rarely in the United States. When they are, critics and readers often respond by attempting to "de-collaborate" them, to use Lorraine York's term (7): that is, they anxiously seek to identify the contributions of particular collaborators, or even to identify the real artist in the attributed pair or group.

Oyl, a chapbook issued in 2000 by Pearl Editions, fits the strictest definitions of collaborative writing. It is the product of extended collaboration by Denise Duhamel and Maureen Seaton, poets who also maintain independent careers of some distinction (I follow their consistent practice of crediting their coauthored works in alphabetical order). In this case, Duhamel and Seaton focus on a cartoon character, Olive Oyl, whose legend has been shaped by many artists in many media; their collection concerns collaboration in a deliberate way and speaks to the permeability of identity's borders. *Oyl*, further, joins a particularly important tradition within coauthorship, the feminist collaboration.[4] In Ede and Lunsford's terms, Duhamel and Seaton collaborate in a "dialogic" rather than a "hierarchical" mode (*Singular Texts / Plural Authors* 67, 133–36). Hierarchical collaboration tends to be "rigidly structured, driven by highly specific goals, and carried out by people playing clearly defined and delimited roles," and led by a senior member of the writing group or someone hierarchically superior to it (133). Hierarchical collaborative writing is widespread in business and the professions. Alternately, the dialogic mode is characterized by a loose structure, fluid roles, and an emphasis on process (133). Duhamel and Seaton often do set clear roles for composition—each person adding lines, for instance, in a prescribed order—but their work strongly emphasizes creation and exploration rather than the recovery of information, the resolution of problems, or seamless final products. For these contemporary women poets, a cooperative writing process is generative and liberating.

While *Oyl* is an overtly coauthored text, "The Book of Ephraim" occupies a firm position as the apparent opposite of such processes: a testament to individual mastery and evidence of James Merrill's singular genius. In fact, it constitutes the first third of a large and complex trilogy, *The Changing Light at Sandover*, which more than any other work proves Merrill's gifts and defines his legacy. I include it here not to overthrow standard editorial and scholarly practices concerning Merrill, much less to undermine Merrill's reputation. In fact, challenges to conventional notions of authorship within "The Book of Ephraim" amplify its substantial fascination and are fundamentally irresolvable. I do intend, however, to build on remarks by many of Merrill's best readers and highlight "Ephraim'"'s collaborative aspects. As Laird puts it, "Instead of dissecting the relationships behind the writing, this study reads coauthored texts as the realization of relationships" (*Women Coauthors* 5). Parsing the exact roles of this work's various contributors would be impossible. However, reading "Ephraim" as the "realization of relationships"—historical, literary, spiritual, and social—enriches and illuminates the work.

"Ephraim" draws on many sources through quotation, allusion, influence, and other modes of intertextuality; the published text is haunted by other versions of the manuscript and projects multiplicity through many avenues. Also, crucially, "Ephraim," like the rest of *Sandover*, is based on coauthored transcripts of Ouija-board sessions Merrill held with his lover and companion, writer David Jackson. Jackson's role in the séances, and in the poem itself, emerges through intermittent references to "David" and "DJ" as characters, as well as through first-person plural pronouns. While not itself a cosigned publication, this poetic sequence is obsessed with the boundaries of authorship. "Ephraim," like *Oyl*, implicitly argues for a conception of poetic voice as intrinsically collaborative and an understanding of identity as fluid.

Once the boundaries of authorship are breached, of course, other dams are bound to burst. In *Writing Double*, Bette London refers to a frequent, sexually charged question often leveled at collaborators: "Which hand held the pen?" (25–26). As London observes, the underlying question is a reductive and hostile one, assuming that collaborative writing is an oxymoron: Who *really* wrote this text? *Oyl* and "The Book of Ephraim" result from different collaborative models, and each suggests a different answer to this simplifying inquiry. Even the technologies involved defy the question. Duhamel and Seaton sometimes compose in each other's physical company, but when e-mails and faxes are also involved, or when one poet speaks a new line or two into the other poet's telephone answering machine, how does one identify the "writer" of any particular textual fragment? "The Book of Ephraim" likewise relies on a technology that obfuscates authorship, the Ouija board. As London observes in relation to other spiritualist collaborative texts, mediumistic practices suggest that the "author" is really a transmitter of messages from the dead or from divine sources, and transcription may regularly be delegated to another party.

Sexuality, too, is very much an issue in these collaborations. Both *Oyl* and "Ephraim" spring from and, to varying degrees, depict a relationship between two people. However, the parameters of each partnership—Duhamel and Seaton, Merrill and Jackson—are utterly different. Paradoxically, of the two texts, the hidden collaboration openly describes romantic partnership, and the overt case of coauthorship circumnavigates sexual questions.

Merrill's relationship with Jackson is not only literary and spiritual but also sexual: "The Book of Ephraim" makes their erotic bond quite clear. Its twenty-six poems, untitled and organized alphabetically by their first letters, are often set in Merrill and Jackson's shared homes in Connecticut and Greece (Jackson was wealthy and Merrill spectacularly so, and they therefore enjoyed unusual leisure and mobility). The complexities of their work suggest both dialogic and hierarchical modes of writing together: the Ouija sessions fully involved both writers, but Merrill controlled their transformation into literature.[5] Their writing relationship both resembles and diverges from what London calls a "dominant model of spousal collaboration" (20) in which the female partner receives little or no credit for her hand in the work.[6] Although stereotypical gender roles do not apply here and Merrill and Jackson could not legally marry—their unsanctioned relationship, in all its intensity and ambiguity, is widely recognized as one of *Sandover*'s most compelling subjects—"Ephraim" clearly emerges from one version of this spousal model.[7] As Alison Lurie alleges in her memoir of Jackson and Merrill, the séances sustained their romantic partnership but also reinforced the growing disparity between their creative statures: Jackson, an unsuccessful novelist, created much of *Sandover*'s material yet receives no byline (135–36). Jackson, in fact, played the traditionally feminine role of medium in his séances with Merrill, while his increasingly famous partner held the pencil.

In *Double Talk*, Wayne Koestenbaum emphasizes how collaborative writing challenges "sexual propriety" rather than its assault on "our dogmas of literary property" (9); in his psychoanalytic approach, desire and shame motivate and shape male coauthorship.[8] London likewise observes that women writing in pairs earned reputations that hovered between "the faintly scandalous and the quaintly domestic" (5). Duhamel and Seaton, in fact, capitalize to some extent on this "prurient response—a desire to make collaboration rend up its bodily secrets" (London 26). In many comments about their own coauthorship, Duhamel and Seaton describe their friendship and the mechanics of their joint writing process, but never address the real or metaphorical eros of collaboration. Allusions to Duhamel's husband, poet Nick Carbó, would seem to defuse that potential tension, but their coauthored poems set it burning again and again. Duhamel and Seaton articulate an array of desires, teasing out the relationship between literary and sexual transgression. Their Olive Oyl, for instance, is stereotypically butch and finally abandons her tempestuous affair with Popeye in favor of lesbian love. Duhamel and Seaton link this change in Olive Oyl's sex life to her literary aspirations, as if bodily and textual pleasure are interdependent.

Both "Ephraim" and *Oyl* revolve around a dyad, the most common model of coauthorship. However, both works challenge the centrality of dyads as well, particularly the normative heterosexual couple. This challenge occurs in the content of the poems. Olive Oyl and Ephraim are flirtatious, even promiscuous, and the poetic representatives of Merrill and Jackson in "The Book of Ephraim" have real affairs as well as spiritual dalliances. All of these poets, further, use sexual experimentation to suggest the permeability of their own literary authority and their unusual processes of composition. In each case, the central pair of writers stands in for a multitude of potential contributors, alive and otherwise.[9] Discussions below indicate some of the ways editors, allusion, and apparently mystical forces have helped shape these works.

This multiplicity contrasts sharply with the conventions of poetic authority. Of all contemporary literary genres, lyric poetry would seem to present the most resistance to a collaborative writing process, or to readings that emphasize the array of voices speaking through single texts. Western high culture traditions differ in this way from other modes. African and Asian poetry often depends on shared authorship, as in the well-known Japanese renku. Whereas oral traditions all over the globe present alternate models of composition and publication, the conventions of the Anglo-American lyric strongly emphasize privacy.[10] Copyright law, established around the Romantic period, economically reinforces the central illusion of the Romantic and post-Romantic lyric: that is, a poem emanates from a single speaker freshly expressing a process of thought or feeling. The idea of voice is paramount in this definition, suggesting that a poem is a unique production analogous to the singular sound of a poet's speaking body. Various formulations of the lyric as a genre emphasize not only the expression of a coherent self but also the relative privacy of the lyric "utterance." For example, although he is discussing objects in print culture, John Stuart Mill describes poems as "overheard" (270). What does a reader "hear," then, when a lyric poem is cosigned, or when scholars discover within it substantial contributions from other parties?

These questions hinge on contemporary understandings of authorship, the "myth of solitary genius," as Jack Stillinger puts it. Recent studies by Linda Karell, Lorraine York, and others recapitulate the history of authorship better than I can in this space, but in brief, feminist criticism, post-structuralism, and textual criticism have reshaped and continue to interrogate the term "author." While human writers persistently muddle along in specific times and places, scratching on pads or dictating to voice-recognition software, "author" has become theoretical shorthand for a function, a social construct, a "repository of meanings" (Karell 4). Authorship, in other words, constitutes a powerful idea for many constituencies, from publishing corporations down to individual consumers, and its myths bear only tenuous, accidental connections to the actual practice of writing. Poetry poses a particularly intense challenge for contemporary criticism, because it depends very closely on the identity of the poet; for instance, while booksellers and college courses systematically differentiate prose fiction and non-fiction, no one categorizes poems this way. Presumably, poems are all true, or false, or beside the point. Certainly, most bookstores carry so little poetry that their offerings don't require subdivision.

None of the books on literary, print-culture collaboration are genre studies. Monographs by Stillinger, Koestenbaum, Karell, London, Laird, and York treat nineteenth- and twentieth-century works of multiple literary kinds, and whereas most include poetry, none focuses chiefly upon the lyric.[11] York, however, does divide her chapters generically, and the section on collaborative poetry offers a helpful start with respect to the most relevant questions. Her overall argument that "collaborators are relentlessly haunted by the question of property" resonates with the "ethos of privacy" developed in the Romantic and post-Romantic lyric (7, 119).[12] Oren Izenberg's "Language Poetry and Collective Life" examines the idea of collaboration as one contemporary movement defines it, but Izenberg ignores many pertinent intellectual and artistic conversations. Most noticeably, he does not cite theorists of collaborative writing outside of Language Poetry's own poet-scholars.

This chapter, therefore, brings insights from recent studies of literary collaboration to the theories of voice discussed in chapter 1. For instance, Sharon Cameron set this entire project seething in my imagination years ago when I read her arguments about Emily Dickinson's "choral voice" (207). Choral voice, or poetic language that joins different voices into resonant unison, is not necessarily the same as collaborative writing. However, the relationship between the texture of multivoiced poetry and the complicated conditions of poetic production anchors my work.

Despite the differences between "The Book of Ephraim" and *Oyl*, these sequences share three central and definitive traits. First, they both focus on the meanings of poetic voice—its resonances and its boundaries. Second, they both implicitly argue for poetry as a site of conversation or, perhaps, negotiation. For Duhamel, Seaton, Merrill, and their uncredited collaborators, lyric poetry is a social genre. Finally, and most peculiarly, all of these writers express a mystical sense of poetry's origins. Poetry must be shaped by human procedures but it remains uncanny, haunted by traces of the supernatural.

"A Vast Chamber Full of Voices": James Merrill, David Jackson, and "The Book of Ephraim"

"No voice is as individual as the poet would like to think," James Merrill observed in 1981 to J. D. McClatchy (*Recitative* 80). In this interview, Merrill discusses his love for "multiple meanings" and "contrasts and disruptions of tone" (79), hazarding that as the role of meter diminishes in American poetry, what must replace it "would have to be diction or 'voice.' Voice in its fullest tonal range—not just bel canto or passionate speech" (80). In this interview and others, Merrill uses the term voice to designate the cumulative effects of diction, rhythm, and a wide range of other aural qualities—what a poem sounds like and how those sounds convey meaning, even personality.[13] To Donald Sheehan, for instance, Merrill argues that "'voice' is the democratic word for 'tone'" and observes, "I notice voice a good deal more in metrical poetry" (*Recitative* 26).[14] Despite this emphasis on sound, however, Merrill goes on to disassociate voice from the poet's speaking body by questioning poetry's sources. He provocatively comments to his poet-interlocutor that diction and formal choices, with all their inherited associations, have a way of "breed[ing] echoes. There's always a lurking air of pastiche which, consciously or unconsciously, gets into your diction. That doesn't much bother me, does it you?" (80).

Merrill's remarks suggest the various possible meanings of voice as a literary term as well as illuminating the complex status of voice in his own work. Voice can mean tone or attitude, a function of vocabulary and stylistic choices. Along the way, the metaphor of voice conjures an illusion of authorial presence, as if every inward sounding of a printed poem constitutes a séance. Voice insists on the poem, too, as an auditory as well as a visual creation, playing upon the traditional meaning of lyric as song. Merrill's poetry, especially in "The Book of Ephraim," manipulates these implications of the term voice in several ways. Merrill's formal verse depends on sound, yet the poems themselves also emphasize their own status as written texts, troping constantly on visual signs, shapes, and symbols. His works alternately invoke and question the illusion of authorial presence. Finally, and most importantly for this chapter, Merrill also challenges voice's connotation of originality, its invocation of the "myth of solitary genius." The singleness of poetic voice, he advises, is wishful thinking. Instead, voices echo, allude, combine, and not just in genre-challenging experiments like *The Changing Light at Sandover.* Breezily, Merrill identifies lyric voice as intrinsically collaborative.[15]

"The Book of Ephraim" plays with many of voice's possible meanings; I focus particularly on Merrill's construction of a collaborative voice and its implicit challenge to the qualities of originality and coherence traditionally associated with the poetic speaker.[16] This lyric sequence both foregrounds its collaborative roots and, paradoxically, testifies to Merrill's own poetic authority, certifying his formal mastery and the uniqueness of his vision. Contact with another world, particularly in one scene of possession, dramatically challenges the integrity of Merrill's poetic self; Merrill uses this conflict to demonstrate the intrinsically "choral" qualities of lyric voice (Cameron 207). This example shows the continuing relevance of voice as a term for poetic analysis, despite its current marginality to scholarly conversation, because its very ambiguity crucially insists on the lyric poem as haunted ground. My discussion of "The Book of Ephraim" begins by describing the collaborative aspects of the sequence, and then investigates the intersection of voice and genre, concluding with readings of sections R and H as lyric poems meditating on the status and nature of poetic voice.

Merrill both provides an illusion of intimacy through voice and simultaneously exposes the lyric speaker as a construction. Perhaps these are contradictory endeavors on Merrill's part, but the tension between them is one of the most interesting features of a consummately interesting work. "The Book of Ephraim" and its uncanny subject matter demonstrate why attention to voice remains a valuable approach to poetry. The term's excess of meaning mirrors the printed lyric's defining effect, that an arrangement of words alone can conjure up a timbre, a body, a presence.

The twenty-six poems of the sequence called "The Book of Ephraim," which originally appeared as a self-contained series within Merrill's 1976 collection *Divine Comedies*, is just the first part of Merrill's imposing poetic trilogy, *The Changing Light at Sandover*. "Ephraim" suits my concerns for several reasons. First, *Voicing American Poetry* is focused on the idea of voice in the lyric poem, and only the first section of *Sandover* can reasonably be called a lyric sequence; I take up the genre question in more detail below. Second, "Ephraim" represents a hinge, a turning point, between Merrill's early and late style and preoccupations, and because it reflects artistic crisis, it concerns the nature, origin, and audiences of poetry. One reason for its different voice, in fact, to echo this chapter's epigraph from Leonardi and Pope, may be its collaborative origins. "Ephraim'"s material was generated in a very different way than Merrill worked when writing "'all by myself'" (*Recitative* 49). Based on séances, "Ephraim" inevitably raises hard questions about life and the afterlife, what role art might play in both, how consciousness functions, and how communication occurs between human beings, or between human beings and others. As Brian McHale puts it, *Sandover* begins with epistemological concerns in "Ephraim" and moves into an ontological mode as the series progresses; in fact, ontological speculations permeate *Sandover* from its very inception (4).

This abecedarian sequence chronicles a supernatural conversation many years long between Merrill, his lover and fellow medium David Jackson, and an array of spirits they contact via a homemade Ouija board. During each session, Jackson would place his right hand and Merrill would place his left on a teacup, which they used in lieu of the planchette packaged with commercial Ouija boards. This pointer would whiz rapidly around the board, selecting letters with its handle. Merrill transcribed these onto paper with his right hand. Strings of capital letters coalesced into messages that Merrill and Jackson attributed to spirits whom they learned to call by name (Ephraim, for instance, is the control spirit during the earlier séances). These conversations ranged widely and wittily over the relation of the mortal world to the afterlife, as one might expect, but also involve gossip, flirtation, complicated discussions of art and inspiration, and dire warnings about the soul-destroying side effects of radiation. While the later parts of *Sandover* consist of dense passages of capital letter dictation from the other world, "The Book of Ephraim" quotes more sparingly from these sources, at least partly because the original transcripts were lost and Merrill must cite from highlights copied into a notebook. Perhaps because

Merrill was less sure of his audience and less invested in the project at this earlier stage, "The Book of Ephraim" also expresses more frequent doubts than the rest of the book about the source of these communications and the validity of their revelations. It is the most conventionally literary portion of the longer work (although it is deeply strange), and attracted wider admiration than the book's later installments.

"Ephraim" trains its attention upon the ambiguities surrounding identity and originality. In "Ephraim," Merrill presents and enacts a social conception of poetry—modeled on elite literary salons rather than a potentially democratic marketplace, but still representing a gathering of voices. Further, "The Book of Ephraim," like the other two sequences and the coda comprising *The Changing Light at Sandover*, is itself a result of collaboration. No part of this sprawling work is officially coauthored: *Sandover* quotes David Jackson and others liberally, crediting them with influential ideas and actions as well as actual words, but only Merrill's name appears on the title page. Nor does the growing body of excellent scholarship and criticism concerning Merrill challenge the solo attribution of his work. Stephen Yenser, Jeffrey Donaldson, Helen Sword, Mark Bauer, Robert Polito, Richard Sáez, Timothy Materer, and other Merrill critics do observe the intertextuality of his trilogy, or of parts of it. That is, they examine how other texts not only influence or inspire but permeate the language, structure, and content of *Sandover*. Merrill criticism also widely acknowledges David Jackson's substantial role in the séances, but very few books and essays leap from this observation to the puzzle of authorship. That is, who wrote "The Book of Ephraim," and does the answer matter?

Several problems arise when considering "Ephraim" or *Sandover* as the product of two writers rather than as a singly authored text. First, Jackson had opportunities to claim coauthorship and never did. Lehman and Berger recruited a piece by Jackson for their anthology of Merrill criticism; in "Lending a Hand," Jackson emphasizes Merrill's transformations of rough and copious source material into a poem that "astonished" Jackson (299). "I'm flattered to think I lent a hand," Jackson adds, "the second hand, to JM's hours of labor" (305). Here Jackson puns not only on timepieces but on his Ouija-session identity of the "hand" or medium to Merrill's "scribe." McClatchy's interview with Jackson for *Shenandoah* in the late seventies is still more illuminating. McClatchy asks probing questions about the sources of *Sandover*, and Jackson describes significant ambivalence about the sessions, especially the strict "lessons" that succeeded years of more playful table-talk. His anecdotes of their first sessions reveal how vital Jackson's participation was to the enterprise (25), and he speculates about how his own temperament and talent must have influenced the

communications (38). However, he conveys clearly that *Sandover* is ultimately Merrill's work. "I get star role in his film," he jokes, but "that David
Jackson is very much JM's creation" (39).[17] Also, while he admits to discussing the raw transcripts at length with Merrill, he attributes their interpretation as well as their poetic transformation to Merrill, and expresses
a sort of cheerful humility about his role in the project. "Mine was a purely
mechanical part to play," he concludes, and comments, "It's not bad being
a footnote in literary history" (41).

Jackson is not merely modest, generous, or loyal, though the latter words
seem to suit his temperament. Jackson, in fact, knew from personal experience how full literary collaboration works. Jackson published short fiction
(one story appears in the O. Henry collection of 1962) and wrote several
novels that never achieved publication. According to Lurie, a comrade in
those years of struggle, Jackson came frustratingly close to real success
(45–46). Further, he tells McClatchy that he tried "several times" to write a
collaborative novel: "Once, I think Larry Rivers and I were going to do a
novel together, each of us write a chapter. I did it again with another friend
of mine, Bob Grimes; we did it paragraph by paragraph" (42). The latter
artistic process is quite different than the production of *Sandover*. Jackson's
comments to McClatchy probably underplay his contributions to *Sandover*,
but do not radically mischaracterize them; he deserves more credit for the
work than he generally receives, but he is not an equal coauthor.

The 2001 publication of *Familiar Spirits: A Memoir of James Merrill and
David Jackson* by Lurie highlights the problem of attribution in *Sandover*.[18]
She argues that Jackson, overshadowed by Merrill's increasing renown,

> was in an essential sense the co-author of *Sandover*, so much of which flowed
> through his hand, and none of which could have been written without him.
> One sign of this was that the messages from the spirits, like David's own
> writing, were in prose rather than poetry. If you believe, as I do, that his
> subconscious mainly guided the cup, more than half of the text of *Mirabell*,
> *Scripts*, and *Coda* was originally composed by him, and only later reshaped by
> Jimmy. (106–7)

She goes on to wonder if Merrill might have been trying to assist Jackson's
career, although "almost everyone who has written on *Sandover* assumes
that it was a one-man job," and also notes the role of the collaboration in
preserving their marriage (108). Finally, she finds their extended obsession
destructive to Jackson—the compensations for Merrill, who won great ac-
claim for his Ouija-inspired work, were naturally greater than they were
for his partner at the board.

Merrill's own comments tend to corroborate Lurie's: "I wonder if the trilogy shouldn't have been signed with both our names—or simply 'by DJ, as told to JM'?" (*Recitative* 68). However, elsewhere he expresses a strong impulse to retain full control over the products of his art, as well as a fear that use of Ouija transcripts constitute "cheating" (*Recitative* 39, 54). Laird, discussing overtly coauthored texts, suggests that "we neither can nor ought to try to tell coauthors apart" (*Women Coauthors* 6). The issue of authorship in "Ephraim," at least, remains irresolvable, especially insofar as it hangs on the question of belief (what or who directed that teacup?). This is, in fact, Merrill's point. Whether or not a poet foregrounds the collaborative process as elaborately as Merrill does, poetic voice remains shifting and multiple, its sources elusive.

The occult element of the poetry is even more difficult to negotiate than the extent of Jackson's contribution. Does any part of *Sandover* benefit from supernatural influence or assistance? Merrill's poems and interviews, as well as the Jackson interview cited above, adopt a variety of subtly contradictory attitudes regarding the spiritual system described in *Sandover;* this negotiation between doubt and faith, as Merrill well knew, remains part of *Sandover*'s fascination.[19]

Few propose that Merrill or Jackson was a pretender, although Lurie wonders if Jackson sometimes deliberately pushed the teacup (91). The very excess and strangeness of the trilogy seem to preclude the possibility that Merrill or Jackson faked the transcripts or consciously invented these occult conversations. Fictional elements do permeate "Ephraim," some acknowledged within the text (such as a failed novel Merrill frequently invokes) and some not (apparently authentic citations to nonexistent books and appearances by nonexistent people). In some ways, however, all this artifice offers a contrast to the séances, making the Ouija material seem more sincere. Foreclosing on the possibility that Merrill and/or Jackson cynically made everything up and played coy for years afterwards makes it even harder to give a full account of *Sandover*'s authorship. Did Merrill and/or Jackson, using the Ouija board, plumb their own imaginations for all this material? Did the Ouija "voices" spring from the underused halves of their bicameral minds, as Julian Jaynes might suggest?[20] If so, their procedure still resembles collaboration by its dispersal of creative control. The Ouija method, therefore, merits at least a small place in this discussion of "Ephraim" as a collaborative endeavor.[21]

These questions have long troubled Merrill's audiences. Merrill won a Pulitzer for *Divine Comedies*, while later installments of the trilogy were unevenly received. The disparity in critical response stems from two factors: the first third handles the material more skeptically than the latter sections; the latter sections contain a higher proportion of capital-letter dictated material, making them seem less original and reducing the interplay between spirit communications and a more familiar world. Many of Merrill's sympathetic readers remain skeptical of or neutral about *Sandover*'s occult elements. Others argue that one must take the poem's claims seriously, even if conversion is not a prerequisite for enjoyment (Johnston 104). An investigation of authorship certainly requires a survey of contributors to the final product, but how should poetry criticism treat the possibility of divine collaborators?

Merrill's own comments indicate mixed feelings about sharing authorship with angels, although he admits to his "religious streak," to use McClatchy's imperfect phrase (Merrill, *Recitative* 70). McClatchy pertinently asks, "Could not the 'they' who move the teacup around the board be considered the authors of the poem?" Merrill replies:

> Yes and no . . . in a sense, all these figures are our creation, or mankind's. The powers they represent are real—as, say, gravity is "real"—but they'd be invisible, inconceivable, if they'd never passed through our heads and clothed themselves out of the costume box they'd found there. *How* they appear depends on us, the imaginer, and would have to vary wildly from culture to culture, or even temperament to temperament . . . what's tiresome is when people exclusively insist on the forms they've imagined. Those powers don't need churches in order to be sacred. What they do need are fresh ways of being seen. (*Recitative* 60)

Merrill casts doubt, here and always, on the particular explanation for the universe that he and Jackson assembled. However, he doesn't express any uncertainty about the reality of sacred powers, or their ability to communicate with human beings. Poetry, he implies, offers a kind of theater for those forces—and theater is a collaborative art.

Authorship is permanently entangled with the genre questions *Sandover* provokes. Is the poetic voice at hand lyric or epic? Some scholars have settled on "epic" as a label for this magnum opus, but their studies acknowledge considerable ambiguity about the genre question. Merrill's champions, inspired by the poet's own allusions but also displaying some anxiety about the status of this challenging book, typically link it to Dante's *The Divine Comedy* and Yeats' *A Vision* in order to certify Merrill's mastery, suggest generic analogs, and establish that Merrill's unusual experience does, in fact, participate in an important literary tradition of spiritual encounter. Charles Berger, writing specifically about the problem of genre, calls *Sandover* an "apocalyptic poem" and a "polyphonic epic"

(183). Timothy Materer asks, is it "an epic, mock-epic, or anti-epic?" (*Apoc-alypse* 2). Other critics, including David Kalstone and Richard Sáez, em-phasize the persistence of lyric episodes even as they refer to the larger work as an epic. McHale categorizes *Sandover* as a "postmodern long poem" modeled on postmodern novels (4, 18–54). In an interview with Fred Bornhauser, Merrill discusses the work as a "romance," though in-sisting that he is "rather shaky as to genres and modes" (*Recitative* 61).[22] Certainly this five hundred and sixty page trilogy, as Merrill himself gen-erally refers to it, unsettles any theory of poetic kinds. Further, the tril-ogy, also including "Mirabell's Book of Numbers" and "Scripts for the Pageant," concludes with a substantial "Coda: The Higher Keys," so even the genre-neutral term "trilogy" misleads.

"Ephraim" in particular, which Merrill first published with a set of unrelated poems in *Divine Comedies* (1976) and did not yet mark as the introduction to an apocalypse-in-the-making, engages the question of genre with a vengeance. Its challenge to genre, in fact, parallels the es-sential ambiguities of voice these lyrics enact. "The Book of Ephraim" interrogates genre because it interrogates voice, and vice versa. Not sur-prisingly, critics have struggled with labels for this most approachable part of the longer work as well. Harold Bloom calls "Ephraim" a "verse-tale"(133); Helen Vendler refers to it as a "long poem" and a "novelistic poem" (134). Polito characterizes "Ephraim" as the most lyric portion of *Sandover*, in which Merrill initially "inhabit[s] the solitary lyric disguise so absolutely that he almost compels us to apprehend Ephraim," the poet's familiar spirit in the séances central to this sequence, "as only a mirror for himself, and the other world as an eccentric manifestation of his narcissistic will" (233). However, according to Polito, by the end of "Ephraim" Merrill depicts his lyric "I" as "a synthesis or consolida-tion. . . . *The Changing Light at Sandover* gains its main path only when the lyric note is no longer sounded" (239). Lyric, by Polito's implicit defi-nition, represents an inwardly focused, unified self, a concept which the company of voices in this work challenges at every turn and which the sequence eventually abandons. One doesn't have to take dictation from the ghost of W. H. Auden to recognize that all poems, even the most ap-parently lyric, are in various senses polyvocal, composite, choral, rife with dissenting discourses, even haunted. As Mutlu Konuk Blasing argues in her analysis of Merrill's "technically closed and rhetorically open forms" (110), this ambivalent heir to generic conventions "dissociates the lyric from notions of a coherent lyric self" and "conveys his postmodern understanding of the poetic self as textual," using and challenging tradi-tion simultaneously (114).

Merrill, in fact, signals his fascination with voice and genre in the very first poem of "The Book of Ephraim," section A, which begins, "Admittedly I err by undertaking / This in its present form" (3). Merrill here discusses the importance of his literary mission, which eventually emerges as a warning against nuclear catastrophe, and worries that his work might find wider audience if expressed through "the baldest prose / Reportage" (3). He recounts his unsuccessful efforts to convert the material of the séances into a novel, though he only cryptically refers to his loss of the physical manuscript by alluding to a separate poem that tells the tale: "(Cf. 'The Will')" (4). The narrative of his creative process, therefore, already cohabits the poem with other discourses. For instance, "A" exercises literary criticism not only in the latter scholarly aside but through Merrill's disparaging comments on the contemporary novel and his knowing mention of Northrop Frye. He also invokes, and arguably employs, the lyric mode not only through irregularly chiming sound, his intimate use of the first person, and the confessional gesture of "Admittedly," but by emphasizing his isolation after abandoning his fictive characters: "I alone was left / To tell my story" (4). In the same poem, Merrill describes his search for a "serene, anonymous . . . voice" from fairy tales and legends for his aborted novel (3). Since his prose had been mannered rather than plain, he switches to a more familiar medium: "In verse the feet went bare" (4). Blank verse is paradoxically homier than fiction for this accomplished versifier. While puns generally emphasize language's dazzling artifice, Merrill's metrical pun in this passage conversely conveys presence, intimacy, and naturalness, the lyric's central illusions.

Section A argues that in Merrill's own case, given his individual aptitudes and weaknesses, this material finds its best expression through lyric poetry. However, by alluding to a multiplicity of modes, this opening poem also ensures any reader's acute awareness of generic conventions and the constructed nature of voice. Merrill continues to destabilize his literary universe by interweaving details from the abandoned novel throughout the sequence—one of three recurrent plots, as Yenser observes, along with the story of the poem's year-long composition and, thirdly, the relationship between Ephraim, Merrill (JM), and Merrill's fellow medium Jackson (DJ) over twenty years of séances (219–20). Even more immediately, however, Merrill juxtaposes his unconvincing resignation to lyricism with the intense theatricality of section B, which introduces what will be persistent dramatic references through diction, including "backdrop" and "properties" (5); section D, in fact, offers a Dramatis Personae. "B," in contradiction to lyric's alleged monologism, also contains the first transcription of a voice from another world, set in disconcerting capital letters because of the single case Ouija boards offer: "HELLP O SAV ME scrawled the cup"

(6). Jackson, too, briefly speaks as a character, crucially pushing the whole enterprise forward: "I slumped. D: One more try" (6). While Merrill emphasizes the mechanism of communication as writing, not speaking, the nature of the "conversation" highlights and surely inspired *Sandover*'s preoccupation with the figure of literary voice. As Johnston puts it, "The very nature of the Ouija, as a form of writing and reading, emphasizes the paradox of a written 'voice'" (94).

Jackson's comments to McClatchy about interpreting the transcripts illuminate this paradox further. "Sometimes we talked over what we thought the tone was," Jackson remarks, and his interviewer responds, "You found that the hardest thing to 'get,' then, was not the message itself, but its tone?" Jackson's answer parallels Merrill's comments about the nature of poetic voice:

> Because the tone's a voice. They would do their best, and when we got punctuation in it, it was a revelation . . . but then we began objecting to exclamation points, which seemed more like a comic strip! But the thing that was always one of the problems to talk over afterwards was, Did you feel that was said in this voice? Or, didn't Wystan seem surprised? (40)

Jackson and Merrill puzzle over tone because the transcriptions are bare of print's many extra-linguistic features: alternation in font and case, punctuation, layout, even line breaks, all of which can simulate vocal changes in timing, pitch, and intensity.

Another element of literary voice is important in "B" and throughout "Ephraim." Section B contains a crucial pronominal shift. While section A exercises the first person singular, its sequel utilizes a plural voice: "our tenancy" (5), "we had each other for communication" (5), "our breathing stopped" (6), and the final shift to third person plural, "enthralled them" (7). While Merrill employs a range of pronouns in "Ephraim," this "we" persists, even to the last sentence of the sequence: "For here we are" (92). Through the first person plural Merrill suggests the collaborative sources of "Ephraim" and bends lyric convention.

Many passages in "The Book of Ephraim" as well as from the larger trilogy illuminate voice as a literary category. For instance, Merrill engages the issue of his own inspiration, and hence the concept of originality, multiple times. In "U," the shade of Wallace Stevens warns the younger poet that "A SCRIBE SITS BY YOU CONSTANTLY THESE DAYS / DOING WHAT HE MUST TO INTERWEAVE / YOUR LINES WITH MEANINGS YOU CANNOT CONCEIVE"(72). Merrill's wit undercuts his indignant demand for clarification when he asks, then, if the poem has been partly "ghostwritten" (72). Merrill's Eliot, who famously collaborated with Ezra Pound, and, according to the spirits, the ghost of Rimbaud on *The Waste Land* (217), offers partial reassurance in "Coda": "THESE WORKS, YOU UNDERSTAND? THAT OTHERS 'WRITE' . . . ARE YET ONE'S OWN" (557–58). This thread of conversation both asserts and undermines traditional lyric definition insofar as it rests on the idea of original poetic voice.

"Ephraim" also emphasizes the paradoxes of presence and absence raised by poetic voice through constant metaphors of talk and speech for the spirit communications. For instance, the ghost of Auden "sounded pleased" about the afterlife (87); JM and DJ value Ephraim's "table talk, his backstage gossip" (55). The recurring trope of the telephone, too, evokes both the intimacy of Ouija voices and the vast distances such whispers may traverse. Occasionally a telephone literally appears, as when the spirits glimpse Merrill's reflection in a glass phone booth (36) and an interestingly timed ringing interrupts the couple's plans to burn the séance transcripts in section Z, resulting in a "bad connection; babble of distant talk" (91). More often, though, the "calls" refer to sessions with Ephraim. Early on, their familiar spirit accuses another ghost of "wasting, just now at our cup, / Precious long distance minutes—don't hang up!" Elsewhere Merrill guiltily confesses to meaning to "call" Ephraim (55), though he somehow delayed, or refers to a Ouija board sitting as a "long impromptu call" (72). The telephone allusions work partly to ground this unearthly contact in the daily trivia of contemporary life. Merrill determinedly and repeatedly subverts the potential grandiosity of his project through such references. Also, since telephones enable closeness with distant friends, transmitting only sound from mouth to ear in a private circuit, they do resemble the simultaneous familiarity and strangeness of the séances. As Merrill and Jackson both point out, their Ouija nights started as a parlor game with visiting friends and, in their absence, provided "company" (Jackson, "DJ" 25). Finally, telephone references reinforce the trope of disembodied voices so central to this sequence and to lyric poetry itself.

At least one section of the poem, however, manifests distinct ambivalence about the weird operations of voice. "R" presents five sonnets elegizing Merrill's friend Maya Deren, the experimental filmmaker and voodoo initiate who features prominently in the sequence. This poem, poignantly remembering Maya's series of strokes, exemplifies what some critics have noted as the elegiac quality of the whole trilogy, which describes vivid contact with the dead and thereby softens loss.[23] The ghost of Maya seems exhilarated to be "YOUNG AT LAST" and directing "AVANTGARDE HALLUCI / NATIONS ETC FOR HEADS OF STATE" (64). She sends a message to her widower affirming her happiness in the afterlife, where she has power ("WE GIRLS HAVE STOPPED A WAR WITH CUBA") and close access to her gods (64).

Merrill infuses the poem, however, with an angrier grief at his country that "never held [Deren] in high enough esteem" (64). "R" begins with a frustration of the elegiac impulse, recording Merrill's difficulty in handling the material: "Rewrite P," it begins imperatively, then describing the golden late summer poem he'd meant to write.[24] "Impossible," he concludes, "So long, at least, as there's no end to summer. / Late September is a choking furnace" (63). The poem expands the "furnace" image into an indictment of over-industrialized American life, including traffic and pollution as "impedimenta of the arch-consumer" (63). This brief sonnet sequence ends with a description of distant sounds coalescing into voices that again reflect critically on mass culture.

> Swelling, sharpening upwind now—blade
> On grindstone—a deep shriek? The Sunday stadium.
> Twenty thousand throats one single throat
>
> Hoarse with instinct, blood calling to blood
> —Calling as well to mind the good gray medium
> Blankly uttering someone else's threat.
>   (65)

A stadium replaces the church in a world emptied of sacredness; the spectators are unified only in their tribal identification with a violent sport.

At the close of "R" Merrill similarly reflects on his own poetic role, particularly on lyric voice as a representation of diverse sources beyond the individual composing the lines. He invokes and to some extent identifies with the mature Walt Whitman, the Good Gray Poet who spoke for and to the American masses, here standing for populist and democratic impulses as they might manifest through literature. In particular, the grindstone image suggests Whitman's lyric "Sparkles from the Wheel" in "Autumn Rivulets."[25] In Whitman's poem, amid the background noise of crowded city streets, the speaker joins a group of children watching a knife-grinder at work. Whitman characterizes himself as "effusing and fluid, a phantom curiously floating, now here absorb'd and arrested" and especially admires not the overt purpose of the labor but its gorgeous by-product, "copious golden jets" of sparks (514). Like Merrill's poem, "Sparkles from the Wheel" presents an image of potential violence against a noisy backdrop of mass culture. In "R," however, Whitman's "loud, proud, restive base of the streets" (515) becomes a dangerous mob and the "threat" becomes far more overt.

Although linking himself with Whitman, Merrill disclaims Whitman's originality by labeling himself not "poet" but "medium." As transcriber and interpreter of Ephraim's messages, Merrill transmits "someone else's threats"—warnings from beyond that find clearer articulation a few poems earlier in "P," the section he wishes to rewrite. The allusion also marks a distance between Whitman's multi-voiced poetry, relaying many conflicting perspectives in order to celebrate American diversity, and Merrill's own work, which expresses far more skepticism about art's capacity to unify people. *Sandover*'s cast of characters resembles the blood-crazed crowd in "R," since in both cases many voices chime together in a synchronized impulse; when in his memoir Merrill calls poetry "a vast chamber full of voices," this image of oneness through multitudes resembles this stadium (*A Different Person* 15). However, "R" demonstrates distinct discomfort with the poet's representative role.

The extraordinary formal qualities of "R" contribute to this sense of ambivalence. Any use of inherited forms places a new poem in dialogue with tradition, and this must be especially true with such a popular vehicle as the sonnet, which Heather Dubrow suggests might be "the most self-conscious and self-referential of all genres" (23). Merrill, however, partly disguises his use of this common pattern. He marks the division between each fourteen-line unit only by an extra space, so at first glance "R"'s text doesn't appear different from the blank verse, irregularly paragraphed, that comprises many other sections. Further, each sonnet divides into octave and sestet and follows a rhyme scheme, but Merrill deemphasizes his rhymes by arranging them further apart than is the norm (abcd abcd instead of abba cddc) and thereby hides the chiming sounds. Finally, the rhymes themselves are unusual. True rhymes consist of vowel-consonant matches, while slant rhymes merely reproduce a vowel or consonant sound. Merrill, however, is particularly expert at the clever variation sometimes called pararhyme: paralleling multiple consonants in words whose vowel sounds don't correspond, such as furnace / fairness in the first sonnet or throat / threat in the last. Perhaps this strategy reinforces the hollowness of grief the poem describes; it may merely prevent the harmonizing music that suggests a consolation in sensual pleasure, even an underlying order in the world, as fully rhyming poems sometimes do. However, the ingenious craft of these love poems stresses the elitism of Merrill's project, addressed to the erudite.[26] It also marks the poetic voice as distinctly Merrill's, witty and clever. If he acts as a medium, in part passively, he also brilliantly shapes the message consciously.

Section H, particularly, exemplifies how central, provocative, and ambiguous voice, the textual figure for authorship, can be in this sequence, and how it records collaboration. Although "H" (26–28) clearly partakes of the larger sequence, using the persistent mirror motif, deploying familiar characters, and even ending with a cliffhanger, it also fits most lyric definitions. This two page poem relies on the music of form, not only through the sporadically coupling rhymes of its longest stanza but through an opening sonnet. It offers Merrill's "voice of wit and elegance" (Johnston 93), composed in part of a worldly vocabulary ("gemütlichkeit," "pied-à-terre") contrasting amusingly with banal phrases ("presto!", "as we shall see"). Lascivious Ephraim delivers the funniest and most frightening line when he advises the couple desiring to view him that they must "DIE" to do so.[27] However, most of section H unrolls in a meditative, vividly sensual tone. As Sharon Cameron requires of lyric by definition, this poem of recollected experience also stops time. The speaker hypnotizes DJ and they invoke Ephraim together; their invocation results in an ambiguous seduction, transcending that spirit's death, two thousand years past.[28]

Merrill situates this weird erotic drama, entertainingly enough, in a "white farmhouse up a gravel road / Where Frost had visited," revising Frost's own eerie domestic scenes, also narrated in pentameter, in an unexpected way.[29] Frost's isn't the only voice, though, chiming with and against Merrill's. Pronouns, again, oscillate between first person plural and singular; the poem quotes not only Ephraim in upper-case but DJ's account of the seduction in italics, which contrasts notably with the speaker's own version. This variation in perspective calls not only memory but experience itself into question, just as all these strategies emphasize the instability of identity. How many people are attending this party, after all, and who's touching whom on that "deep black couch"? Presence and absence become this poem's central issues: JM and DJ desire an impossible intimacy with Ephraim, that invisible author they've met only through written language, and their own situation deliberately mirrors the reader's, so dependent on the mirage of poetic voice.

D's apparent possession by Ephraim even allows the first sounding, as opposed to scrawling, of a spirit's voice:

> No cup would move, this time. D's lips instead
> Did, and a voice not his, less near,
> Deeper than his, now limpid, now unclear,
> Said where he was was room for me as well.

"Voice" here constitutes Ephraim speaking through D "speaking" through Merrill. The ventriloquism suggests the choral voice Cameron identifies in Dickinson's hymn-based stanzas, although Merrill achieves it through a trope of possession while Dickinson experiments with mismatched pronouns ("ourself," "themself," etc.), among other strategies. The strangeness of "The Book of Ephraim" rests not only in its spiritualism but in its un-nerving use of a familiar lyric trope. "Pure lyric" cannot emanate from a pure speaker, because all poetry partakes in collaboration, and all seem-ingly individual voices constitute thrilling, but momentary, apparitions.

Several recent books address the unnerving effects that spiritualism has had on nineteenth- and twentieth-century literature. Materer's *Modernist Al-chemy*, for instance, examines how occultism inspires modern poets from Yeats to Merrill; Johnston focuses rather on occultism as poetic practice. *Writing Double*, London's exploration of women's collaborative authorship, grants substantial attention to the automatic writings of mediums as col-laboration. Merrill is far from the first to claim to transcribe new lines from deceased poets. As Sword argues in *Ghostwriting Modernism*, her study of the intersections of modernism and spiritualism, mediums and spirits un-settle "boundaries between self and other, absence and presence, materiality and spirituality, life and death" (xi). While only a fraction of spiritualist-era literary production seems haunted in a literal manner, such paranormal material can bear on other major preoccupations of twentieth-century poetry.[30]

As all of these critics observe, spiritualist practice also calls authorship into question. To write from occult sources is to surrender writerly control. In Merrill's work, moving from the openness of the séance to the relatively solitary shaping of formal poetry deepens his engagement with the prob-lem of poetic voice. In Ede and Lunsford's terms, one method is profoundly dialogic and the other is hierarchical. The supremely artful maneuvers of "Ephraim," therefore, could reinscribe as well as challenge the specter of the solitary poetic genius. The poetic universe of "Ephraim," after all, is defined by oppositions, mirror images, locked into interdependence. The sequence testifies both to an individual's vision and the intrinsically poly-vocal nature of poetry. Poetic voice helps to stage this encounter.

In "Ephraim," Merrill presents himself as an ambivalent reader of occult texts. Ephraim sometimes seems vividly real, sometimes a bizarre and exotic fiction. Likewise, a lyric poem renders a version of the author that consists only of patterned words yet can seem utterly present in that the rhythms briefly possess a reader with the result that minds (and in Merrill or Whitman, even bodies) seem to meet. "H" particularly dramatizes this layering or blurring of self, but the whole sequence puts poetic identity, and therefore the idea of voice, under interrogation. Further, Merrill's sexual metaphor for the experience of reading lyric poetry emphasizes pleasure as the motive for literary encounter. If de Man is correct in thinking that the illusion of presence defines lyric as a mode (55–56), and Merrill is correct in thinking that barefoot presence is the lyric's special attraction, all the more reason to keep voice in the critical lexicon.

Denise Duhamel, Maureen Seaton, and Oyl's Third Voice

In their individual works, Maureen Seaton and Denise Duhamel challenge the boundaries of lyric poetry differently than Merrill, but at least as radically. For instance, they experiment with structures as various as sonnet, Oulipo verse, prose poem, and slam poem; their material likewise ranges widely, from sexual violence to mathematics to children's toys; their tonal shifts, even more so than Merrill's, can be dramatic, moving through graphic humor and passionate invective to the surreal dislocations of collage forms. Many of their pieces forge alliances with other genres, from the contemporary visual arts to (in Duhamel's case) stand-up comedy. Each poet puts different languages, modes, and perspectives into conversation with one another.

By practicing an open and various poetry with attention to poetic processes and poetry's audiences, Seaton and Duhamel suggest that poetry is inherently a social form rather than a private one. This social conception of poetry and innovative ethos culminate in their coauthored work. Their jointly signed book, chapbooks, and poems pivot on their understanding of lyric poetry as a site of conversation and cooperative play. Their coauthorship displaces the lyric ideal of original expression in favor of charged, provocative explorations of the nature and limits of poetic voice.

Duhamel and Seaton give several accounts of their collaborations in interviews and short essays. Their comments on the process veer between practical descriptions of the logistics of exchanging lines and intensely mystical interpretations of the experience. Sometimes they refer to poems themselves as independent agents, possessing a "third voice" that feels eerily present even at a joint reading of a completed work ("Thoughts on the Collaboration" 132). Discussing the genesis of a specific piece, "Ecofeminism in the Year 2000," they write, "From the beginning, we were conscious of the specific energy of the poem itself, that third voice between us—of goddess, higher power, the unconscious communal mind of women—and how the poem could operate as a metaphor for the planet if we allowed it to write itself, so to speak" (130). Duhamel and Seaton cast themselves as mediums; they depict collaborative composition as a sort of technologically facilitated séance involving telephones, answering machines, e-mails, and faxes.

Poems by Duhamel and Seaton often draw on autobiographical material, especially trauma, in a way that echoes the so-called confessional work dominant during their poetic educations. However, their interviews, prose, and poems themselves debunk the idea that lyric poetry constitutes personal expression. Instead, they suggest that poetry is dialogic in its functions and in its origins. How can personal expression exist, after all, if one's conception of authorship, and even personhood, is radically open? Every poem, according to Duhamel and Seaton, manifests a conversation among multiple individuals, texts, and possibly supernatural forces. This chapter investigates their dialogic poetry, beginning with comments about their first co-authored book, *Exquisite Politics* (1997), but focusing mainly on their subsequent chapbook, *Oyl* (2000). Throughout these works, they display a profound investment in lyric poetry as a genre and in voice as an idea. Paradoxically, collaboration does not disable these terms, but it does lend them richer and more ambiguous resonances.

The introduction to *Exquisite Politics*, their first book-length collaboration, uses the form of a script or conversation to illustrate the authors' writing process. Both in form and content, it suggests a dialogic rather than hierarchical mode of composition. This brief piece, however, differs from most of the poems that follow in two ways. First, its tone is formal and expository, while the poems that follow tease, berate, mourn, and fantasize, manipulating a wide range of registers. Second, every paragraph of the introduction is attributed to one of the two poets, each identified by her full name on the first page and last name only in subsequent comments. The latter move is especially striking. Why does the introduction highlight each passage as the intellectual property of a discrete individual, while the book as a whole submerges such difference?

This problem gets at the heart of the coauthored lyric as Duhamel and Seaton practice it. Their prose and interviews characterize collaboration as transgressive play, in which each poet is emboldened by the protective cover her partner provides; the most daring passages belong simultaneously to both and neither of them, given the "third voice" resulting from their labor. While one of the poems from their first coauthored book, "Baby Democrats," does tag each passage by author informally by "D—" and "M—," instead of full or last names (EP 50–54), most of their productions are monovocal. That is, most poems by Duhamel and Seaton efface the origin of individual words, sections, and lines, although they do contain visible traces of the collaborative process—their poems could pass as the creations of a solo consciousness, but become still richer read as collaborations. This blending of language, or refusal of authorial boundaries, contributes to the defiant glee of their poetry. Collaboration forms part of an ethic and an esthetic favoring experiment, a testing of all possible rules.

However, while coauthors may feel empowered by collaboration, many individuals and institutions either reject it or struggle to accommodate it. By the time Tia Chucha Press issued *Exquisite Politics*, Duhamel and Seaton had already achieved significant success in their individual careers. Duhamel had made a name for herself through performances at the Nuyorican Café, had seen poems anthologized in the *Best American Poetry* series, and had published six books and chapbooks with small presses; her collection of Barbie-inspired poems, *Kinky* (1997), was issued in the same year. Maureen Seaton had also published three award-winning volumes, including *Furious Cooking*, winner of the 1995 Iowa Poetry Prize. Their solo successes underwrite the creative and professional risk co-authorship entails. Their individual achievements, moreover, persisted during and beyond their subsequent collaborations, the chapbooks *Oyl* (2000) and *Little Novels* (2002) issued by Pearl Editions. Both Duhamel and Seaton continue to publish with increasing prestige, both win grants and prizes for their poems, and both now hold academic positions. Maureen Seaton directs the Creative Writing Program at the University of Miami, while Duhamel, fourteen years younger, is Associate Professor of English at Florida International University.

External pressures certainly shape collaborations. Few literary journals, presses, and contests welcome coauthored pieces, and any humanist seeking academic work, raises, and promotions knows that committees may not consider such work fairly. Duhamel and Seaton inscribe the introduction to *Exquisite Politics* with such concerns by carefully elucidating the history and nature of their collaboration, a process joyfully occluded by the poems themselves.

DENISE DUHAMEL: We didn't know what would come of our collaborations—if we would ever try to publish them or read them publicly. . . . In the beginning [around 1990], we agreed upon certain ground rules: at first we worked in syllabics and were not allowed to change anything about the other's lines, though we kept open the option of changing/adding/eliminating end punctuation in any given line that preceded the one we wrote; and we decided upon the number of lines before we began each poem. We chose loosely defined "topics" before we began, but our collaborative poems (like the poems we wrote individually) often grew to have lives of their own, ones we didn't expect.

MAUREEN SEATON: Together we undertook projects that were either really wild (witches' spell sonnets), emotionally challenging (our childhoods, ex-loves, etc.), or intellectually challenging (writing in forms, using rhyme schemes). . . . It seemed appropriate to be outrageous as a team because being a team is already outrageous, at least in some circles. (11)

Explanatory introductions like this one, focused on the writing process, are rare in contemporary poetry collections. The very fact of collaboration is its implicit justification. This preface forestalls hostile questions, mediates between the poetry and its readers or evaluators, and emphasizes the rigor of this mode of work. Duhamel notes that she and Seaton wrote together for six years before they were "ready to assemble a book length manuscript" (11), and that their methods included work in "month long periods during the summer, in a pretty much 9–5 fashion" (12). The overlap between friendship and joint labor also emerges strongly, emphasizing the book as a feminist collaboration without ever mentioning the word "feminism." As Seaton describes it, "We're committed to women in our individual work but it's heightened when we collaborate. . . . We're not unaware that we're doing something 'unusual,' even taboo for women in our society" (11–12).[31] The book's title foregrounds politics, they imply, because dialogic collaboration is itself a political act, undermining conventions about property, work itself, and the nature of creative talent. That is to say, nobody truly works alone; play is serious business; originality is a chimera.[32]

Their coauthored introduction, finally, offers some helpful observations about how voice might be understood to function in a coauthored poem. Seaton comments,

> Sometimes I struggle to perceive the identity(ies), voice(s) of our poems. At times the voices ring clearly and definably as either Denise's or mine. Other times there is only the voice of the poem and ours are subsumed. That is what feels most spectacular about collaboration, that creation of a third person, but I'm not always objective enough to see/hear it. And then, lately, I'm not sure how important it really is to create the new voice. (12)

Seaton struggles here with the dominant view, especially in the 1990s, of lyric poetry as voice-based. She also identifies voice with individuality, even personhood, as if together Seaton and Duhamel construct a coherent character speaking through the poems. This is not, in fact, how any of the poems in *Exquisite Politics* sound. Arguably, a distinctive voice percolates through them, by which I mean certain qualities of language and preoccupations in content—not only politics and sexuality but wit and formal ingenuity (the book contains a wide range of forms, from prose poems to sonnet crowns). Certain poems, too, adopt a collective and/or representative voice in the political sense, channeling and parodying the hackneyed rhetoric associated with various public positions (see "Exquisite Candidate," "Exquisite Incumbent," and "Exquisite Communist," among others). However, on the whole, the poems of *Exquisite Politics* feel less integrated than the later collaborations of Duhamel and Seaton, because so many pieces consist of alternating parts.

An interview with Maureen Seaton conducted by Neil de la Flor refines this point. In the on-line journal *Scene 360*, de la Flor begins by asking Seaton about her work with literary collage, and then asks about her various forays into collaborative work (like Duhamel, Seaton has collaborated with various visual and literary artists):

> N: What is the magic that occurs when two or three poets get together and create a piece of writing with a uniform voice? Are the poets mimicking each other or is there a deeper undercurrent that the collaborators are tapping into?
> M: Maybe the muse. Just waiting for a couple of ripe collaborators to come along and tap the well, the spine, the cistern, the minds of the goddesses and gods. That third voice, a little bit you, a little bit me—then, who's that? It feels that way when you write solo too, don't you think: you and the poem, then: hey, who's that? . . .
> N: But is it a merging of voices, of spirits, of purpose, or is it just dumb luck?
> M: With another poet or writer it's just upped, that's all, the energy goes up a notch, sometimes way up. (9)

"Magic," "goddesses and gods," "spirits": both de la Flor and Seaton express a mystical attitude about poetic creation that often appears in discussions of voice. For Seaton, the sources of poetry are already mysterious. Collaboration may enable a freer access to those deep wells and cisterns, but the process is fundamentally similar.

According to this conversation with de la Flor, Seaton does not prioritize coherence in a finished poem. Fittingly enough, her solo poetry, like her collaborative work, is full of dislocating leaps and often produced by Surrealist methods. Particularly given her recent work in collage—her newest book, *Venus Examines Her Breast* (2004), is entirely collage-based—Seaton would seem more likely to sympathize with the experiments of Language Poetry than with the so-called "workshop poem" or "voice-based lyric." However, Seaton's work and her comments about it tend to short-circuit this false dichotomy. "Voice" implies the coherent identity of a physically present "speaker," linear temporality, singular expressiveness, and poetry as an aural rather than a visual art. Certainly Seaton and Duhamel overturn all these expectations. However, as a term and as an idea, voice remains important to

Seaton. Crucially, it suggests conversation, a moment-to-moment exchange between two or more collaborators, a solo poet and her sources, the poem and its audience, or all of these.

The idea of voice also permeates Duhamel's solo poetics. Her success in Spoken Word venues derives in part from the oral energy of her printed work; these poems are often conversational, daring, and funny. Her recent collections, however, obsess over poetry's visual elements. In *The Star-Spangled Banner*, for instance, various poems forge similes with symbols ("its *a* all swirls, looking like @" [5]); focus thematically on vision and its failures to "read" the world correctly ("The Little I know about Eyes," [9–11]); refer repeatedly to modes of textual production ("How Much is This Poem Going to Cost Me?" [16–17]; and discuss typographical symbols like the tilde and the breve (5, 59). Duhamel's latter work exhibits self-consciousness about how voice might operate in a printed text—how sounds, like "The Star-Spangled Banner" misheard by an imaginative child, generate poems that invoke sound but may rarely be spoken physically. These paradoxes, central to poetic voice, give Duhamel's accessible work intellectual heft.

Given the individual interests of Seaton and Duhamel, it's not hard to imagine how they came to produce *Oyl*. The chapbook's central character, the heroine of *Popeye* comics and cartoons, represents an ideal intersection for two feminist poets who are fascinated with female stereotypes, sexuality, and the boundaries of gender. Both poets have demonstrated an urgent interest in beauty myths and female empowerment. Providing ample material for such investigations, Olive plays both rescuer and damsel in distress. The formal variety of *Oyl* is characteristic of Seaton, and its brash, sexy wit echoes Duhamel's other work. This offbeat subject for poetry also suits Duhamel's abiding and productive obsession with popular culture and Seaton's commitment to the visual arts. All of these comments may imply greater difference between their sensibilities than actually exists—Seaton, after all, writes poems about the pop star Madonna, and Duhamel about Goya—and as this chapter emphasizes, jointly authored poems cannot and should not be divided into piles of separately created lines. Nevertheless, the particular artistic success of *Oyl* rests partly in the felicitous fit between the material and the artists.

Another factor makes Olive Oyl a particularly apt subject for a collaboration. This singular character is already coauthored. Duhamel and Seaton highlight Olive Oyl's complex origins from the beginning of their chapbook, commencing with the following explanatory note:

One story goes like this:

   Olive Oyl was birthed from the pen of Elzie Crisler (E.C.) Segar in the
year 1919 into a brand new comic strip commissioned by *The New York Journal* entitled "The Thimble Theatre." She remained its high-strung heroine
along with her father, Cole Oyl; her brother, Castor Oyl; and her pickle-nosed
boyfriend, Ham Gravy until 1929, when Popeye staggered off his ship and
stole the strip. . . . Max Fleischer animated the whole gang in 1933, helping
to make spinach the American metaphor for muscle; and Robert Altman put
the crew in a movie in 1980 and called their seaside home Sweethaven.
Through it all, Olive and Popeye broke up and reunited uncountable times.
And after seventy years, in February 1999, King Features Syndicate announced that the wacky wayward couple finally tied the knot.

   That's one story. Here are the others . . . (7)

This fragment of poetic prose, framing its names, facts, and dates with
rhyme and alliteration, emphasizes how many artists have contributed to
the myth. Importantly, giving credit does not entail giving priority to one
version over others. The poems that follow, Duhamel and Seaton indicate,
offer histories of Olive Oyl that are no less valid than the original one. The
introduction also presents Olive Oyl as a sort of feminist recovery project.
Her "birth" is coincident with suffrage for women in the United States,
and, they note, her original power was eclipsed by the advent of heterosexual romance. Significantly, Duhamel and Seaton dedicate their chapbook
to "Mae Questel (1908–1998), for giving Olive a voice" (3). Questel literally
gave Olive a voice by reading her lines for the cartoons, but in this context
the phrase also obtains a political resonance. *Oyl* re-empowers its epony-
mous heroine by exploring her "life" and relationship with Popeye, and finally liberating her from the latter. It reinstates Olive, in fact, as the star of
her own show.

   Seaton describes the origin of *Oyl* more pragmatically in an e-mail interview with Estee Mazur and Richard Ryal: "I said [to Denise], Would
you PLEASE write some Olive Oyl poems with me and she said sure. I'd
wanted to write Oyl poems for years but whenever I tried, I'd miss Denise's input. It was fate" (5). *Oyl* springs from other sources as well. John
Ashbery's sestina about Popeye, "Farm Implements and Rutabagas in a
Landscape," is an important precursor. The chapbook also refers apprecia-
tively to collaborations within the New York School of Poets, surrealism,
Language Poetry, encyclopedias, television, and popular music of different eras.

The dedication and headnote of *Oyl* foreground how many artists have participated in Olive Oyl's story. The chapbook as a material object, however, is the result of a wider collaboration than its by-line indicates. As McGann argues in *The Textual Condition*, a text is always a social object, enabled by the contributions not only of authors and readers but of editors, designers, publishers, distributors, booksellers, and others. The paratextual elements of *Oyl* are relevant here not only because they testify to the role of collaboration in this or any publication, but because they contribute significantly to *Oyl*'s meanings. As in *Exquisite Politics*, a tension exists between the free play of artists composing together and the necessary work performed by poetic authority. Book design attempts to establish that authority through tactile and visual elements, as well as to help the book find a reading public by advertising its contents; paradoxically, however, it multiplies the number of contributors to the book and in subtle ways shapes its total message. Just as the poems in *Oyl* push mightily at the boundaries of the lyric, but also reinstate them, the chapbook as a material object both constructs authorship and challenges how authorship is traditionally constituted.

Oyl is published by Pearl Editions, an independent press with a feminist history.[33] The press began with *Pearl* magazine, founded in the mid-1970s by Joan Jobe Smith, then an undergraduate at California State University in Long Beach; the first version of *Pearl* focused on women writers and artists. Smith resurrected *Pearl* in 1987 with the help of coeditors Marilyn Johnson and Barbara Hauk. Like many independent literary presses, it publishes a magazine along with some books and chapbooks which are either solicited or selected through manuscript contests. *Oyl* and its successor, *Little Novels*, are inexpensively produced saddle-stapled chapbooks, about forty pages long and priced cheaply at eight dollars. Editor Marilyn Johnson designed both.

The physical production of *Oyl* mirrors the irreverence of its contents in that all elements of the chapbook demand that a reader adjust any expectations associated with the high-culture art form of "poetry." The red card-stock cover and bright yellow fly-leaf belong, aesthetically, to mass culture (they resemble ketchup and mustard, colors the McDonald's restaurant chain uses in its omnipresent marketing). Large swirling O's, typeset as dropped capitals on several interior pages, constitute another significant visual motif. Nikki McDonald identifies these recurring o's with orgasm (5); while the poems do not announce this equation in any transparent way, they do use the character "o" as a figure of eros and connection. Appropriately, in lyric tradition "o" heralds apostrophe, a figure of speech that reaches after impossible union with absent people or inanimate entities (and sometimes with the poem's audience). Occasionally "oh" appears in *Oyl* as an exclamation of surprise (10) or love (36); Seaton comments to McDonald, referring to the surrealist language game of Oulipo used in several poems, that "it was the 'O' that attracted us" (3). Finally, in this collection's closing poem, "The Origin of Olive Oyl," the character "o" seems to represent the embedded curves of fetus, uterus, mother, world, suggesting unity and wholeness (37). Johnson's design gives the "o" additional prominence, interpreting it as one of *Oyl*'s central tropes.

The most unusual and prominent aspect of this collection's design, however, is the use of illustration. Four line drawings of Olive Oyl, dispersed throughout the book, are credited to "Cobalt," a friend of the authors. Marilyn Johnson writes,

> I simply received the drawings (which I loved) along with the manuscripts and incorporated them into the design of the books.
>
> For the cover of OYL, I took Olive's face from Cobalt's full-page drawing at the end of the book, framed it within the "O" and colored it for a "comic-book" effect. My idea was to surprise the reader at the end with the *entire* picture—not just the new spiked hairdo already seen on the cover, but Olive complete with black leather jacket and sheathed dagger, flexing her new-found feminist muscle. (e-mail to the author, 16 July 2005)

Johnson refers to the largest image of Olive, appearing near the end of the chapbook, just before the author biographies. This version of the protagonist sports a fair amount of studded leather, a phallic dagger in her belt, spiky hair, and a piratical scarf knotted around her brow. She poses in profile, body-builder style, her left arm flexed upwards in a fist. The female symbol marks her surging bicep. Most of the other illustrations represent Olive borrowing different personas, paired with mock encyclopedia entries casting Olive as a series of famous women: "Olive of Troy," "Olive Magdalene," and "Olive, Queen of Ancient Egypt." The final illustration, different in style and unsigned, is a caricature of the poets "jogging in Central Park" with outsized heads, dark shades, and identically pert bodies running in bare feet. Duhamel and Seaton confirm that it was contributed by a different artist; "I don't know his name," Duhamel writes, "but he was an artist working in the park" (e-mail to the author, 28 July 2005).

Seaton expands on their relationship with the artist Cobalt, now known as Thalo, in another e-mail message (25 July 2005).[34]

She is a talented young woman whom I first met in a poetry workshop in Chicago circa 1993. We became fast friends and have kept in touch over the years, even with her move to the Pacific Northwest and mine to South Florida. She originally drew and painted Olive Oyl pictures as a gift to me because I just loved Olive! (In fact, the cover/final image of the book, Oyl with headband, leather jacket, knife, and muscle, is one of those early drawings.) Denise enthusiastically agreed that the book would be even livelier with illustrations, and Marilyn was open to the idea as well. (A bold move in the poetry world!) We sent Cobalt the manuscript and she sent us back delicious new drawings. Marilyn incorporated them into the design of the book in a very organic way. We were all very happy with the results!

Cobalt's first contributions occurred at a very early stage in the project; her re-imagining of Olive through drawings, in fact, preceded and possibly influenced Duhamel's and Seaton's interpretations of the cartoon figure.

Johnson and Cobalt might, therefore, be considered additional collaborators in *Oyl*, even though their contributions do not determine the actual words of the text. Butch Olive, in particular, crystallizes many attributes of the poems, because she represents a funny new vision of a familiar image, recognizable yet outrageously different, and highlights the sexual transgressiveness of Duhamel and Seaton's poetry. The very presence of illustration emphasizes Olive Oyl's original medium as well as the boundary-play this book engages in. Finally, it radically deflates the pretentiousness of poetry itself. The visual appeal and simplicity of such line-drawings belong to popular culture, and particularly ephemeral forms of it such as newspapers cartoons, sidewalk artist-hustlers, and doodlers of all stripes.

The medium of the chapbook itself also suits these poems well, and not only because the sequence is shorter than a typical poetry collection. Chapbooks, literally "cheap" books, were sold in Europe in the sixteenth, seventeenth, and eighteenth centuries, and in the colonial United States, by itinerant dealers or chapmen. Although eventually superseded by magazines, they were a crucial vehicle for popular literature of all kinds, from ballads and tales to news and advice, and were often illustrated by woodcuts. Chapbooks are rarer today, but some independent presses still publish them, often as the prize in manuscript contests; they serve as a step towards a first full-length book for some poets, and thus possess less authority, formality, and prestige. As formerly, chapbooks cost less than other books, though not by as wide a margin. All of these associations fit well with Duhamel and Seaton's poems, which ally themselves with the ephemera of popular culture and defy the stereotype of the poet as a high-minded loner, creating art in pain and isolation.

This chapbook, like Merrill's poetry, engages voice and authorship by investigating the limits of lyric poetry as a genre. *Oyl* includes so many poetic forms—old and new, associated with a wide range of schools and traditions—that its very range constitutes part of its message. It presents received forms including a villanelle, a sestina, a pantoum, and a cento; blank verse and free verse; prose poems imitating encyclopedia entries; Oulipo verse; and interviews and dialogues. Duhamel and Seaton thus celebrate the multiplicity of Olive Oyl, a coauthored character who possesses different meanings for her many interpreters. The repetition of some of these forms at patterned intervals discourages a linear approach to reading or even to biography. The use of footnotes, in one case longer than the poem itself, contributes to this effect and gives the book a scholarly or mock-scholarly cast. However, the virtuosic display of *Oyl* also represents its chief means of asserting poetic authority in a traditional sense. The authors may seem to have too much fun with a light subject, and the fact of their collaboration may seem inherently anti-poetic, but they certainly possess significant knowledge about their genre and substantial skills in its methods. Perhaps none of these pieces would "pass" at a New Formalist cocktail party, but they would certainly confuse the bouncer.

The word "voice" only appears once in the book, and it refers to Popeye. The penultimate poem, "Caprice," tells of Olive and Popeye's prolonged affair (35–36). It is a sestina and its end words, repeated with slight variations, touch on many of the cartoon's verbal and visual motifs: spinach, boot, Olive, order, skinny, and haven ("Sweethaven" was the name Robert Altman gave to Popeye's home town). The most significant variation is "virgin" substituted for "Olive" in the first stanza; the substitution literally refers to the cold-pressed oil Olive drizzles on endless spinach soufflés, but it also suggests the protagonist's sexual inexperience at the relationship's onset. Shortly afterward, Popeye "lower[s] his voice a scratchy scale or two, order[s] / her to kiss him," and subsequent lines detail "the kinky games they sometimes played with spinach." Although Duhamel and Seaton reserve the word "voice" for Popeye, they nevertheless emphasize Olive's increasing empowerment. As the sestina progresses, Olive becomes attracted by feminism, marches in a pride parade, and falls in love with a woman. The repeated word "order" chronicles her transformation, first referring to domestic and sexual commands she receives from Popeye, next "a protection order / against iron-enriched greens," then Amazon.com "orders / for every book published by Firebrand Press," and finally mutual, non-hierarchical play between lesbian lovers: "They ordered / each other around like siblings." Although "Caprice" recounts Olive finding a voice through feminist and gay liberation movements, it does not depend on sound as a strategy or figure. It is far more invested, in fact, in visual media such as political placards and revolutionary books, as well as Olive's romantic forays via internet.

However, many of the poems in *Oyl* do depict conversations. Sometimes poems merely contain short quotes or brief references to speech, as "Caprice" does; "Olive's War Effort," "Melvina, Paulina, and Lunt," and other poems also employ this strategy. Two pieces, "Oyl On: Sex and Chocolate," and "Oyl On: Voodoo Dolls and Zombie Slaves," align alternating verse paragraphs against different left-hand margins, suggesting the interplay of two voices, although not neatly divided into clearly defined points of view. Three shorter pieces, "A Love Poem," "After Couples Therapy," and "A Sex Poem," comprise dialogues between Olive Oyl and Popeye that are formatted as scripts using the initials "O" and "P." These poems consist of accusations and commands, often unsynchronized, as if the lovers cannot hear each other or acknowledge the other's point of view. In "A Sex Poem," these commands are ecstatically erotic (starting with "Shiver me down. Blow me timbers" [29]), while elsewhere they connote less friendly emotions. Frequently, too, the lines verge on unintelligibility: "P: I stays loyal on top of the sewer of yer cursked hair" (26). Duhamel and Seaton mirror the dialogic process of their own compositions through these poems, and they also transcribe the distinctive accents of the cartoon characters as far as possible. In fact, the dialog poems perform paradoxically, invoking both conversation and its failures, mimicking the characters' speech patterns and disrupting them with peculiar non-sequiturs.

The longest and richest poem in dialog format is the first one in the collection, "Interview with a Comic Strip Diva." This piece stages a three-way conversation between MS, OO, and DD, prefaced by an italicized sentence: *"We sat down with Olive Oyl in her home in Chester, Illinois. We were struck by the graceful reserve with which she served us herbal tea, her quiet yet sparkling generosity"* (9). Both the caption and the title submerge us instantly in celebrity culture, praising and promoting Olive in the manner of a million interviews in women's magazines. The word "Diva," associated with opera, emphasizes her cultural power, her individuality, and also her voice. Mae Questel's memorably nasal, harshly accented, high-pitched voicing of Olive may differ from the tones of famous sopranos, but Duhamel and Seaton do locate a valid resemblance. Olive's status, like many an opera diva's, rests in her individual "body," its shape and sound.

Performing the same role as "Baby Democrats" in *Exquisite Politics*, "Interview" is the only poem in *Oyl* in which the puppeteers emerge from behind the curtain.[35] While it brings the authors into overt conversation, it also dramatizes the "third voice" of their collaborative poetry more fully than ever before, and in a way that contrasts comically with the head note. Olive's answers exhibit neither "graceful reserve" nor "quiet yet sparkling generosity" but instead a straightforward feistiness, as illustrated in the opening exchange:

> MS: Ms. Oyl, you've been called the skinniest thing in boots. Do you find this interferes with your self-esteem?
> OO: Did you ask General MacArthur that? Nancy Sinatra? Betty Boop?
> DD: Are you concerned at all about America's obsession with the private lives of celebrities?
> OO: I've never had sex with Clark Kent. But that doesn't mean I won't if I get the chance. (9)

Duhamel and Seaton's Olive Oyl is quick to challenge the terms of a question, forthright about her sexual appetite, and well-versed in both high and low culture. She is also defiantly hybrid. Her first answer links military figures with entertainers, human beings with cartoon characters; later she compares herself to New York School poet Frank O'Hara and alludes to surrealist artist Meret Oppenheim. She ends the interview with the question, "Why can't I be it all? Pen and ink legs with human hair or Meret Oppenheim's teacup covered in fur, the way art has sex with life and vice versa" (10). This comment stresses Olive's collaborative origins and her participation in many media. It also posits a complex relationship between "art" and "life": not expression, not representation, but copulation. If art can have sex with life (and vice versa), neither can be illusory or wholly self-contained. Duhamel and Seaton shake the foundations of identity. Olive Oyl, or the "third voice" of collaboration, is in some fundamental way as real as the living artists.

"Interview with a Comic Strip Diva" represents voice through its format and refers to it in its title; it also engages the definition of poetry itself through two exchanges. In the middle of the interview, DD asks OO, "Speaking of the New York School of Poets, do you align yourself more with them or the Beats?" This odd question highlights how genres intersect at this juncture, since two poets are writing a poem that imitates a magazine interview (which is already a conversation converted into print) about a comic strip/cartoon/movie character. The New York School of poets, further, various as its members were, had strong ties (and sometimes collaborative artistic relationships) with stars the New York School of painting, while the Beats both through name and practice engage music, particularly jazz. OO's answer repudiates even these inclusive categories: "You can't imagine how boring it gets in all these boxes, each strip's linear predictability" (9). Through this conversation, Duhamel and Seaton convey strong skepticism about the usefulness of poetic labels, including, it seems, the label of "poetry" itself. A book of poems might indeed resemble a linear sequence of little boxes, reflecting frustrating confinement for the artist(s) and dull predictability for readers.

A further comment attributed to OO, however, qualifies this apparent dismissal of genre: "I believe in performance *and* page. My goal is to bust through genre restrictions—strips, 'toons, feature films" (10). Duhamel and Seaton convert OO's boredom into positive energy and a will to challenge the boundaries of genre; the word "bust" connotes not only breakage but female sexuality. Olive Oyl is busting into a new genre with this very piece, and OO's remark, appropriately, also engages lyric definition in a specific way. The first sentence refers the criticisms commonly leveled at Spoken Word poetry—that it sounds great live but falls flat on the page. As contemporary poet Bob Hicok retorts, the converse is also true: much of the poetry that succeeds on the page falls flat on stage. Should either fact exclude a piece from the definition of poetry?[36] "Interview" argues for eros rather than competition, championing a flexible and adaptable conception of poetry ("double-jointed" [10]). Duhamel and Seaton's Olive Oyl anticipates Charles Bernstein's argument that poems can exist in multiple media, and that neither performance nor page should automatically have priority as any poem's best, truest, ultimate version (*Close Listening* 8).

Arguments for more capacious understandings of genre—and even arguments for "busting through" it—do not, however, equal an argument against genre. Even this prose interview, Duhamel and Seaton assert, is a poem. They publish their collaborations with this label and use the term on their acknowledgments page. "Interview" establishes its poetic lineage, defends a broad definition of poetry, and classifies itself as a poem. Duhamel and Seaton follow it with an array of pieces rich in sound play, patterned by traditional poetic schemes, and persistently engaged with tropes of voice, speech, and dialog. The conventional solitariness of the lyric is refracted into many voices. Further, even when they establish the fiction of an individual voice (as in OO's distinctive outrageousness), its origin is strangely unstable. Where do Olive Oyl's lines come from? How many authorial partners has she enjoyed? After all, as OO states in "Interview," "I am not monogamous. There are millions of monogamous people, but I am not one of them" (9).

Duhamel notes to MacDonald that she has "hope for poetry" because of its "brevity and beauty," well-suited to shorter attention spans (6). Seaton adds in the same article, "I like new definitions and bigger umbrellas" (6). Years later, corresponding with Mazur and Ryal, Seaton identifies the primary pleasure of poetry as "connection" (1). Seaton told de la Flor the following about her poems: "I believe I wrote them all with the muse or in partnership with the poems themselves, that everything I do happens in a synergy of relationship" (5).

Interestingly, this provocative chapbook has had a subsequent life as the basis for further collaborations. Shortly after its publication, Emily Rems adapted and directed *Oyl* for Banshee Productions. The one-act play featuring no fewer than ten Olives, played by both women and men, opened in the spring of 2001 and had three successful runs in New York City: at the WoW Café Theatre, The Hudson Valley Writer's Center, and Off-Broadway at The Culture Project. As Mazur and Ryal suggest, "The Banshee production of *Oyl* off-Broadway took collaboration and collage to another level, didn't it? Now you had to collaborate with actors, the dramaturge, the producer, director, and the stage hands, just to name a few" (5). Seaton responds,

> In the case of Oyl's off-off Broadway debut, however, we writers just handed over the poems and Emily Rems did the rest. We were thrilled with the production, absolutely dazzled. At one point, I felt tears well up because I'd wanted to hear Oyl's empowered voice since, oh, maybe the '80s, and there were ten Oyls on stage booming her words to the world. (6)

The metaphor of poetic voice again becomes embodied, this time multiply and with more power. Duhamel and Seaton received the coauthored character into their poetic relationship, and hand her forward gladly into new ventures. Comic strips may be unlikely inspiration for the lyric, and innovative poetry is certainly an unlikely basis for theater, and yet the conversation continues to circulate and strengthen.

If poetry is a social enterprise, according to these poets, what role do poetic audiences play in the party? Merrill tells one interviewer, "It's madness to think of an audience. It's madness also not to think of one. . . . That sense, however dim, of mutual endeavor is the indispensable thing" (*Recitative* 58–59). Chapter 5 takes up this question by documenting the live delivery and reception of poetry in various contexts, with special attention to the National Poetry Slam. Collaboration and conversation dominate Slam poetry, both as trope and in practice. For the print poetries of Merrill, Duhamel, and Seaton, however, readers only enter the "talk" by proxy. The latter poets position themselves simultaneously as creators and as audiences

entertained by, sometimes even possessed by, other agents. In some fundamental way, then, print poetry cannot contain audience response. The
open conversation must close for the book to see publication. The figurative nature of voice remains a limit for printed poetry, although often a
welcome one. Poems on the page cannot complete the circuit between poet
and audience unless or until the poem is physically voiced.

VOICE ACTIVATED

CONTEMPORARY ACADEMIC POETRY READINGS
AND THE NATIONAL POETRY SLAM

The United States has been enjoying a sort of poetry renaissance. Currently the "poetry slam," an event where drunken audiences hoot down sensitive poems about dying grandmothers or inevitable divorces and bestow twenty-dollar prizes on scatological doggerel, is sweeping the nation. It's an amusement that seems to be a goldmine for saloon keepers too sophisticated for "hot Buns" contests. It has recently been possible to find at least three such events every week in different venues—even in a city like Houston. Perhaps, for a new generation, the poetry slam is the equivalent of the Beatnik coffeehouse scene. Not!

—Lorenzo Thomas, *Extraordinary Measures*

There can be no such thing as a poet who is a bad reader of his or her own writing, because only the poet can give you the unique experience of hearing the writer read the work. . . . Short of falling down drunk or bursting into tears, it can't go wrong, because however you read is what people came to hear.

—Katha Pollitt, in *The KGB Bar Book of Poems*

What is most commonly said about Slam poetry—that it's not as good on the page as it is live—is true for most though not all of the work. What people don't notice, or admit, is that the opposite is true. Much of the poetry that gets published is no good on the stage.

—Bob Hicok, *Caffeine Destiny*

Poets have publicly sounded their own poetry in an astonishing variety of ways since 1950. They have performed in a range of venues, including universities, bars, bookstores, and festivals. They have reached many kinds of audiences from bohemian, activist, and academic circles. Finally, they have voiced their work with different goals, such as earning a living, promoting a cause, or celebrating a community. I began work on this chapter, however, wondering about the ubiquity of one mode of poetry performance—what I refer to throughout as the contemporary academic poetry reading. Where did it come from and whose interests does it serve?

Peter Middleton, in one of the very few books that examines this practice historically, describes the ritual of the poetry reading as follows:

> A person stands alone in front of an audience, holding a text and speaking in an odd voice, too regular to be conversation, too intimate and too lacking in orotundity to be a speech or a lecture, too rough and personal to be theatre. The speaker is making no attempt to conceal the text. Signs of auditory effort in the audience are momentarily lost in occasional laughter, tense silences, sighs, and even cries of encouragement. Sometimes the reader uses a different, more public voice and refers to what is being read, or to some other information of apparent interest. No one talks to the reader. No one proposes a second take. (25)

In the current academic version of this event, "cries of encouragement," in fact, are fairly rare; the audience is typically seated in orderly rows and behaves quietly. The ritual also prescribes a podium, a glass or bottle of water, and a microphone, but no other props.[1] The room is lit as a classroom would be, and in fact it may be a classroom. The speaker's costume is some variation on the humanist professor's—dark or neutral colors, probably rumpled. The men have open collars and the women wear interesting jewelry. The hair might be a little longer or weirder than what one sees at a suburban office park, but not by much.

The origins of this kind of poetry reading are not hard to divine. It evolved largely from the model of the academic lecture rather than, say, the recital or exhibition, although it credentials the creative writer just as the latter activities serve as recurring qualifications for other artists employed by universities. Whom it serves, however, requires a more complex answer. The academic poetry reading benefits, primarily, the insiders to academic poetry's institutions: the poets, editors, and teachers who profit from the conventions of the academic reading circuit. This is not the same as calling such readings pointless, narcissistic, or exploitative. The amounts of money involved are, after all, relatively small and hard-won; earning a living this way is quite difficult. Po-biz is no field for hungry entrepreneurs. Further, academic poetry as an umbrella term is almost ridiculously capacious, potentially including any work produced by poet-professors and/or published by university presses and in university-sponsored journals. Even when the performance conventions are identical, the poems voiced may differ radically. Academic poetry readings can serve audiences well, even when pleasing audiences is not the primary goal of any of the organizers or participants. Anybody who has attended a lot of them has encountered many mediocre performances, but has also heard at least a few poets deliver memorable work in mesmerizing ways.

The more I learned about American performance poetries since the 1950s, however, the more my questions altered. Why, given the innovations in poetry performance over the last six decades, have academic poetry readings changed so little? I also became increasingly interested in how, where, and why contemporary poets voice their work outside of colleges and universities, where the audience for poetry remains large, eager, and various, even if those audience members are buying very few books. Oral publication is tremendously important in contemporary poetry. As other critics have observed, a poet who succeeds as a performer, whether on slam or academic circuits, in bars or independent bookstores or festivals, probably reaches far more listeners through readings than readers through book sales. Embodied voices attract audiences.

Most of this chapter focuses on one alternative to academic poetry readings: spoken word poetry, the populist movement of the late twentieth century that includes poetry slams and jams, and whose works share features with the lyrics of popular music, especially rap. A recent National Poetry Slam (NPS 2005) and the experiences of one participating team serve as the main texts. Slam poetry engages all the meanings of poetic voice that this book has explored: its emphasis on the poet's presence, its relation to song and vernacular speech, its connotations of singularity and originality. It both exploits and challenges the association of poetry with voice, and it does so with the explicit agenda of reclaiming poetry from teacher-scholars like me. Nevertheless, slam did not emerge suddenly as a novel alternative to the stale commonplaces of academic reading practices: it resembles and is indebted to other counter-culture poetic modes. Further, slam is becoming an institution in its own right, with some of its most well known practitioners pursuing and achieving academic credentials, publication, and employment.

The most important context of spoken word is the history of American poetry reading since shortly after World War II. In the sixties and seventies, poetry readings were meant to be revolutionary; during these eras oral poetries and anti-academic performance philosophies penetrated universities. By the nineties, poems were voiced in academic settings in ways that had become highly predictable. In the years since, a spoken word aesthetic has also infiltrated some academic poetry performance. This chapter therefore begins the history of voiced poems in the United States since the late forties, and then analyzes the contemporary academic poetry reading and its various subgenres, using the 2006 convention of the Association of Writers and Writing Programs (AWP) as a case study. Through such contrasts, slam emerges not as the cure for an academic style of voicing poetry, nor as the nemesis of university-sponsored art, but as one manifestation of a recurrent set of questions in American verse culture. It compels poets and audiences to consider the boundaries and purposes of poetry: what does a good poem sound like? Is it primarily an oral or a textual event, or both, or something else entirely? Who should voice it, where, to whom, and how? Finally, why should anyone listen?

The American Poetry Reading since 1950

Michael Davidson observes that literary history often centers on "inaugural moments" that become mythic (*The San Francisco Renaissance* 1). Sometimes these moments are textual: the seizure of part of *Howl*'s second printing by U.S. Customs, the anthology wars of the late 1950s and early 1960s, the founding of Third World Press and the Women's Press Collective, the publications of manifestoes, the rise and fall of various magazines. More recently, these inaugural moments have been electronic: the establishment of archives such as PennSound and UbuWeb; on-line literary magazines; the proliferation of blogs and listservs creating virtual poetic communities. Some of the most important inaugural moments of American poetry since the fifties, however, involve neither print nor the internet but instead center on live performances.

Readings, recitals, and performances can be hard to recover and study, as the introduction to this book emphasizes. However, poets and critics sometimes begin their careers inspired by a public poetry reading;[2] great performers have catalyzed the founding or development of poetry centers and reading series; through readings, activist poets have fought for poetry's central role in public life. Any one event has a limited range of influence, because relatively few people attend it. Its effect, however, may be amplified through broadcast (as in Robert Frost's recitation at John F. Kennedy's inauguration) or enthusiastic first-person accounts that are printed or circulated by word of mouth (as in Dylan Thomas's tours or the Six Gallery reading of 1955). Even more frequently, a famous reading occurs in a context of other, similar events; it may epitomize a trend that is experienced by large numbers of people. The proliferation of feminist poetry readings in the seventies is a good example of the latter—"being there" involves not attendance at one specific gathering but participation in the culture of independent presses and bookstores that fostered so many of these occasions. Further, critics and poets tend to recall different "firsts," a range of radicalizing experiences, depending on their geography, generation, access to poetry readings, politics, and taste.[3] Does the importance of a reading depend on how many people attended, or the freshness of its conception, or the skill and daring of the performers, or just on one person publishing a powerful account of it? If those are all reasonable criteria, and I believe they are, the list should be very long, and should vary according to the readings and experiences of its compiler.

Appendix A of this book offers such a list of foundational, legendary, influential, or notorious public poetry soundings, with the caveat that such inventories must always be subjective. My catalog begins with Dylan Thomas, who like Millay fused poetry performance as theater with poetry performance as a spectacle of personality. While Millay played the femme fatale, however, Thomas ran variations on the charismatic drunkard, the gifted bard in a tailspin—a role that attracted many other actors in the fifties and beyond. Donald Hall describes Thomas as a "starting point and emblem" of the contemporary poetry reading ("The Poetry Reading" 65). Thomas's tour, however, might be more accurately described as a cultural pivot or turning point. George Economou, for example, describes it as the "swan song" of the kind of poetry reading he witnessed at the Poetry Center in New York in the late fifties: "something of a cross between lecture and a dramatic-reading. Proscenium or podium oriented, they emphasized the distance between poet and audience" (655). Whether they represent a beginning or an ending, Thomas's performances, like other antecedents of the contemporary poetry reading, were sometimes billed as lectures and bore limited resemblance to the contemporary phenomenon. Thomas had received elocution lessons in childhood and always demonstrated a strong affinity for theater; he broadcasted for the BBC before ever venturing abroad. His voice was rich and trained and audiences on both sides of the Atlantic found his performances riveting. Like Millay, Thomas combined unusual dramatic skills (for an accomplished poet) with notoriety and charisma, so that his readings were an exhibition both of skill and of celebrity presence. Unlike Millay, Thomas recited poems by a range of authors before concluding with a few of his own pieces; in this way, his performances resembled the actor-recitations popular in the nineteenth century.

Poetry readings become increasingly prevalent, at least in cities, from the mid-fifties onwards, partly through the establishment of the Poet's Theater in Boston and Poetry Centers in New York and San Francisco. Other institutions developed in tandem. Betty Kray showed inspiration and initiative in developing college reading circuits; in this enterprise, she met substantial resistance from colleges themselves. Her leadership at the Academy of American Poets starting in 1959 involved promoting the poetry reading as an important aspect of the art. John Malcolm Brinnin, also a director of the Poetry Center of the Young Men's and Young Women's Hebrew Association in New York and an important early proponent of poetry readings, handled Thomas's American engagements for a commission of fifteen percent. Although talent agencies had existed for decades, by mid-century they began brokering poetry readings.

Other poetic institutions were also created in the fifties and began to shape poets' careers. The Poetry Center at San Francisco State University, for example, was founded in 1954 by director Ruth Witt-Diamant, thanks to a bequest from W. H. Auden.[4] The San Francisco Renaissance is, in fact, one of the best documented regional scenes, especially in regard to its lively readings at bars and galleries. Many other bookstores, presses, arts communities, and reading series sprang up in the sixties: the Poetry Project at St. Mark's Church and Beyond Baroque, created during that decade, continue to be hubs of poetic activity.[5] Arts funding opportunities expanded dramatically in the late sixties and early seventies, sometimes supporting such endeavors (Norris 39–40). As Kim Whitehead, Kathryn Howd Machan, and others write, feminist poetry performance, sponsored by a range of feminist bookstores and presses, gained steam in the sixties and attracted loyal audiences, although some of them have since ceased operations.

During the 1960s and 1970s, antiwar poetry, Black Arts, feminist poetry, and ethnopoetics advocated the power of oral performance to build community and inspire social change (see Rothenberg's "New Models, New Visions"). Like events associated with Black Mountain and the San Francisco Renaissance, these revolutionary performances were often manifestations of a bent for experiment that extended to printed poetry as well—these movements all subverted conventions concerning the proper materials, purposes, and strategies of poetry. The incorporation of Buddhist chants and mantras by readers including Ginsberg and Anne Waldman also demonstrated a hope that poetry readings could genuinely transform both poets and audiences, producing physiological changes in the body that could yield insight or quiet riotous crowds. Many, but not all, of such events occur on the East and West Coasts, reflecting the pre-eminence of New York City and San Francisco in American poetry during these decades. Most of these poetry readings, finally, pose a fairly explicit challenge to what was, by the late sixties, the standard way of sounding poetry, the kind of academic reading described in this chapter's opening pages. Perhaps counter-academic readings became just as formulaic as the university style of presentation; free verse protest delivered from a political platform is not necessarily more poetically powerful, or even less predictable, than the kind of poetry it resists. Still, the existence of parallel practices put pressure on the dominant model and made visible the academic poetry performance style as a not-inevitable choice. The academic poetry reading, by implication, reflects certain prejudices about what a poet looks like and how he or she sounds, as well as clearly demarcated boundaries between art and political life.

Performance experiments in large and small cities are crucial to the history of poetry in the United States. Nevertheless, the whole story of poetry's soundings does not occur there. From within a lively urban scene with its own factions and aesthetic imperatives, the national poetry landscape can seem distorted, full of waste lands where, in fact, poetry in different modes may be thriving. The full history of the public poetry reading must include what happens in city galleries and Poetry Centers but also what happens in suburban bookstores and bars, on less-than-hip campuses, on radio and television and the internet. For example, little colleges accepted the poetry reading as a practice more reluctantly than urban audiences did, but did not simply mimic city reading culture with a ten-year delay. Instead, they welcomed some practices and resisted others, and continue to endorse an idiosyncratic poetry canon.

As a brief example, at my home institution of Washington and Lee University, located in a small southern town out of commuting range of any major city, soundings of poetry by its authors were quite rare before the end of World War II.[6] According to the undergraduate newspaper, there were several public lectures about poetry but very few performances by poets themselves. Headlines indicate a few exceptions: Vachel Lindsay was "well-received" in 1921, Carl Sandburg gave a lecture-recital in 1923, and Frost "interpreted" his poems in Lee Chapel in 1941. After faculty and students returned from World War II, the community began to host a range of literary visitors under the auspices of "The Washington and Lee Seminars in Literature," a series founded in 1952.[7] Nearly all the speakers, including the poets, gave titled lectures. For instance, John Ciardi spoke on Dante in 1956 and Jarrell on "The Poet and the Public" in 1957. This began to change in the 1960s, when some programs simply designated the event as "A Reading"—as for Frank O'Hara in 1961, Muriel Rukeyser in 1965, and W. S. Merwin in 1968. This fragmentary evidence suggests that the campus reading tour was, in the sixties, just beginning to be the sanctioned way for American poets to build academic reputations and followings. Visitors began to adhere to the professional roles for which they increasingly seemed best credentialed: poets recited and scholars lectured. In this way, not surprisingly, Washington and Lee trailed well behind developments in urban literary culture but reflected closely how the academic poetry reading was becoming an institution.

Changes in English departments during fifties, sixties, and seventies reflected increased student interest in studying contemporary literature, the explosion of creative writing as a discipline, and, as David Wojahn puts it, "fatter budgets . . . in part because of funding from newly founded organizations such as the National Endowment for the Arts" (277).[8] Washington and Lee, even in its relative isolation from research universities, mirrored these shifts. In 1950, faculty and students founded the literary magazine *Shenandoah*. After James Boatwright became editor of that journal in 1964, readings by prominent poets occurred on campus with increasing frequency. Arthur and Margaret Glasgow also established an endowment in 1960 "for the promotion of the expression of art through pen and tongue" and a committee has since drawn upon that fund to bring creative writers to campus, generally several per year.[9] In the sixties Glasgow readers were entirely white and male and often Southern; student poetry readings also proliferated. The poetry of protest that galvanized communities up and down both coasts from the sixties onward did reach Washington and Lee: the first "Poetry Be-In" occurred in 1969 and in 1973, a symposium of five women writers—Mary McCarthy, Denise Levertov, Carolyn Kips, Barbara Deming, and Penelope Gilliat—drew fascinated crowds within the all-male campus. Ishmael Reed was the first African-American poet to accept an invitation, in 1974, and Ginsberg read here shortly afterwards. The 1980s and 1990s saw a greater proportion of European poets, including Czeslaw Milosz, Tom Paulin, and Piotr Sommer, and many Irish writers, and after a recent festival of Native American writing, there is much interest here in establishing such gatherings on a regular basis. The Glasgow Endowment, in short, has sponsored mainly East Coast academic poets, those with advanced degrees and/or university jobs, but there is usually some esthetic, ethnic, and geographical diversity in the roster.

The character of these events has changed only slightly from the sixties to the present. The physical spaces are more or less the same: the formal pews of Lee Chapel for the biggest events and a range of classrooms and small auditoria for the rest. Poetry readings based in these spaces partake of the conventions of academic lectures; the poet stands on a stage and speaks from behind a podium to rows of quietly seated students, faculty, and community members. Generally these writers read from books and manuscripts, proffering occasional glosses or background information on the poems in a more extemporaneous manner. In the past two or three decades, a few poets gave lectures as well as readings or participated in panel discussions. However, the conventions of the readings themselves remained stable at this little liberal arts college and throughout much of the United States.

While poetry readings were very numerous in the eighties and nineties, most performers who found their way into colleges and universities during these decades were not trying to challenge preconceptions about how poetry readings sound and what they can do.[10] I attended many memorable poetry readings during this time but they tended to focus on distinguished poets who had been performing for decades: Ginsberg singing Blake in a chapel at Rutgers College in the late eighties; a centennial celebration for Walt Whitman at which Adrienne Rich and James Merrill read unforgettably, one apparently in pain and the other seemingly spry in a dapper green suit; Seamus Heaney charming vast multitudes at Princeton University, simulcast in giant screens in an overflow auditorium; and, in 2004, an utterly radiant Lucille Clifton at the second Furious Flower festival of African American Poetry at James Madison University. For the most part, the eighties and nineties saw a widening rift between the academic poetry reading and alternative modes, whether activist, theatrical, or populist. Far fewer readings, tours, and festivals have been canonized, debated, or gossiped about on a national scale—outside, that is, of the spoken word phenomenon, which has garnered a great deal of press without yet sending significant numbers of stars out to the boondocks on national reading circuits.

Grassroots poetry scenes began to expand again in the early 1990s, as Joseph Harrington (170–73) and Christopher Beach attest (123); Dana Gioia asserts that "the most surprising and significant development in recent American poetry has been the wide-scale and unexpected reemergence of popular poetry—rap, cowboy poetry, poetry slams, and certain overtly accessible types of what was once a defiantly avant-garde genre, performance poetry" (6–7).[11] If academic readings have become an increasingly settled institution at colleges across the country, have any of these alternate approaches to poetry performance—the festival, the happening, the rally—also had such a lasting influence? The answer seems to be that while the oral poetics of the fifties, sixties, and seventies encouraged academic poets to read differently, this effect faded or was repudiated in later decades. Poetic counter-cultures of the eighties and nineties, meanwhile, have influenced university programming, but their existence has not yet had much effect on how professor-poets perform.

This may change, as I discuss below. Meanwhile, many of the most compelling poet-performers among young academics are alumni of Cave Canem, a workshop for African-American poets founded in 1996, or associated with the Dark Room Collective, a group of African-American writers founded in Boston in 1989, or spoken word alumni more generally (these identities can overlap). Such groups include many writers with deep investments in poetry as sound; Cave Canem, in fact, advertises itself as bringing together writers "schooled in MFA programs or poetry slams."[12] As affiliates and graduates of these communities filter out in to colleges and universities, they bring along a dedication towards poetry performance as a craft in its own right. Other poets may end up responding positively to such competition or, perhaps, see their on-campus reading options diminish.

The Contemporary Academic Poetry Reading

Critiques of contemporary American poetry readings emanate from opposing perspectives—positing that such events are conservative and dull, for instance, or conversely, that by being entertaining they pander to audiences in a manner that betrays the work. Constructing the latter kind of polemic, David Groff argues that good poetry is inherently visual and is always misrepresented in oral performance:

> But even if the poem takes on a fresh life when it's delivered in the voice of its maker, it loses more than it gains. Attending a poetry reading has as much in common with reading a poem on the page as reading a screenplay has to do with seeing a movie. Only when we acknowledge that a poem performed is no substitute for a poem read in private will we truly advance the cause of the poetic word.

More commonly, critics oscillate between declaring that public poetry readings shouldn't occur at all, and wishing simply that they might be better. Judith Shulevitz prefers recordings over live recitations and laments various aspects of the academic reading as ritual:

> [T]he recitation of difficult verse in a strange, singsongy voice; the rambling preamble about the experience that led to the epiphany that led to the idea that led to the poem; the knowing murmurs that accompany the hint of a joke, whatever the punch line. . . . It is hard to imagine an appreciation of serious poetry being deepened among readers who witness these faintly embarrassing speech acts. (34)

Jeffrey McDaniel, contrasting a lively reading honoring June Jordan with a less engaging event, recalls:

> A dozen years ago I went to some Lannan Foundation-sponsored dinner before a Louise Glück reading at the Folger Shakespeare Library in Washington, D.C. The topic of poetry as performance came up. Glück said, emphatically, "The poem should remain on the page." An hour later she was on stage, reading her work to a large audience, in a voice that was different—more breathless—than the voice she had been using at dinner. Perhaps Glück's statement should have been: "Poetry should remain on the page unless you're being handsomely rewarded for it."

As McDaniel observes, many writers who express skepticism about the value of readings or even contempt for the enterprise nevertheless accept paying gigs. Sometimes critics mourn the dispersal of readings' former revolutionary energies, as when Hank Lazer posits that "In part because of [its] anecdotal and personalized format, the dominant version of the poetry reading has become an ossified prop for a certain kind of brief lyric" (66). Lazer and others, such as Naeem Murr, do hope that the ritual can be resuscitated. Murr frames this faint optimism, however, with a "taxonomy . . . of potentially harmful readings," including debacles of personae such as the drunk backwoodsman, the sexpot, the stand-up poet, and the "Abstruse Inflictors" who use the event to punish their benighted audiences.

Hall argues both positions—that readings fail poetry, that readings can save poetry—in "The Poetry Reading." The negative portion of his essay cleverly echoes *Howl*'s opening wail: "I have seen Robert Frost make coo-material for the coo-ers; I have heard Robert Lowell play his audience with the skill and vulgarity of Ed McMahon" (72). From this point of view, readings are advertisement disguised as entertainment and hence vulgar; they prostitute the intimacy of silent reading, in which "the mind's voice speaks to the mind's ear" (72). On the positive side, the same money can free poets from the demands of teaching and encourage travel. Readings also provide "tentative publication" for nearly finished work and remind poets that their art is rooted in the human body (75–77). Playfully repulsed and idealistic by turns, Hall rehearses most of the major arguments for and against what he calls the "standard college reading" (66), and finds that they center on economics. Should poetry be pure of commerce? Or is answerability to audiences crucial to its vitality, even its survival as an art form?

This conflict mirrors the basic tension at the heart of academic life at the beginning of the twenty-first century: what role does, or should, money play in education? To what extent are faculty service-providers for student-consumers? The parallel isn't accidental, and it need not destroy universities or poetry, although a good balance between economic urgencies and intellectual and artistic life is hard to find and harder to maintain. Colleges and universities, however, with their constituent departments and presses, are not the only institutions shaping poetry readings. The Association of Writers and Writing Programs, the chief professional organization for creative writers in higher education, holds an annual conference that not only exemplifies the practices of academic poetry readings, but to some extent establishes and reinforces them.

As the organization's web site states,

> AWP was founded in 1967 to support the growing presence of writers in higher education & thereby foster new generations of writers & new audiences for literature. Founded in 1967 by fifteen writers representing thirteen creative writing programs, The Association of Writers & Writing Programs has grown to include 22,000 individual writers, teachers, & students & 330 college & university creative writing programs in the United States, Canada, & the United Kingdom.[13]

I attended the 2006 AWP annual conference—held in Austin, Texas, and attended by thousands—in order to sample a wider range of academic readings than is available in my small town. I found that, even though I had never attended the AWP before, these were completely familiar. I had attended most of these kinds of readings at various home institutions, including the public university I attended as an undergraduate, the elite research university I attended as a Ph.D. candidate, and the liberal arts college where I have taught since. The quality of the performances exhibited the same range: dreadfully dull, intellectually galvanizing, emotionally moving, disparate in mood and audience, but never particularly surprising.[14]

Most of the events occurred in the conference hotel or the adjacent convention center over the packed days of concurrent sessions. The readings I attended included:

- Group readings (three or four poets) sponsored by literary magazines and occurring in a curtained-off corner of the Book Fair amphitheater. At these events professionally dressed poets read from books at podia, using amplification. These poets displayed little affect and some nervousness; their framing patter was minimal. The silent audience members were mostly white and female. These readings were the least rewarding and the most sparsely attended of any I visited.

- Panels comprised of short talks and readings by several poets. These took place in hotel meeting rooms, which were far quieter than the Book Fair. Two, for example, were sponsored by book series, Camino del Sol and Crab Orchard; another honored a new anthology of poets from Cave Canem. At these, poets and editors generally spoke from books and notes, but most read expressively, emphasizing rhythm and performing dialog—this may be because all three specific groups are unusually sympathetic to spoken word, populist traditions. The participants in these panels acknowledged audiences more comfortably via eye contact and verbal comments than did the Book Fair readers, and those audiences were considerably warmer. For example, when audience members laughed at a line in Gina Franco's poem at the Camino del Sol event, she interrupted herself to cry, "It's true!" At the same event, Maria Melendez began, "Boy, you are a good-looking crowd" and recited her first poem from memory.

  At the Cave Canem reading, when Cornelius Eady remarked, looking out into the crowd, "So many black people," loud laughter erupted. Each poet introduced the next at this panel, enacting how members of Cave Canem support one another professionally and artistically. Vocal styles varied widely here, from Eady's intense whisper to Patricia Smith's virtuoso performance, which itself contained booming passages and sotto voce asides.

  The latter two events attracted minority writers who generally work in geographical isolation from each other. The Crab Orchard Book Series did not so obviously gather a generally dispersed community for a rare celebration. Nevertheless, the packed room was eagerly receptive. Victoria Chang exemplified how the academic style of presentation, which purports to focus attention on words or ideas instead of bodies, can work well: a few deadpan asides delighted her listeners, but she delivered her poems well without pronounced theatrical elements.

- Readings hosted outside of hotel sites. The feminist bookstore Book-Woman was packed for several poets published by Red Hen Press. By choosing this venue, the publishers brought an urban, counter-culture feel to the fringes of an academic conference. The poets took turns perching on a stool while audience members, seated on the floor or on folding chairs, munched hors d'oeuvres and sipped wine.

- Featured readers in the Hilton Grand Ballroom. This was a very large space: I couldn't see, for example, whether the light stripe across Naomi Shihab Nye's shoulder was long hair or a scarf. Nevertheless, Nye and Tony Hoagland were animated and energized. Audience members seemed delighted by them (and also by the comically misspelled captions projected for the hearing-impaired).

Despite the range of skills and styles displayed at the AWP, most of the readings I saw there adhered to the norms observable at colleges and universities. Poetry readings tend to be indoor events. Staging signifies that the poets are experts, physically separated from their audiences, often elevated by a stage and supported by a lectern. They control the microphone. Audiences, disciplined into rows, participate only affirmatively. Most importantly, poets perform the fact that they are not performers. Readers may wear street clothes or business clothes, but avoid any suggestion of costume; I saw no AWP poets strumming mandolins, carrying props other than books, or manipulating the lighting; they may read expressively but without the dramatic ranges of pitch and intensity that characterize theater productions. A few, like Camille Dungy, recite signature poems from memory, but most simply read, and although their asides may be scripted, such remarks seem to be spontaneous or at least casual. Most of all, AWP readings seem to disembody the poet and the poetry. Many of the stages were too narrow to permit pacing, much less theatrical blocking, but with the exception of a few poets crossing over from slam, authors tended to plant their feet in one place anyway, limiting physical movement. This effacement of the poet's physical self, particularly the lower body, reflects the uneasy professionalism of academically sponsored art. This impersonality may also spring from discomfort with confessionalism's legacy and the stereotype of the "workshop poem" as narcissistically self-expressive. In any case, poets did not display emotions at their readings but instead tended to manifest intellectual detachment, if not in the poem's words then through carefully neutral delivery.

When a few poets alluded to their bodies during AWP events, they produced an interesting dissonance in the ritual. Victoria Chang mentioned a new pregnancy during her reading, drawing all eyes to her abdomen, but in fact her self-presentation in dark street clothes was self-effacing; paradoxically, she drew attention to the irrelevance of the poet's body by mentioning her own. Chang's anti-performance performance also resonated with her hyphenated identity. Her work repeatedly invokes the dichotomized worlds implicit in the label "Asian American" but refuses to choose sides—it alludes, for instance, to Emerson and the T'ang Dynasty, emphasizing connection as well as conflict. Readings by some of the Cave Canem poets likewise addressed race, but Toi Derricotte framed the panel by celebrating Cave Canem as a place where black poets "don't have to write about race all the time." At the Red Hen reading, the roster of female readers and the location in a feminist bookstore highlighted gender, but the participants drew attention to poetry's embodiment in other ways. Cynthia Hogue, for example, read poetry reflecting a serious illness and spoke about how pain affects one's cognitive capacities. Physical experience, she thereby emphasized, can be an invisible, interior event, fracturing one's sense of self and therefore the voice of the poem.

Poetry readings by authors embody language forcefully. Surely, too, this is one rationale for the AWP conference—to manifest editors, authors, and audiences to each other, to embody literature and correspondence, to foster live rather than electronic conversation among artists. By definition, panels that gather authors of one race and/or sex assert that the writer's body affects poetry. Even such events, though, manifest counter-pressures. These stresses may be social and institutional, but in some cases they also emanate from the complexity of the poetry itself, its ambivalent negotiation of the human condition. Insisting on the freedom of language from bodies, even when that freedom is qualified, is a defining aspect of the AWP ritual and of the academic poetry reading more generally.

Crossover poets like Patricia Smith participated in some of these readings, pushing at their conventions in a potentially transformative way. One of the last official events at AWP 2006, too, was a showcase of slam poets. This occurred at the nearby convention center, at the tail end of the conference, as if not quite under the AWP umbrella, although slam poets have been reading at these conferences for years now. The presence of the showcase, in conjunction with a lively panel on slam earlier in the gathering, suggests how slam, once a sort of outlaw, populist strain of American poetry, is gradually moving towards the academic mainstream—to the unease of both parties.[15]

Slam Poetry as an Institution

Slam poetry, meaning work recited by its authors at competitive poetry performance events, often sounds less transgressive than familiar. This aural art possesses many antecedents in both its style and its material, including Beat poetry, the Black Arts movement, Confessionalism, ethnopoetics, the poem-talks of David Antin, and many other authors and movements. It also echoes contemporary musical forms from jazz to hip-hop.[16] In fact, slam poetry's familiarity is inextricable from its innovations: slam seizes contemporary poetry, redefines its audiences and goals, and sounds and embodies it for public consumption. It manages to offend and delight various listeners, moreover, through its very orality and its insistent populism—qualities that have characterized poems from many places and eras and hardly constitute radical experimentality.

Even as it affirms the rootedness of poetry in sound and the human body, however, slam challenges literary conventions, in particular, the conventions of the academic reading and the implicit definition of poetry advocated by those events. Slam is deliberately conscious of its listeners, because its audience is physically present during a poem's "publication" by performance. Moreover, because of the judging system, slam poets try mightily to please their non-specialist addressees. And too, slam rebuts a post-Romantic definition of lyric in terms of its refusal of "solitude." It constitutes, in fact, a kind of team sport. Slam is often performed in collaboration with others; it is received and evaluated by participatory audiences; and sometimes slam poems are composed jointly. As Maria Damon observes, slam rewrites the privacy of the "lyric scene into a site for public discourse" (326). In short, slam is all about poetic voice in its various senses.

Slam poetry is an inherently social, dialogic poetic form, although many tensions spring from its sociability, including conflicts over ownership, identity, and poetry's very purposes. The National Poetry Slam of 2005 reveals some of the ways poetry can help foster community, as well as the ways that slam's conventions, and perhaps poetry itself, press back against cooperative endeavor. The team I treat most closely is a delegation of five from Four Corners—the only area in the United States where four states touch—Arizona, Colorado, New Mexico, and Utah—and a region located on Navajo Nation lands. The members of this team expected to lose and they did, for various reasons. Their marginal position emphasizes all the advantages and problems with poetry as a team sport.

Slam is often slammed by literary critics, as it hopes to be.[17] While this chapter responds in part to Charles Bernstein's advocacy of "close listening" in his collection of that title, any academic treatment of slam could be accused of listening *too* closely. The poets I cite at the end of this piece, for instance, might say I am over-hearing their work, applying a kind and intensity of attention inimical to their goals. Further, this chapter analyzes not the best of slam, as in a literary-critical rescue operation, nor the strangest work, as in an anthropological study. Instead, I test the meanings of poetic voice for slam on the works and experiences of a single, marginally successful team, in order to show how poetic sound and poetic performance inspire and worry even the writers at contemporary poetry's ragged edges.

Slam's pleasures, its proximity to stand-up comedy and other unpoetic performance modes, urge audiences to consider what poetry can be and what it can do. The works delivered at NPS 2005 engage all of the big ideas that trouble contemporary poetic communities: authenticity, originality, and identity; poetry's "multiform existence" in various media; the role of sound in form and genre; poetry's potential to instigate social change; and the materiality of language. From Four Corners, the borders, territories, and anthology subheadings of contemporary poetry don't seem wholly rational or helpful—in fact, they seem quaint. Slam both manifests and encourages a shift in the cultural meanings of poetry, as Joseph Harrington argues (171). It does so, however, not only by being interesting as a phenomenon but by emphasizing poetry's most appealing aspects. Adalaide Morris and others have argued for poetry as the most "sound-saturated" literary genre (5), seeking to "activate words in the dimension of sound" (Rasula 286), and slam is above all an aural form. Further, as Kathleen Crown puts it, all spoken word returns to "voice and presence as fundamental principles of lyric poetry" (216).

The history of slam has been covered more completely elsewhere, so I treat its sources briefly and focus on its current conventions. These practices emphasize the movement's repudiation of professionalism in the poetry world. Further, slam as a poetic form illuminates the fraught question of authorship. The necessary presence of the author's body seems to guarantee an aesthetic of personal expression, and yet the prevalence of group pieces emphasizes that no voice is original and that what may purport to be expression is always, in fact, performance. This chapter concludes with an account of the gathering from the perspective of the members of the Four Corners team, who competed in the nationals for the first time in 2005. Their experiences and their poems demonstrate the sociability of slam as a lyric mode that invites collaboration and demands a high level of involvement from its addressees.

Spoken word institutions are impermanent, ad hoc, borrowed on the cheap—in short, neither academic nor textual. Articles on this poetic mode do appear in scholarly and popular venues, but very few books take it seriously, and poet-professors tend not to accumulate tenure credentials on the slam circuit the way they might by reading at the annual AWP meeting.[18] Many web sites offer some information on spoken word, and a few television programs and documentaries feature performances. Glossy anthologies offer printed samples, and occasionally a slam poet moves into academic publishing venues, or just publishes an inexpensive book with a friendly press.[19] The material venues of spoken word poetry, however, are most importantly the bars, cafes, and theaters in which such poetry finds its audiences. These sites and conventions are inseparable from the poetry's meaning.

Poetry slams, or competitive poetry performance events, only constitute a portion of the spoken word scene. While the origins of the former are complex and contested, all sources agree that Marc Smith played a major role in its inception. According to Poetry Slam, Inc., the non-profit organization that promotes slam and oversees some of its annual competitions,

In 1986, Smith approached Dave Jemilo, the owner of the Green Mill (a Chicago jazz club and former haunt of Al Capone), with a plan to host a weekly poetry competition on Sunday nights. Jemilo welcomed him, and the Uptown Poetry Slam was born on July 25 of that year. Smith drew on baseball and bridge terminology for the name, and instituted the basic features of the competition, including judges chosen from the audience and cash prizes for the winner. (PSI Poetry Slams Inc. FAQ: Poetry Slam)

Other poetry events in Chicago and elsewhere, starting in the late seventies, established a climate for slam and helped to cultivate a style of poetry and performance that would flourish later. "The Incomplete History of Slam" by Kurt Heintz, a web-published history of slam's origins in diverse Chicago venues, credits not only poets but also a punk rock ethos for the early scene. Heintz chronicles a couple of infamous poetry boxing matches in various Chicago venues, and it is one of those organizers, Al Simmons, who brought the idea to New Mexico, where the Taos Poetry Circus operated, beginning in 1982. Meanwhile, under Smith's leadership at the Get Me High Lounge and later at the Green Mill, this combative mode of performance evolved into slam. Bob Holman, Gary Glazner, and others eventually exported the phenomenon to other cities, partly as a way to draw customers to bars and clubs. Again, poetry readings have an economic motive.

Slam as a phenomenon repudiates academic dominance over poetry, although the conflict between performance and academic poetry may not be a permanent state of affairs.[20] Marc Smith created a judging system that values amateur reaction to a piece much more highly than expert appreciation. However, because slam requires organization (certification, registration) and possesses a major national festival, gathering its most talented practitioners to one site over several days, it in fact constitutes an alternate literary institution to academia, and may be better suited to scholarly treatment than other spoken word scenes.[21] The National Poetry Slam, originally a two-team competition, first convened in San Francisco in 1990. It migrated annually to different cities from coast to coast before it landed in Albuquerque in 2005. National slams earn coverage from local media and internet blogs, but do not receive attention on a national stage, probably because they are, by design, not particularly lucrative for anyone. However, for an energetic community of poets and listeners, "nationals" remains an event of tremendous importance.

NPS 2005 was the biggest to date, and many of the participants felt that it was particularly well-organized, but it followed an established format. It began with two nights of competition in seven or eight venues. Bouts occurred simultaneously so that no one person could enjoy the whole scope of the event.[22] Seventy-five teams of three to five people each competed, including delegations from various cities distributed through twenty-eight states, Canada, and France. Large cities with multiple certified slam venues sometimes sent multiple teams. For example, New York City had four, designated "Brooklyn," "NYC Louder Arts," "NYC Nuyorican," and "NYC Urbana."

In Albuquerque, the slam was effectively advertised, and a strong local team had evidently primed lively audiences. The venues were packed, sometimes well past a building's official capacity, with spectators lined up along the walls and camera operators perched on tables. The early events occurred in a range of cafés and smoky bars. Audiences included many young bohemians and a few of the cultured middle-aged and older people who attend academic poetry readings; most of these patrons were white.[23] Teams and their friends and managers, however, were so diverse in race, age, gender, and fashion preferences that the excited crowds seemed strikingly various. Although slam rules prohibit costumes, performers' hair, clothing, and accessories signaled a range of clashing sub-cultures with one factor unifying the crowd: no one sought to dress like a professional of any kind.[24]

The competitive element of poetry slams depends on highly ritualized procedures overseen by the emcees and policed by every competing team. Policies involving the judges, some of which are formal and others tacit, are among the most crucial. For each bout at NPS 2005, five judges were chosen from the audience, usually by the emcee quietly circulating and making selections. When all five were selected they stood on or near the stage while the emcee issued group instructions and the competing teams were invited to look them over. Each panel that I observed included one white-haired man and four younger people; every group contained men and women and at least one person of color. Sometimes one judge's slot was filled with two people conferring together and presenting a joint score. The emcees themselves were experienced performers and sometimes the very sound checks were poetic.[25] Every bout also featured one "storm poet," or unaffiliated competitor, between the second and third rounds. The only other person to appear on stage was the "calibration" or "sacrificial" poet, on whom the judges initially tested their scoring impulses.[26]

The "official emcee spiel" is one of the best-rehearsed institutions of slam and many audiences know it by heart. Just before the competition, the emcee delivers a short speech describing the slam rules, exhorting the judges to remain consistent in their scoring and not to be swayed by the audience, and exhorting the audience to try to sway the judges. The spiel is interesting in several ways. First, although it is "official," the full speech is not available through the most accessible "official" source: the web site of Poetry Slam, Inc. Second, while Albuquerque emcees did deliver roughly the same announcement, slight variations sometimes shifted the emphasis in significant ways. For instance, some emcees instructed the audience to judge poems based on "performance, content, and originality," while others dropped the tricky term "originality." This alteration could affect scoring, especially in relation to unique or surprising pieces. Thirdly, the spiel sets a precedent for audience participation that goes well beyond the representative votes of five amateur judges chosen from the crowd.[27] At one telling juncture, each emcee describes slam's founding by Marc Smith, at which every single audience, unprompted, shouts the challenge, "SO WHAT?" In the content of the spiel, too, the emcee urges boisterous communication. At the 2005 national slam, this translated into polite attention to the poems themselves but vigorous booing for low scores, and wild cheering for high ones, especially tens. Some performers in some venues elicited, or at least received, a call-and-response from the audience: rhythmic clapping, approving remarks during pauses. At some other venues, most famously at the Chicago Green Mill, audience response is ritualized into snapping, stomping, or cutting verbal rejoinders.

In 2005, twenty teams survived the first two days of competition to compete in Friday's semi-finals, occurring at 9 P.M. in four venues (preceded by group pieces and haiku showcases). These bouts operated by the same rules as the earlier ones. The Championship Finals, on Saturday night at the Kiva Auditorium at the Convention Center, was a somewhat different affair, although the basic slam structure persisted. The final event was long, beginning at 8 p.m. and lasting until after midnight, while the previous bouts occupied only about ninety minutes when emceed efficiently. The event also included miscellaneous performances by musicians and non-placing teams, and extended vamping and many speeches praising generous contributors. However, the most striking difference was the formality of the upscale venue, a sold-out theater seating 2400, the aisles spiked with very professional camera gear, and a giant screen on stage to broadcast performances into the wings. In the finals, the grungy rituals of slam met the polish of commercial theater. The result was sometimes successful, sometimes uncomfortable, and less tensely entertaining than the minor bouts. This last event illustrated, in fact, a phenomenon that Julie Schmid and others have observed: "the increasing institutionalization and commodification of the movement" (637).

Slam as a Poetic Form

Jim Coppoc declared at the slam showcase at the 2006 AWP that slam is not a genre but a gimmick or a party game.[28] Nevertheless, several critics have sought to describe slam as a form, or at least to describe its most common strategies. While Ron Silliman views slam as a conventional "free-verse presentation of sincerity and authenticity" (362), Beach finds slam parodying "the workshop poem," critiquing the latter on socioeconomic grounds (132). Damon likewise stresses the political dissidence of slam that she finds to be rooted, at its most successful, in "some kind of 'realness'—authenticity at the physical/ sonic and metaphysical/ emotional-intellectual-spiritual levels" (329). Tyler Hoffman also analyzes the political subversiveness of the slam esthetic, stressing its "pluralism" and "dialogism" and comparing it to Bakhtin's notion of carnival (49–50). Susan B. A. Somers-Willett notes the prevalence of a slam subgenre she calls the "identity poem" (52), arguing that "the authenticity that slam audiences reward is at least in part contingent upon the performance of identity that takes place on slam stages" (53). Schmid writes,

> It is impossible to define an overarching slam poetry aesthetic. However, the majority of slam poems tend to be narrative—often times written in the first person—and in iambic tetrameter and trimeter. End rhymes are usually eschewed by veteran slam poets. However, many performers tend to rely on more subtle sound patterning—internal rhyme, alliteration, assonance, consonance. Beyond these more traditional poetic devices, volume and timbre of the voice, blocking (the way a poet moves on stage, and the poet's ability to connect with an audience) are integral parts of the slam poem. (639)

Schmid's characterization of slam as a poetic form is arguable at several points: for example, while accentual and accentual-syllabic rhythms do occur in these pieces, and iambs can be clearly audible, "tetrameter and trimeter" are harder to identify in the absence of a visual line. Nevertheless, slam's strictures in some ways resemble those of any other lyric shape. Instead of occupying a prescribed number of lines, a slam poem must occupy a prescribed number of minutes. Visual line breaks do not shape meaning, but pauses do. Some slam poems sound like free verse, but others deploy rhyme and alliteration in the accentual rhythms of hip-hop prosody. Like sonnets or ballads, too, slam poems possess conventions concerning content, examined below.

Spoken word poetry cannot rely on graphic elements as printed poetry does, but physical performance offers an ample new vocabulary to compensate. Occasionally a poet appears on stage with notes or a typescript, but high-scoring performers like the ones who appear at nationals tend to memorize their pieces, right down to the timing, pitch, and volume of individual syllables. This becomes especially evident at the finals, in which the top teams are permitted to repeat pieces from earlier bouts. Slam poets block pieces theatrically, moving upstage and down to emphasize points, pacing and leaping from left to right, performing stage falls, and making effective use of gesture, posture, and facial expression. A performer's craft involves not only the control of breath, voice, and body, but also technical expertise such as how to manipulate a microphone. The most overused gesture at the 2005 nationals involved using microphone cords as mock-nooses—surely stretching the "no props" rule.

All these dramatic elements emerge particularly clearly in group pieces, which the members must choreograph and perform with exact coordination. Group pieces are also the most inventive (or gimmicky) in their staging. For instance, at the 2005 Nationals, a San Antonio team poem about teachers and students posed one poet on another's shoulders for the entire work. Other teams positioned a member or two offstage to shout timely remarks, or designated one key performer to jump onstage part way through a poem, as in an effective production by Austin on the short-lived triumphs of a high-school nerd. The second-placing team, from Charlotte, N.C., specialized in such group poems, including one about a mother beaten to death. In that effort, three men narrated the episode from the stage while the mother character, supposedly hiding in a closet, spoke from a concealed position at its foot.

Some elements of printed poems are stripped away or downplayed by slam pieces, in part because of the effects of competition. For instance, slam poets rarely announce titles, epigraphs, or dedications, much less offer explanatory notes, since these subtract from the allotted time. Little space exists for improvisation, banter, or response to a particular audience. Also, since slam poems cannot be reread before they are evaluated, their meanings must be clear after just one performance—or, at least, their wordplay must be wildly entertaining. The fact that the judges are amateur, not poets themselves, exerts a powerful influence on the poems as well. At the 2005 Nationals, judges tended to reward intensity. Loud, fast poems delivered with a display of outrage scored well. Many of the most successful pieces concerned abuse, rape, and oppression, although inspirational poems (we can and must overcome abuse, rape, and oppression) often received high approbation as well. I heard several hilariously witty poems that pleased both the judges and the larger crowd, but these tended to receive slightly lower marks than the desperately heartfelt variety. Other slammers may have appreciated the rare, soft-spoken, lyrically meditative piece, or third-person narrative poems, or other variations on the standard, but the amateur judges tended not to.

Many poetic subgenres were visible in the 2005 nationals, including elegy, persona poems, prayer poems, and tributes to inspiring figures including Harriet Tubman, Tom Waits, and tough mothers. Social protest recurred frequently in group and individual pieces. Anti-war feeling ran high throughout the four-day gathering, but American consumerism was also targeted for critique by several teams and individuals, as were hip-hop for its sexism, drugs for their destructive force, and the racism of U.S. institutions such as the media. Certain strategies of language and verbal performance also punctuated the nationals. Slang and obscenity were commonplace. A number of poems were bilingual, including phrases from Spanish and Tagalog, but only the French team performed entirely in a language other than English (accompanied by PowerPoint translations). Some group pieces very nearly constituted a capella songs, combining vocals with percussive noises. The rules permit no instruments beyond the human body, but poets were highly resourceful in exploiting the musicality of lungs, skin, muscle, and bone. Many individuals belted out parts of their poems melodically, or musically quoted other songs. Oral poetics might seem to prescribe a high degree of repetition and frequent use of refrains, but while these devices did occur, they were surprisingly rare, especially in individual pieces. Strong exceptions were the anaphoric poems of Anis Mojgani, the co-winner with Janean Livingston of the Indy Poetry Slam Championship for 2005.

The majority of the poems, further, were framed as personal. These poems used the first person and the "I" persona seemed to be autobiographical, given that it closely resembled the physical speaker in race, gender, or other characteristics. I documented 112 poems over several evenings, not including unrated pieces such as the calibration performances. By my reckoning, at least 68 contained personal references to the poet or poets. If my sample is representative, more than half, possibly two thirds, of the slam poems delivered in Albuquerque were presented as personal expression.

This figure does include a range of modes. Some slam poetry opens with a strong "I" and veers through narrative into other situations and strategies. Many pieces, however, participate strongly in the conventions of so-called confessional poetry. Spoken word significantly postdates this literary mode of the late 1950s and early 1960s, which is print-based and deeply formal, yet shares confessionalism's concerns with childhood and family, trauma, and addiction. More importantly, slam, like confessionalism, encourages audiences to identify the speaker with the poet. Both modes depend centrally on the performance of authenticity—the manipulation of textual and/or physical conventions that suggest sincerity, factual accuracy, and expressiveness. Post-confessional poetry, especially its free verse varieties, has a smaller presence in literary magazines now than it did in the 1980s and '90s, but slams make its continuing appeal abundantly clear.

Decades after the term "confessionalism" was coined to describe Lowell's *Life Studies* pejoratively, however, the markers of authenticity have mutated slightly. Spoken word's theatrical nature also complicates the comparison. In performance, poetic tone is not an illusion created by diction, syntax, punctuation, and other printable elements; instead, it joins such factors to the physical qualities of voice and presence. Fast, loud poems succeed because they play to a contemporary understanding of poetry as a deeply personal expression of inner conflict. When gesture, pitch, and timing convey grief, rage, and other strong emotions, the words seem more authentic. Slam poems are more obscene in diction than confessional poetry because words like "fuck," "shit," and "asshole," when uttered with intensity, are easily recognizable codes for unaffected, uncensored feeling. When uttered casually, the same words signify frankness, even intimacy, which resonates with the anti-pretentiousness of slam. The anti-corporate hair and dress of most slammers, and the nature of the venues, contributes to these effects.

Autobiographical poetry tends to rely on tropes of speech, the author figuratively "speaking" to an audience even when his or her "voice" is purely textual. However, in spoken word venues, authorial presence is literal and guaranteed: by the stringent rules of slam, a competing piece must have been composed by its performer, and a group piece must have been composed by at least one member of the team. Of course, many poems that seem deeply personal could be partly or entirely fictive. When Carlos Gómez of Louder Arts, New York City, recounts administrative censorship of his high school teaching, he could be conflating details of different episodes for dramatic effect; it is less likely, although still possible, that he never experienced such censorship at all, or that he actually works as an airline steward or a tax auditor. When his teammate Rachel McKibbens, in a letter-poem to her mother, draws gasps with the line, "Mom, I miss the back of your hand," listeners cannot readily check her credentials as a survivor of abuse. However, the presumption of autobiographical truth-telling is strong, and these master performers are utterly convincing.

Because gender and race, however, are relatively visible identity markers, their role in slam authenticity is particularly important. I heard relatively few poems about sexuality: heterosexual sex is a popular subject, but I noted only three pieces concerning homosexuality or transgender identity, and none focusing on lesbianism or bisexuality. However, I counted twenty-four poems addressing what it means to be a man or a woman in light of social and familial expectations. A similar proportion (just under a fifth) focused on racial identity, with a quarter of those poems exploring the complications of being mixed-race. Again, my estimate may be conservative, given that many poems concerned culture, politics, class, and other subjects that intersect substantially with race. Many poems, of course, addressed both race and gender; black womanhood was a particularly prevalent subject in Albuquerque. Somers-Willett, focusing on the 2002 national contest, likewise remarks that marginalized identities are often the subjects of successful slam poetry, and further that "the most commonly rewarded of these identities at poetry slams, at least at a national level, is black identity" (58).

Gender and race may be central subjects for slam because spoken word is attractive to many artists at the margins of mainstream literary establishments. Those mainstream literary establishments, while far more inclusive than formerly, still demonstrate the superior cultural power of white people, heterosexuals, and men; while many women now edit important magazines, for instance, they are rarer where the money concentrates. These subjects also fuel the intense emotions slam thrives upon. Whatever the reasons, poems about racial inequalities, sexual violence, white male nerdiness, and black female beauty accrue power in performance because they intensify audience attention to the speaking body. When Joshua Fleming jokes about his own obesity, we can visually confirm it; when Ragan Fox refers to himself as "gay and lispy," we register his physical performance of homosexuality; when light-skinned Aaron Cuffee recounts how airport officials refused to believe that a black man could be his father, we must notice the poet's coloring, his hair, his features. Not only the context of slam poetry, but often its very content, insists on words' embodiment.

It makes sense, given slam's dependence on the poet's body, voice, and presence, that more than half of the poems I heard used self-referential language. By this I mean not just the use of first-person pronouns, but direct references within the performance to performance. These include comments on the status of a piece as a poem, allusions to the poem's own peculiar qualities, describing the situation or condition of the artist while composing the piece or declaiming it from the stage, and specific addresses to the present audience. At first this surprised me; metapoesis is a feature of postmodernism and seemed ill-suited to the assertive populism of spoken word. If slam, performed in accessible settings and judged by non-slammers, eschews the professionalism of academic poetry and seeks an ordinary audience, why would it deploy this strategy so heavily? Why would the nature of poetic inspiration, say, be interesting to people who are not poets or literary specialists?

One answer might be the DIY aesthetic that slam borrows from punk rock: slam aims to be a meritocracy, with no participant inheriting his publishing contacts or buying the slam equivalent of a prestigious diploma. Slam invites anyone in the audience to wonder if he or she could do that too. Given the charges of unfair practices swirling around academic poetry— teachers selecting their students as contest winners, for instance, and various other rumors made infamous by Foetry.com—this commitment to openness is probably instrumental in slam's popularity.[29] Spoken word provides audiences and attention without requiring connections or major financial investment. Self-referentiality as a strategy, therefore, demystifies the origins of poetry and emphasizes slam's potential inclusiveness.

These metapoetic allusions, further, draw attention to the literalness of voice and presence in a slam venue. A book of poems read silently, or for that matter a CD played over headphones or downloads through an iPod, can create a powerful illusion of intimacy with the absent artist. Spoken word poetry, however, insists that the real poem exists where composer and audience are literally present to each other. Voice becomes not a metaphor or an ingenious typographical trick, but actual sound waves in the air, created by nearby bodies. Audiences can not only hear the poets but watch them sweat, and in their passage on and off a nearby stage, touch and smell them. As Crown describes it in an essay on Tracie Morris, "By focusing on the persona of the poet who takes the stage, spoken word poetry seems at times to exalt the authoritative *presence* of the poet's body and the esoteric *aura* of the poem's voiced body prior to any technology of reproduction" (216).

A live slam poem is not more *real* than the printed or recorded variety. All constitute performances in different media. These performances inevitably deploy conventions and create fictions, even when a deeply sincere poet means to tell the truth about her experience. The ubiquity of self-reference in slam, in fact, suggests an energizing tension between the artifice of poetry and the overwhelming vividness of real presence. If a performer discusses what poetry means to her in a performed poem, she both draws attention to the nature of the form and invites us to think of her as a fallible individual, with aspirations that the poem at hand may or may not reach. Many NPS 2005 poets also referred to "writing" their pieces, which both asserts originality and highlights the divided nature of performed verse. Christopher Michael from Austin, for instance, wittily compared his compulsion to "write poetry" to drug addiction while he performed withdrawal by hunching over tensely, rubbing and scratching obsessively like someone in physical pain. His piece raises the question of what urge performing the poem satisfies, as opposed to composing it on paper. Which version, for that matter, *is* the poem? Is it the original typed lines, the transcript in the playbook, a best performance? Is it the lasting version collected in *Bum Rush the Page* (Medina) or recorded for *Def Poetry Jam* on HBO?

Group pieces also do their part to destabilize conventions of poetic expression slam otherwise depends upon. Pieces delivered by two, three, or especially four or five people are more patently theatrical than solo performances. The lines must not only be composed but they must be designated, and performers must collaborate on timing and blocking. At the Albuquerque Nationals, these pieces were common and popular. Excluding the Group Showcases (team pieces only) on Friday and the Indy Competition (individual pieces only) on the final night, I documented ninety-three poems, thirty-four of which were group pieces. These often elaborate numbers enlivened rooms; judges rewarded them generously. The proportion of team to individual poems was largest in the ultimate event. During the Team Championships Finals, in which Albuquerque, Charlotte, Fort Worth, and Hollywood competed, eleven out of sixteen poems were group performances. Charlotte, in fact, performed only team pieces, as they did the previous night in their semi-finals bout.

Several group performances I observed manifested some anxiety about how individual writing contributions should be credited. This is an old controversy, relative to slam's short life. In his documentary *SlamNation: The Sport of Spoken Word*, which chronicles the 1996 Nationals in Portland, director Paul Devlin pays considerable attention to slam star Taylor Mali (Providence), who presents himself in the film as a cannily ambitious slammer, the consummate strategist. Indeed, Providence eventually wins the title, but Mali's approach triggers argument at the annual "slam family meeting" held before the finals.[30] Danny Solis, then a member of the Austin contingent, raises a question about the authorship of group pieces leading to the hypothetical result that "one poet could conceivably write four pieces and just have the team be like actors to perform that person's writing." A flurry of questions and comments follows about the "poetry police" and whether such poetic malpractice has occurred within "a team that will be in the finals tonight." Mali intervenes: "I think everyone's talking about Providence here," he guesses correctly, and describes the rules concerning this point as a "gray area." Mali eventually satisfies the group, more or less, that "all four members of our team had a part in writing our group piece," but not before Marc Smith (aka "slampapi") lectures him about the dishonor of exploiting gray areas for one's own gain. This conflict illustrates dissonances in slam culture. As Daniel Ferri (Berwyn) puts it in the same documentary, competition "provides a focus for community . . . and the seeds of destruction of that community."

This collision of strong personalities also indicates the fraught status of authorship in slam, as in other poetic communities. Authorship is generally an economic problem, although money plays less of a role than prestige for many slam poets. Very few poets can build a livelihood on slam success—the prize of $2,000 to the winning team is small, given the size of the teams and cost of travel, and a slam championship is considerably harder to parlay into tenure than the Yale Younger Poets Prize. Solis' remark indicates how much slam depends on the presumption of original expression and the priority of textual rather than oral composition: slammers must not be merely "actors" but "writers." Later in the documentary, Mali describes how the idea for the contentious piece originated with him, but the group composed the words together. Does the poem, then, consist chiefly in those fixed words? One or more people have to create the staging—is that not part of the poem? Slam rules indicate that performance must be judged as well as content. Why isn't performance, then, an intrinsic part of a slam poem? Collaborative poetry has been and remains a "gray area" for slam.

Mali's performance in 2005 (his last time at nationals, he announced to mass skepticism) echoed this nine-year-old controversy. When his current team, NYC-Urbana, presented a group piece, one member, Chad Anderson, began by stepping up to utter a rare explanatory remark: "I wrote this piece." The team allotted precious seconds to state one writer's authorship from the outset—perhaps so that no one would credit Mali and imagine that he was dominating his current team for strategic reasons. Further, Urbana wasn't the only team to refer to the process of composition. Other group poems incorporated allusions to authorship, suggesting that collaboration, or the relative lack of it, remains a potential source of conflict.

Some of the collaborative pieces I witnessed were significantly less "poetic" than individual efforts. Their language was looser, less witty or intensely loaded with meaning, and there were fewer oral traces of the poetic line as a structuring principle. However, if these are faults, they were not peculiar to team performances. Many moving, urgent, and high-scoring pieces exhibited moments of predictable word choice, tired imagery, or tangled syntax, even during finals night. Clichés uttered with perfect seriousness during NPS 2005 poems include "inner child," "paints a picture" (oh, so many times), and "it's like cutting out a part of myself." Unlike the editors of prestigious literary journals, slam audiences do not regard fresh and economical language as a priority, or at least they do not punish cliché when the overall piece is powerful.

In fact, some of the most memorable and challenging pieces were presented by multiple artists. One example was Berkeley's third-person account of violence against a transgender person. Their piece incorporated an incident from an earlier performance: "The first time we read this poem . . . someone shouted from the audience, 'She had a dick.'" A team member hidden in the audience shouted the last four words in a way that implicated the current audience. I admired the complexity of this piece, especially its alternation between pronouns claiming and disclaiming identification with the victim. Preceding the championship bout, Hawaii also delivered a provocative piece comparing the United States invasion of Iraq to the United States invasion of Hawaii (though another mock-hanging by microphone cord was a low point in this poem). Along with individual triumphs by Anis Mojgani, Janean Livingston, Ragan Fox, Rives, Evy Gildres-Voyles, Cassie Poe, Christian Drake, Kimberly Zisa, and many others, group poems were some of the most exciting features of the 2005 nationals and remain one of slam's most unique offerings.

Significantly, the parent organization of the National Poetry Slam, Poetry Slams Inc., later announced that as of 2006, individual and team competitions would be separated into different events. This does not preclude individual pieces performed by members of teams, but "storm poets" are no longer be accepted, and the "Indy" award at Nationals is now offered only at the Individual World Poetry Slam Championship (iWPS), hosted during February in a different city than the National Poetry Slam (NPS). The change answers a logistical problem caused by the number of teams now participating in nationals (seventy-five in 2005, with an upper limit of eighty). However, it also recognizes a difference between solo and team competitions. Since the nationals will now concentrate on teams, the institutions of slam have declared their primary allegiance to slam as a social form. This commitment to dialogue involves not only the accessibility of audiences to poet and vice versa, but also camaraderie and collaboration between poets themselves. Inevitable competitive tension undermines this. The 2005 Championship Finals ended with an emotional protest from the second-place Charlotte team, whose members had been troubled by backstage booing, or the perception of booing, during their entries. Several people at the event told me these crises always erupt at nationals, which is why slam should not be referred to simply as a "family" but more correctly as a "dysfunctional family." They also compared this minor crisis favorably to the previous year's "debacle" in St. Louis, praising the 2005 chairperson Danny Solis, who had produced the biggest and possibly the best-advertised and organized NPS yet. In any case, judging by friendly conversations among strangers on shuttle buses, and the hotel parties that died down around five in the morning, slam has attracted the most gregarious poets in the Western world.

The Four Corners Team

During the 2005 NPS, I studied one team particularly closely to learn more about poetry performance from the competitors' point of view. I followed up afterwards by e-mail questionnaire, seeking their reflections on poetry generally, their experiences in and attitude toward performance, and their responses to nationals. Their comments uphold my perception of slam as a profoundly and intrinsically social form, for many a first entry into poetry. The group from Four Corners also exemplifies how slam appeals to a diverse range of people. Team members range in age from nineteen to forty-five; two are male and three are female; three are parents. Some of them became poets in high school, while others came to poetry later, by chance. They work in a variety of service jobs and professions including health inspector, teacher, library director, and desk clerk. By race they include white and Navajo, and the youngest by fifteen years, DJ Mydas, identifies as "half Mexican, half Cajun." Their tastes, influences, experiences, and educations vary widely. They are nonetheless a cohesive group, some of whom traveled and roomed together in order to stretch their tight budgets. Coming to Albuquerque meant taking vacation days from their regular jobs and negotiating child care.

Scott Nicolay, the Four Corners Slam Master, was instrumental in organizing the team. He possessed previous experience in performance poetry through the Taos Poetry Circus and through co-founding the National Youth Poetry Slam in 1998 with Elizabeth Thomas. Although he never attended NPS before registering as a competitor in 2005, he won the 2004 Four Corners Slam and served as slam master for this group from that time to the present, sharing duties with his most experienced team mate, Amy Mullin.

About creating the team, Nicolay writes,

> My original goal was to help organize an adult Navajo Nation team and attend as coach, but our venue on the Reservation closed in Dec. Restarted in Farmington. The team only fell into place after I was asked to bring a group of poets to a poetry festival in Telluride, CO and recruited Tish and Zoey. Amy and Mydas joined shortly after our return and suddenly we had a team. (e-mail to the author 23 Aug. 2005)

His comments acknowledge both motive and happenstance, as well as the interstate geography that shapes this group. The NPS program identified them as representing the city of Farmington, but they preferred to be called Four Corners. Nicolay explains:

Zoey and I are from Shiprock, Amy was living in Aztec, NM—but is moving to the Caribbean soon. Mydas lives in Durango, CO. Only Tish lives in Farmington, and she doesn't much identify with it. Our venue is in Farmington. We were repeatedly identified as Farmington because the organizers were from our state and are predisposed to think of Farmington, rather than a regional identity, as many of us do . . . (e-mail to the author, 24 Aug. 2005)

Months later, reflecting further, he adds:

I deliberately use Four Corners to reflect a regional, rather than a local, identification. It is also the same region that was the heartland of the Ancestral Puebloan (Anasazi) culture, and later still, of the Navajo . . . 4C is not a set of borders, but an intersection, a crossroads, a frontier, a cartographer's conceit that somehow bull's-eyed a sacred heartland. (e-mail to the author, 7 March 2006)

Their team name also represents some resistance to slam conventions—even though those conventions themselves spring from resistance to the poetic status quo. Most other teams identify with a city, or a club or group name within that city. "Four Corners" still takes government borders as its starting point, but it also emphasizes connection through a common landscape rather than government-designated categories.

My correspondence with Four Corners often involved all the teammates simultaneously, and exchanges could be hilarious, full of intentionally outrageous boasting and mutual congratulation (the latter mostly from Nicolay, who flooded my electronic mailbox with comments flippant and serious, including parodic news releases such as "Four Corners Team French Fries Frogs," referring to their higher final placement than the French team). Their remarks further illustrate the sociability of slam. Zoey Benally writes, "I started performing poetry because Scott said that my stuff was good enough to be performed. I always thought my stuff wasn't really poetry, but lo & behold it was. Before Scott introduced the idea of performance, I had only a handful of friends that I showed my stuff to" (I draw this and subsequent quotes from an interview in Appendix B, unless the passages are otherwise attributed). Tish Ramirez remembers that "At the first slam I went to, Zoey signed me up." DJ Mydas admits that "i don't work well with others," but at the nationals "actually felt like part of a team for the first time since i can remember." Amy Mullin, a veteran slammer, expresses more reservations about the group's dynamics than other members, yet even she writes positively about the overall experiences and praises her team members as "brilliant."

Having built their repertoire and relationships in local venues, the Four Corners delegates were inspired by nationals and, to various degrees, skeptical of its prestige as well. None of them expected a triumphal march onto the finals stage, and indeed, they didn't score highly enough to enter the semi-finals; this was an experimental venture and an opportunity to learn. Further, as Mullin writes, "There's a saying about the foolishness of trying to win a slam with poetry." Some of them, nonetheless, were surprised by the obtuseness of the judges. DJ Mydas enjoyed the community he found there but comments, "sometimes it's not the best poem that wins, sometimes it's just the loudest or fastest or smartest-sounding poem." Benally echoes this: "I guess the big learning for me about slam is not to take the scores seriously. . . ." Nicolay and Ramirez seem less disturbed. As Nicolay puts it, "My experience was really all positive, other than drawing the first slot in both our bouts, but that's part of the game, and is funny in a kind of cursed way," referring to the lower scores usually received by the earliest performers. Ramirez adds, "It was a charged environment when you heard a poem that moved you. . . . It really was not a competition, just an opportunity to share values, art, feelings, thoughts, dreams." Listening, according to Ramirez, could be as powerful as performing. Marc Smith is idealistic when he refers to the slam community as a family, but both slam's resonance and its rivalries do spring from a sense of connection among poets, and between poets and their audiences.

Over two evenings Four Corners delivered six poems: one solo piece by each team member and a group piece performed by four of them (DJ Mydas' schedule made it difficult to include him in practice sessions). Their team piece, "The Dream Factory," was closely based on a poem Mullin had written and performed alone, but that she and her teammates considered well-suited to collaborative presentation. It mimics the style and diction of commercials for discount stores but takes a surreal enterprise as its subject, the hawking of dreams for every customer and every occasion. Interestingly, it challenges the standards for group pieces that Danny Solis proposed in 1996; Nicolay, Benally, and Ramirez were essentially actors performing Mullin's words. The latter three poets, however, also describe jointly composing other collaborative pieces for other occasions. They reminisce about a poem they performed in Telluride that involved throwing condom packages at audience members in homage to a raucous annual fair in Shiprock. Benally describes collaborative work as "more fun to create than solo poetry," and Nicolay finds that a sense of community is fundamental to all artistic production. Nevertheless, the ethos doesn't perfectly fit the practice in this case, since the process for "The Dream Factory" does not constitute full coauthorship, and individual pieces by team members sometimes achieved better responses.

Two of the poems delivered by team members—one by Benally, one by Nicolay—illustrate the nature of the slam poem as a form. Benally was the lowest scoring poet (23.9), largely because she appeared first on the first evening, but judges may also have penalized her for drawing occasionally on notes. However, a head injury sustained in a 1998 car crash both spurred Benally to begin writing and makes it exceptionally difficult for her to commit language to memory. She presents herself differently, too, than many of her fellow performers. Her manner exhibits none of the self-aggrandizing loudness that makes so many slam poets such raucous company. She comments on her own dress in her blog account of NPS 2005: "i looked slightly yuppie conservative in a Wal-Mart sorta way compared to all the characters milling about."[31] However, keeping a blog, as she does, requires a certain amount of extroversion, and she expresses a serious commitment to poetry, while for her friend, Tish Ramirez, poetry is a means to social and spiritual ends.

The untitled poem Benally delivered (in conversation she referred to it as "the roadkill poem") is lyric in tone and style of delivery, also unusual for nationals. The poem uses narrative, but in fragments. It juxtaposes brief stories about different car accidents involving pet dogs and cats. The material could be sentimental. However, Benally's poem, from its very first line, invites a level of identification between human beings and animals that is uncomfortable; the feelings it provoked, at least for me, were more interesting than reflexive sympathy for vulnerable creatures. When I first listened to it, I recognized linguistic intensity, but didn't know whether the poem's ultimate thrust was misanthropic or something more complicated. Good lyric poems in print compel re-reading; in this case, I felt eager to *see* the poem I had heard but not fully grasped.[32]

Benally's piece is comprised of multiple interrelated stories evoking drivers, vehicles, and animals in vivid descriptive detail. Its gruesome particulars are crucial to its effect because they undermine the sadness of the material. Slam poems typically invite us to identify with victims—neglected children, abused women, people who suffer discrimination for color, accent, baldness—and such poems score highly because, paradoxically, it can be pleasurable to identify with a victim (as opposed to being a victim). Our sympathy with damaged creatures reassures us of our own goodness; briefly, at least, we can enjoy blameless anger against fully deserving foes.[33] What if, however, we are also the oblivious driver leaning forward to apply lipstick? What if we must admire "beautiful carrion" along with "glossy black crows," well-fed on death? What if part of the poem's pleasure lies in lyrically gory imagery: the "burgundy smear" of blood on asphalt, "soft flesh" under the wheels, "twisted yellow carcass" contrasting with a "freshly waxed king cab"? Benally's aesthetic creates pathos but also implies her and our complicity with the killers.

Benally provided me with a visible version of the roadkill poem and it rewards examination. The first line, in particular, had been easy to miss in performance, and yet it gives away part of the poem's agenda: "His wrist hangs, drying meat, over the steering wheel." The meat comparison insists on the animality of human beings, how even as predators we are also mortal and vulnerable. Benally's strong focus on sensory images is unusual in slam poetry, but the lack of transitions between each story is even more surprising. These strategies leave a considerable amount of work to the listener. Even the punctuation of the opening line, while perfectly clear on the page, is hard to follow aurally: an overt simile, "like drying meat," would render the comparison significantly clearer.

In performance, Benally's voice rises in pitch and volume towards the end of the poem, when she yells "GET HOME STUPID DOG!" The emotion is patent, but the poem's interest lies much more in the details of language that are difficult to perceive during a first hearing.[34] Benally acknowledges this when she writes that I "still have not decided where I fit within that [the slam] world." In this piece and generally, Benally is mediating between very different audiences. She delivered her roadkill poem to an urban bar crowd, although Benally wishes for other listeners: "Most of my poetry is for Navajos. I am defining my reality as a Navajo woman who grew up in a border town at the juncture of the 20th & 21st century. I am defining my reality and not accepting the definitions imposed upon me—noble savage, drunk indian, conquered people." Slam does overlap with Benally's goals: it offers populist art with an anti-racist tradition to a diverse audience. However, its means will probably remain inadequate to Benally's ends and ill-suited to her strengths.

Nicolay's solo piece, "mascot," is a more typical slam poem, adhering more closely to the conventions of the mode, although it didn't score much more highly (25.0). Nicolay describes how he drafted "mascot" "on the plane coming back from the 3rd Annual National Youth Poetry Slam in San Francisco," although he sometimes composes in his head or partly on the computer. If he had ever preserved "mascot," however, in a computer file, he had since lost access to it and had to retype it for me from memory. He notes that

this was the first poem I wrote specifically for the slam. . . . In writing a deliberate slam poem, I was thinking of composing something political, with
humor and certain types of repetition that seem to me to be effective in the
form. Where it fails somewhat is its length—it is probably too short to be
really effective, as most successful slam poems seem to cram a six minute
poem into three minutes. (e-mail to the author, 26 August 2005)

At sixty-four lines of varying length, "mascot" is shorter than many slam
poems, but considerably longer than the average lyric published in literary
magazines. Nicolay transcribes it with phrasal line breaks, conceiving the
poetic line as a unit of breath as well as meaning.

"Mascot" satirizes the American practice of identifying some athletic
teams with images of indigenous peoples. It begins:

> I wanna be a reservation
> high school
> football team mascot
>
> I want my big nose
> big head
> made into a cartoon . . .
>
> so I can strike fear in the hearts of the opposing team
> as I leer at their cheerleaders from the field house wall

The poem goes on to imagine alternate team names, progressing from "the
Crownpoint Crackers / or the Rough Rock Rednecks" to fiercer and more
specific indictments of European-American behaviors:

> or how about the Lake Valley Land Thieves
> or the Rock Point Rapists
> or the Moenkopi Murderers of Pregnant Women, Children,
>   and the Old and Defenseless.

"Mascot" concludes by forecasting how "the locals / across the reservation
border" will take offense, and offering this twist:

> and then let every Native American man, woman, and child
> rise up as one and say,
> Thank you!
> We thought we'd have to wear these

god
damn
things
forever.
            (e-mail to the author, 25 August 2005)

In diction by turns biblical and heretical, "mascot" casts itself as a last, desperate ploy to redefine behavior many Americans refuse to acknowledge as racist.

The ending of "mascot" also ventriloquizes Native Americans, fusing its voice with a native one in its final sentences. In its shifting identifications, its refusal to let the audience identify simply with racism's victims, "mascot" resembles Benally's poem. Unlike Benally, Nicolay relies on scathing humor instead of sensory detail and wields a far more overt ideological agenda. However, the effect is once again to suggest the listener's possible complicity in prejudice. In several self-referential lines, Nicolay offers up his own Anglo face and body as a model. For instance, he suggests how to simplify his profile for a colored logo:

> make it livid white
> all except my eternal five o'clock shadow
> make that blue.

In performance he demands, in second-person address, that we examine him visually, re-imagine him as a cartoonish image of savagery. Stereotyping is explicitly a communal activity in which audience members participate.

Nicolay, like Benally, is not wholly committed to slam as a poetic outlet. He expresses vital interests in "concrete poetry, pseudo-tribal, science fiction haiku, slam, avant-garde epic," and admits, "I still get a kick out of writing unperformable slam poems, such as those that include hieroglyphs and concrete elements, or are simply too esoteric" (e-mail 23 August 2005). Slam nevertheless provides a vital sense of community to poets working in isolation from academic support, and it does so in a non-exclusionary fashion. Academic poetry can be intensely pleasurable to write, read, and listen to, and yet it demands erudition from its audiences and, from its writers, adherence to occluded, rather than overt, rules.[35]

In overhearing slam, in listening too closely, I frame and moderate my delight in it; I indicate that, in multiple ways, I know better. Nor would my case study, the Four Corners team, constitute the best of slam by popular or academic judgment. However, the work of its members shows that even in individually authored and voiced poems, slam is a social form, designed with respect for its listeners. Slam reveals that poetry has never been an art of solitary voices. Poets always have sought audiences, although sometimes with great ambivalence, and consciousness of those audiences has always shaped the work. And, further, poets do labor together in many types of relationships (as mentors, editors, coauthors, and comrades of all kinds) with results that range from intense conflict to great art.

Slam also suggests that poetry remains a site of cultural conflict, as it was in the Vietnam War era and its liberation movements. What Gioia identifies as a "new bohemia" in American poetry, noting that "over the past decade bookstores like Chapters in Washington, D.C., or Cody's in Berkeley have presented literary programming equal to that of major universities," is not that different from the old bohemias of San Francisco in the fifties or Greenwich Village in the twenties (28). Certainly newer, more flexible institutions, like performance series and presses, will always be closer to poetry's vanguard than universities, which must be controlled by the slow process of curricular change and the even slower credentialing of experts in emerging fields. It is by no means clear that universities will always support the arts, or that therefore the academic poetry reading could be considered secure, but so long as the latter exists, it will rarely be as revolutionary, or even as lively, as its bar and café counterpart.

Nevertheless, college poetry readings can shape what poetry means for generations. Is the poet a tweedy expert edifying captive students against their collective will? Is she an entertainer, a performance artist, a dissident? Or is the poetry reading ceremony, rather than theater, "a ritual affirmation for the existence of this community of poetry readers" as Stern offers, hypothesizing that "to hear the poet is to overcome one's own anonymity, to overcome the loneliness which the printed page cannot overcome"? (77–79). Is it a "public tuning," as Bernstein suggests, for poems that "do not follow received or prefabricated forms"? (6). Poets and audiences at alternative sites know why they're in attendance: because they want to be, because it's fun or marginally profitable. A hundred years ago, educators knew why students must voice poetry: to train their memories, to develop poise and eloquence. Universities and colleges at the present moment, however, do not agree on a rationale for all the work and expense of the poetry reading circuit, instead manifesting an embarrassed reluctance to examine any of its conventions. Poetry needs to be voiced physically and to be listened to. What we're listening for, however, is changeable, contested, and contradictory.

RESONANCES

Arguing that "conclusions are at best a bad idea," David M. Posner writes:

> The problem, as anyone who has attempted to finish a book knows, is that writing a book is more than anything a process of discovering what one ought to have written instead. The real work of a conclusion, then, may be to conceal this uncomfortable fact from both author and reader, while simultaneously persuading the same audiences that we have in fact written the book that we would have written had we only been learned or smart enough. (179)

A book on voice in twentieth-century American poetry could certainly sound very different than this one. I have mentioned many writers and movements glancingly whose productions could have been central here, such as Robert Frost, Carl Sandburg, Vachel Lindsay, Amy Lowell, T. S. Eliot, Marianne Moore, Charles Olson, Gwendolyn Brooks, Allen Ginsberg, Anne Waldman, Amiri Baraka, Jerome Rothenberg, Judy Grahn, Denise Levertov, Alice Notley, Ron Padgett, Joy Harjo, Tracie Morris, Patricia Smith, and many, many others. Instead, I chose Millay, Hughes, Merrill and Jackson, Duhamel and Seaton, and the performers of the National Poetry Slam 2005, because their work both exemplifies and challenges various meanings of poetic voice. It is equally true, however, that I have been studying voice because these disparate writers, whose work I admire and enjoy and want to think about, teach me that voice is a complicated and resonant idea.

I end my haunted monolog with the same theme—that voice is a powerful notion in American poetry, more lasting than the various literary fashions it has periodically codified—but I hope this motif has become more resonant. In physics, resonance occurs when a sound or musical tone is echoed by another body. For example, when a musical note is sung, a nearby violin string will vibrate at the same pitch. Resonance has many other meanings: in phonetics, for example, it refers to the quality of voice caused by sound vibrating in a body cavity such as the pharynx, mouth, or nose. Applied to poetry studies, this word could emphasize the source of voice in the body or the communication of sound from one body to another. A poem in live performance carries that oscillating force between physically present individuals; a recorded, manuscript, or printed poem transmits some aspects of that force over great distances of space and time. The term voice suggests this resonance as it vibrates with its own multiplicity of connotations.

The cover image of this book, a photograph by John "Hoppy" Hopkins of Ginsberg reading in London, shows just how far the reverberations can carry.[1] As if to return the gift Charles Dickens and Fanny Kemble gave to the United States in their influential nineteenth-century reading tours, Ginsberg and others galvanized London through a 1965 performance at the Royal Albert Hall. Some aspects of the event are captured in this image—the grandeur of the oval space, postures of attention and distraction among the audience members, Ginsberg's hairy intensity over an open notebook, bouquets of cut flowers heaped anyhow on the stage. Several American poets associated with the Beat movement were in England that spring, and when Ginsberg's friend Barbara Rubin discovered an unbooked night at the prestigious venue, she and others began arranging an international poetry reading—"The First International Poetry Incarnation."[2] A large group of male poets participated, representing several countries, including Gregory Corso, Lawrence Ferlinghetti, William S. Burroughs, and Allen Ginsberg from the United States; Adrian Mitchell, Christopher Logue, Spike Hawkins, and Michael Horovitz from England; Alexander Trocchi, Tom McGrath, and George MacBeth from Scotland; Anselm Holland from Finland; and Simon Vinkenoog from Holland. Chilean author Pablo Neruda had been booked for the event but was unable to participate (Schumacher 447). Somewhere between five and eight thousand people attended as audience members, including Indira Gandhi, who sat in a front row. Ginsberg performed last, choosing to read the poems "Who Be Kind To" and "The Change" before "leading the audience in a session of mantra singing" (Schumacher 448). By many accounts, the readings were of mixed quality, and yet the event served as a significant "catalyst for the burgeoning London arts community" (Miles 372).

Ginsberg wrote "Who Be Kind To" just three days earlier for this occasion, and not surprisingly, his paean to human compassion is also a warning about distancing technologies and a celebration of embodied voices. "Be kind to yourself," "be kind to this place," "be kind to your neighbor, "And be kind to the poor soul that cries in a crack of the pavement because he has no body" (*Collected Poems* 367–70)—this anaphoric chant asks for peace and erotic communion in a time of war and suffering, ending by announcing a revolution and looking with hope towards the next millennium. Parts of the poem stress how television, radio, and "the hard voice of telephones" create and confirm human isolation. Books work the same way. Ginsberg finds the Bible and its prophecies similarly alienating in that they inspire fear and suffering among believers. The same distancing technologies, however, can also connect people over time and space. At a train station, for instance, "the bearded stranger of telephones" is met by a smiling friend. Even more powerfully, amplified, recorded, and broadcast music joins the people of the world together in a common psalm. Ginsberg had just been to Liverpool to hear the Beatles, who in this poem "raise up their joyful voices and guitars / in electric Afric hurrah." They are part of a movement, according to Ginsberg, that "reechoes amplified from Nottingham to Prague." Even the human heart is a sort of "red transistor / in your breast": deep inside one's body, one picks up distant signals, an empowering, life-affirming rhythm. In "Who Be Kind To," such eros has the power to heal a damaged world, to overcome a kind of death-in-life Ginsberg finds in modern existence:

> lackloves of Capitals & Congresses
> who make sadistic noises
> on the radio

Suffering comes from being disembodied and only loving presence can redeem us.

"Who Be Kind To," recited by Allen Ginsberg to thousands in the middle of the sixties, stresses what embodied voices have the potential to *do:* create community through ritual, inspire peace, call audiences to arms in a sensual rather than a military way. On the pages of Ginsberg's fat, posthumous *Collected Poems*, dated and glossed in end-notes, its voice is only a disembodied echo, much like the broadcast "ghosts and demons" the poem laments and deplores. It was composed for performance in a specific venue, so it seems incomplete without physical voice, like an empty carapace or a shed skin. However, this is Ginsberg's point: "Who Be Kind To" works as a telephone does, and like any poem in print, has equal potential for isolating and joining the individuals at either end of the wire.[3] Voice and presence have a strong spiritual aspect, too. We must

        end the cold war he has borne
        against his own kind flesh
        since the days of the snake.

That is, we must pray to and worship each other, the poem insists, and not distant abstractions like God the Father, if we want to experience paradise again. Technologies for transmitting voice, for Ginsberg, can create pain and division, but have equal potential for fostering unity.

    Underlying the disharmonies over poetic voice as a critical term, likewise, powerful questions and possibilities resonate. Some of the disagreements about voice among poets, critics, scholars, and theorists spring from conflicting ideas about what poetry should be or do. Finally, the vagueness of voice's meaning, its slippery quality, interests me even more than the esthetic conflicts that the word's use often encodes. I find that voice remains an important word in the poetic vocabulary not despite but because of its latent contradictions—poets and readers often deploy the term to conjure community, to acknowledge inspiration from undervalued sources, and to emphasize the pleasures of sound. I am confident, for all these reasons, that sound and voice in American poetry will remain topics of spirited conversation.

A SELECTED LIST OF PUBLIC POETRY SOUNDINGS SINCE 1950

Early 1950s: Dylan Thomas stars in multiple U.S. reading tours, speaking in museums, libraries, community centers, and on campuses.

1952: John Cage stages a "happening" at Black Mountain College, a mixed media event including poetry readings by Charles Olson and Mary Caroline Richards (who recited Millay from a ladder), paintings by Rauschenberg, dance by Merce Cunningham, music, and lectures (Duberman 11, 350–54).

1954: Betty Kray, then director of the poetry program at the YHMA in New York, seeks funding from the Rockefeller Foundation for two projects: (1) to support public readings by younger poets and (2) to create college reading circuits. When she moves to the Academy of American Poets in 1959, she brings these programs with her (Norris 25, 53–54, 59–60, 192, 226).

1955: Allen Ginsberg, Michael McClure, Gary Snyder, Philip Whalen, and Philip Lamantia read at the Six Gallery in San Francisco; this event is best remembered as the first public performance of *Howl*. Kenneth Rexroth presided over the event and Jack Kerouac, according to his own fictionalized account, passed jugs of wine through the assembled crowd and shouted "'Go! Go! Go!' (like a jam session)" (13). Before and after this date, poets were sounding their work in a great many Bay Area venues, but this is the event most often remembered and retold.[1]

1961: Frost recites "The Gift Outright" at Kennedy's inauguration when the sun glaring on the snow prevents him from being able to read "Dedication." The inauguration is broadcast by radio and television.

Norman Mailer, out on bail, reads a poem full of sexual imagery at the YMHA Poetry Center in New York City, and the outraged organizer pulls the curtain down in the middle of the show (Norris 109–10).

1962: Howard Nemerov, Muriel Rukeyser, John Crowe Ransom, John Berryman, Louise Bogan, Gwendolyn Brooks, W. D. Snodgrass, Allen Tate, Frost, Langston Hughes, Randall Jarrell, Ogden Nash, and many others read at the National Poetry Festival at the Library of Congress. (The proceedings, published in 1964, include not only the poems but the poets' framing remarks, which are sometimes extensive.)

1963: Ginsberg begins singing mantras as poetry readings (Morgan 375, 392).

1964: Amiri Baraka and others establish the Black Arts Repertory Theatre / School in Harlem. It collapses within a year, "but by 1968 there was a nationwide network" of such groups, "usually the site of readings rather than fully staged dramatic productions" (Thomas, "Neon Griot" 308–19). Lorenzo Thomas documents such centers in Chicago, and Houston, arguing that this is a "genuinely national movement" (312).

1965: The Berkeley Poetry Conference is held, where the godfather of postwar American poetry performance and author of "Projective Verse," Olson, shares the spotlight with Ginsberg, Robert Duncan, and Jack Spicer. Libbie Rifken characterizes Olson's poetry performance as "billed as a reading but identified by the poet himself as a talk (and later derided as a filibuster)" (131).

A famous non-reading also occurs this year: Robert Lowell publicly refuses Lyndon Johnson's invitation to speak at a White House Arts Festival as an act of protest against American involvement in Vietnam.

1966: Robert Bly and David Ray organize American Writers Against the Vietnam War, "orchestrating protest readings, demonstrations, and draft card burnings" (Kalaidjian 130; Von Hallberg 117).

The Poetry Project at St. Mark's Church in the Bowery is founded; it sponsors series of readings and workshops.

1966, 1967: The first two Black Writers Conferences occur at Fisk University in Tennessee, organized by John O. Killen. At the second, especially, younger poets associated with the Black Arts Movement take center stage (Smethurst, *The Black Arts Movement* 76, 332–33, 379; Clarke 28).

1968: Beyond Baroque, a bookstore that sponsors readings and workshops and becomes an important center of gravity for poetry in Southern California, is founded in Venice.

Anne Sexton begins reading with a backup rock band, Her Kind.

1969: Judy Grahn co-founds the Women's Press Collective with Wendy Cadden, beginning only with a mimeograph machine. She distributes mimeographs at Bay Area poetry readings, building a wide underground audience.

Late 1960s: David Antin begins improvising "talk poems" at his readings (see Perloff, *Poetics of Indeterminacy* 288–339 on the development of this oral form).

Anne Waldman begins to experiment with spontaneous oral poetry performance (Charters 2.531).

The "poetry in the schools" movement springs up as a result of contemporaneous work by several arts and teaching organizations, including Betty Kray from the Academy of American Poets, the Teachers and Writers Collaborative, and California Poets in the Schools. Kray also arranges readings in libraries, parks, and other outdoor spaces (Norris 35–38, 165–67).[2]

1970s: Feminist poetry readings occur at coffee houses, bookstores, women's festivals, and political rallies (Whitehead 9, 30–32).

1971: Woodie King Jr. produces "Black Spirits: A Festival of New Black Poets" in New York City and follows it with a record album and print anthology (Thomas, "Neon Griot" 312).

1975: The University of Wisconsin-Milwaukee sponsors the First International Symposium on Ethnopoetics. At this event, "poets, performers, and scholars of performative genres met, debated, performed. . . . The participants were invited to define 'ethnopoetics' and to present ethnopoetic performances" (Victor Turner 337).

Miguel Algarín moves his poetry salon from his East Village living room into an Irish bar, soon rechristened The Nuyorican Poets Café. This becomes a lively venue for slam as well as other performance arts by the late 1980s.

1976: The Grand Piano reading series begins at a coffeehouse on Haight Street in San Francisco. During its three-year run, it fosters a strong sense of community among writers identified with the Language Poetry movement.

1977: Ginsberg and Lowell give their only joint reading, hosted by the Poetry Project at St. Mark's Church in New York City. Gregory Corso shouts hostile questions to Lowell before Corso is persuaded to leave.

1978: Marie Hara, Arnold Hiara, and Stephen Sumida organize the "Talk Story" conference in Hawai'i and thereby "launched a renaissance in local Asian American writing" (Schulz 351).

Charles Bernstein and Ted Greenwald found an influential Saturday afternoon reading series at the Ear Inn in New York City. The series is still running, although it has been refashioned by many curators.

1979–1980: Al Simmons stages poetry bouts in Chicago; for one of them, the poets Anne Waldman and Ted Berrigan dress up in boxing gear. These events inspire the Taos Poetry Circus (1982–2003), held in New Mexico, which culminates annually in the World's Heavyweight Championship Poetry Bout.

1982: The Center for Research on Women at Stanford sponsors a conference for the fiftieth anniversary of Sylvia Plath's birth; Rich, Grahn, Lorde, Levertov and many others speak and read, and Marjorie Perloff exposes Ted Hughes' alterations to Plath's *Ariel*. This gathering exerts a powerful influence on feminist poetry criticism.[3]

Early 1980s: Hedwig Gorski, who coined the term "performance poet," begins broadcasting poetry by live radio from Austin, Texas, with the accompaniment of a jazz band, East of Eden.

1985: The National Cowboy Poetry Festival is first held in Elko, Nevada; it continues to occur annually, as do similar gatherings at other western sites.

1986: Marc Smith begins to emcee the Uptown Poetry Slam at the Green Mill in Chicago.

1997: David Lehman and Star Black start a free reading series at the KGB bar, a small, communist-themed site in the East Village (Lehman and Black xix).

2002: New Jersey Poet Laureate Amiri Baraka reads "Somebody Blew Up America" at the Geraldine R. Dodge Poetry Festival in Waterloo, New Jersey, stirring up intense controversy and demands for his resignation.

Russell Simmons takes his HBO series, *Def Poetry Jam* (taped live before an audience at New York's Supper Club), to Broadway. In this series of shows, nine spoken word artists perform individual poems and group pieces.

2006: At a formal New York City reading and panel discussion by Marc Doty, Philip Lopate, Rick Moody, and others in honor of the fiftieth anniversary of *Howl*, protesters from the Underground Literary Alliance shout hostile remarks. One is ushered out by a security guard, but at the intermission, the panelists cajole him back in (Aviv).

2007: The day after a shooting rampage at Virginia Tech, Nikki Giovanni speaks at a memorial service to rousing cheers of "Let's go, Hokies!" Variously referred to as a speech and a poem, her piece, "We Are Virginia Tech," quickly becomes a popular YouTube download.

This list, compiled from print sources and conversations with poets and literary critics, includes only events at which authors sound their own work (although they sometimes perform other poetry as well).[4] Many memorable events during this period are therefore omitted, such the ninetieth birthday celebration for the Brooklyn Bridge (Norris 165–66), at which various poets read work by Bishop, Crane, Whitman, Zukofsky, and others. Robert Pinsky's Favorite Poem Project is likewise an important event in poetry performance, but it focuses its on-line video and audio archives on readings by non-poets.[5] Other performance art events use sound differently, such as The Typing Explosion, whose members dressed in 1960s secretarial outfits to type collaborative poems based on titles selected by audience members (Glazner, *How to Make a Living as a Poet* 135–40). The noise of clacking keys, bells, and horns played an important role in these performances, but members of the group did not read the results aloud.

FIVE POETS FROM FOUR CORNERS: AN INTERVIEW, AUGUST 2005

Slam culture favors collaborative processes among team members, within its organizational structures, and in a performance style that encourages audience participation. I therefore compile the answers below by question and not by individual, emphasizing the conversation they reflect, although the process of collecting replies was far more unruly than this linear document can represent. I originally sent my questions to the team's Slam Master. He forwarded them to other team members and they responded individually, sometimes copying each other on their replies. I have edited their responses lightly: I corrected inconsistencies in spelling and punctuation, for instance, except when they constituted authorial style. I also offered each poet the chance to revise his or her answers when publication became an option (I received only one brief addition). Our long-distance conversation was frank and informal, and I use the poets' first names or stage names to reflect this.

Team Members
Scott Nicolay (42), K-12 Gifted Program Coordinator
zoEy benally / Twyla Zoann Benally (35), Environmental Health Specialist
Tish Ramirez / Patricia Ramirez (45), District Sanitarian
DJ Mydas / Benjamin D. Stalcup (19), Front Desk Clerk, Econo Lodge
Amy Mullin (32), Medical University Library Director

When/why did you start composing poetry?
Scott: High school. Inspired by Wm. Blake.
zoEy: I started "composing" poetry sometime in the fall of 1998. I was in a car

crash in the spring of 1998. I whacked my head on the left side. Before the crash I was all about math. I would find patterns and numbers in everything. There were colors, taste, touch and personality associated with each number. I remember that I liked the flavor and smell of 27 best. When I was bored I would amuse myself with square roots and cube roots. When I shopped for groceries one of my favorite games was to keep a running total of all my purchases in my head. When I got to the checkout, the final challenge was to calculate the total, including tax, down to the penny and have the amount ready for the cashier before she said it. After the crash, after whacking the left side of my head, all the math was gone. It was horrible. I couldn't keep lists of names, list of numbers, lists of anything in my brain. I couldn't add three numbers. I felt like a mere mortal—all my math superpowers were gone. I was like Superman after he visited his ice castle and was exposed to kryptonite radiation.

One night several months after the crash I was sleeping. In my dream these words kept barging in and ruining my dreams. It was the same words over & over. They weren't being spoken—the words were just there. The words drove me nuts and woke me up. I couldn't go back to sleep because every time I closed my eyes, the words were there, impatiently tapping their feet, and with deep resentful sighs of annoyance. Finally I grabbed a scrap of torn envelope. I felt around for a pen (I have a very small house—400 square feet—everything is within arm's reach) and scribbled down the words in the dark. I hooked the pen over the envelope scrap and tossed it on the floor and fell back to sleep. After this, poems would just come.

I don't really write or compose the poems. The poems are just there. The stanzas might be mixed up, and the lines might not be as cool as they could be, but everything is there. All I have to do is write the poems down and edit them. I run into poems everywhere—I kinda imagine them to be like spider webs stretched across paths. When I run into them, I am given the poem if I am humble and ready to receive.

Tish: A few minutes before the first slam I went to.

DJ Mydas: around 16, serious stuff a year later

Amy: Second grade, if not earlier.

When/why did you start performing poetry?

Scott: College. Once barricaded myself in the college radio station and read Blake, Ginsberg, A. D. Hope and Hawkwind lyrics over a variety of instrumental space music, Brian Eno and such, for two hours. Later, open mics with my own work, occasional feature reader, eventually performing in Coaches's Slams at youth slam events.

zoEy: I started performing poetry because Scott said that my stuff was good enough to be performed. I always thought my stuff wasn't really poetry, but lo

& behold it was. Before Scott introduced the idea of performance, I had only a handful of friends that I showed my stuff to—Karen, Chris, Tish, Bert. After I started performing my poetry, I found that I actually enjoyed the performance aspect.

Tish: Zoey signed me up.

DJ Mydas: around 17 . . . decided to back up my shit-talking and show i could do more than write bragging rhymes

Amy: Second grade: reading a poem about Christmas during Mass. Adulthood: first public reading was at my 26th birthday party after 5 bottles of red wine. Started going to open mics and getting features shortly thereafter.

Have you performed poetry in non-slam venues?
If so, how is it different?

Scott: Crowd sometimes does not know how to respond to poetry as well, most of the poets don't know how to perform very well. Slam raises the bar a little. On the other hand, some slam audiences expect more of a dog and pony show and may not be as open to all varieties of poetry.

zoEy: Non-slam poetry venues and performances are cool, mellow because in these venues it is only about the poetry. The audience is more relaxed and the competition element is not there. Slams are more exciting. I guess the big learning for me about slam is not to take the scores seriously. Slams are a nifty poetry venue, but only for a certain type of poetry. I have found that my style of poetry doesn't necessarily fit with the slam world. Scotty tells me that it's a type of poem just like haiku and sonnets. I understand his logic, but still have not decided where I fit within that world. Right now I am at the edge of the envelope and haven't decided if I am in a position to push.

Tish: Two venues. Crowd was very receptive.

DJ Mydas: yes . . . some of the pressure is off . . . and in some cases there was a good Q&A afterwards where i get to talk about my two favorite subjects: myself and my work . . . plus, it's easier to connect with the audience sometimes in non-slam venues

Amy: I prefer it. I can do quieter, gentler stuff that requires more attention from the audience. With a longer reading I can craft a set list that takes the audience on a journey.

What slam experience did you have before
the 2005 nationals?

Scott: Co-organized the Taos Poetry Circus and World Heavyweight Championship Poetry Bout in 1991. Founded first youth poetry slam team (Navajo Nation) in

1995. Co-founded New Mexico Youth Poetry Slam Championship with Anne MacNaughton of the Taos Poetry Circus. Co-founded the National Youth Poetry Slam in 1998 with Elizabeth Thomas. Won 2004 Four Corners Slam. Slam Master of Four Corners Slam from December 2004 to present (shared duties with Amy Mullin).

zoEy: Shiprock Slam, Andrea Kristina Slams & San Juan College Slam.

Tish: Just the slams I went to in San Juan College: the one Zoey signed me up for, one at SJC on poetry day, and the one where Scott qualified.

DJ Mydas: Just read at a couple of high school slams . . . any other slam/open mic i heard about and felt ready for . . .

Amy: Started slamming in Albuquerque in '99. Won the first slam I competed in: Poetry n' Beer when it was at Burt's Tiki Lounge. Went on to co-found the Albuquerque Slam Council in 2000, laid the groundwork for the '05 Nationals. Was on the SlamAmerica bus tour in 2000. Slammed at the Green Mill in Chicago, the Taos Poetry Circus and the Nuyorican in New York. Hosted numerous slams in ABQ and Farmington.

What attracted you to competing in the nationals?

Scott: My original goal was to help organize an adult Navajo Nation team and attend as coach, but our venue on the Reservation closed in December. Restarted in Farmington. The team only fell into place after I was asked to bring a group of poets to a poetry festival in Telluride, Colorado and recruited Tish and Zoey. Amy and Mydas joined shortly after our return and suddenly we had a team.

zoEy: The excitement of trying something new is really what drove me to practice my stuff for Nationals. This indicates a big commitment from me. An additional side effect of the crash is that it is extremely difficult for me to memorize stuff. For the National Slam I had to practice my poems daily. I practiced two miles / thirty minutes on the way to work and two miles / thirty minutes on the way home from work. I practiced in the shower. I practiced anywhere I could.

Tish: Scott signed us up.

DJ Mydas: Heard from a friend that there was a qualifying slam for the four corners team in farmington . . . me and a friend (not the same friend) drove out to farmington, i won and joined the team . . . but as far as wanting to compete in nationals, that was never a question . . . there r very few things i'm good at . . . and slam poetry was one of the places where i felt like i fit in (at least a little bit) . . . i was going to go watch the national slam in ABQ anyway . . . so i figured, y not try to be in it too?

Amy: It was a dream I had for several years. Unfortunately, I never made an Albuquerque team despite making the semi-finals three years in a row. I moved from Albuquerque to the Four Corners area in 2003. Met Scott Nicolay at the 2004 San

Juan College slam, and slowly (and lazily) worked with him to help build a slam community and get a team together.

Describe the experience, positives and negatives.

Scott: My experience was really all positive, other than drawing the first slot in both our bouts, but that's part of the game, and is funny in a kind of cursed way. It was great to perform to packed, enthusiastic houses, to be part of a great team, to see old friends from the slam world and beyond, to finally move out of the coach role into national competition. To have people come up and thank me for my poem. The Nerd Slam was the funniest thing I have ever seen in my life, and the poetry was great. I'm still laughing.

zoEy: Positives: a) Working & performing with a team. b) Supporting and receiving support from my team members. c) The Nerd Slam was awesome! I loved the nerd slam. After attending the nerd slam I have ascertained that I am a vector borne disease nerd. d) The feeling of being recharged from hearing and seeing all the poetry. e) Not scoring 21 during the first bout. I knew being the very first poet was bad—the judges ALWAYS score the first poet low. I was went up there afraid that I would get all 7–s. Fortunately my score was not as low as I had imagined it would be. f) The stellar organization of the entire National Poetry Slam event. Negatives: a) Drawing the number one slot for both bouts. Scotty did an amazing job with his mascot poem. It was bad that he also had to be first in the bout. b) Watching beautiful women being let into the slam venue after they told us that fire code occupancy had been exceeded. As an environmental health specialist this was as disturbing as a food handler wiping snot away with their hand, adjusting their shoe with a finger on that same hand, and then making me a sandwich.

Tish: It was a charged environment when you heard a poem that moved you. You heard so many bad works of art, then came to realize that you didn't have to worry about your own stuff. It really was not a competition, just an opportunity to share values, art, feelings, thoughts, dreams, and so forth.

DJ Mydas: where do i start? . . . saw some of the best poetry i've ever seen . . . got to spend a few last days of summer with a good group of people . . . actually felt like part of a team for the first time since i can remember . . . after the nerd slam, i was glad to be able to tell people (convincingly) that there is no way i am a nerd . . . jumped into a few ciphers (first time . . . remember, i grew up in white america) . . . we didn't win, but we didn't care . . . realized that sometimes it's not the best poem that wins, sometimes it's just the loudest or fastest or smartest-sounding poem (JUST BECAUSE U MENTION EMMITT TILL AND MEDGAR EVERS DOESN'T MAKE YOUR POEM ANY GOOD!!!) . . . oh, yeah . . . i would also like to mention that i was able to meet and fall in love with my future wife, Ms. Mayda Del Valle.

Amy: I honestly hate the competitive aspect of slamming. I have "slam" poems, which fit neatly into the three minute, over-the-top slam aesthetic. But most of my best pieces aren't slam pieces. Low audience scores have taught me that. There's a saying about the foolishness of trying to win a slam with poetry.

What I like is the ability to perform in front of a really large attentive audience. Sometimes the Nationals can give you that. Back in the day I was more into schmoozing and hanging with the poets all the time, doing round robins for hours. I think the Nationals came about three or four years too late for me to enjoy them that much.

Our team had brilliant poets with complex pieces. It would have been nice if we had more than one slot for each person to really show their stuff.

Describe your role in the team and/or relationships with other members.

Scott: My role is a combination of Captain Kirk and the Village Idiot. It is my job to beam down to unexplored slam venues first and get punched in the face by hostile aliens. To make strategy decisions about order and poem selection, to coordinate group efforts on and off stage, to work with team members to hone their work into competitive dynamite.

zoEy: My role in the team was that of the adrenaline junkie slacker. I adore all my team mates.

Tish: I work with Zoey, then I met Scott, then Amy, finally Mydas. Other than Scott as the team leader, we really don't fall into roles . . . none that I can pick out. We have different styles of poetry; perhaps that is our role and relationship. Essentially we're all from different points in the span of life.

DJ Mydas: as the newest member of the team, living a ways away from the rest without a car, i'm still getting to know the rest of the team . . . which, of course, is one of the best things about friends . . . as far as my role goes, i guess i'm the latino voice, the teenage voice, the hip-hop voice and any other label u can think of . . . but i try not to use my "role" to guide my writing . . . i just hope i can be me

Amy: I was kind of the assistant coach, I guess. Did a lot of the organizing and scheduling for fundraisers and rehearsals. At times Scott and I didn't see eye-to-eye on things like poet order or poem choice, the strategy. I had to be the bad cop to his keystone cop.

It was the first nationals for all of us, but I'd been hanging around the slam scene for long enough to know a couple of things. After spending years around disciplined professional slammers, Slam Serious had been drummed into me, and the laid-back attitude of the team was sometimes hard to understand. I expected to rehearse every day for months, but we didn't really start rehearsing until a couple of weeks before (I think).

I got along well with the other team members. All great poets and performers. It was great to see them take a huge leap from Four Corners performances to excellent Nationals performances. They also helped me see different things in my poems and perform these moldy oldies in very new ways.

I liked working with this team, although most teams go down together and stay through the whole thing. Our team was more a collection of individuals that met up at bouts. I really missed that camaraderie. I wound up hanging out with Indie competitors when the team left, because just about everyone else there had a team.

How do you compose—where, when, why?

Scott: Usually driving or hanging around at the local coffeehouse, although no longer with the aid of massive doses of caffeine as before. Often I compose completely in my head, or I start from a partial handwritten draft and refine it on the computer. Sometimes a poem is complete over several stages, even over months or years. I rarely make major changes after a poem is "complete," but I may tinker with it years later. Some poems I send out on paper or the Internet and forget about almost completely, especially haiku, which I feel should be composed quickly and scattered like seeds. At other times I pay famous writers such as Stephen King and Alice Walker to write poems for me, and I sign my name to them without ever getting around to publishing them—this is the main reason I am always so broke.

zoEy: I keep my mind open & am ready to receive poems at any moment. I carry an arsenal of pens and a book with plenty of blank pages. I try not to taint poems with judgment. I try to limit gerunds, articles and similes. I try to keep the voice active. I am not afraid to scribble stuff out. I am not afraid to crumple paper & throw it away. I am not afraid to laugh out loud at what I have written down.

Tish: The mood or fleeting inspiration pushes me to write, anywhere, anytime, because the urge is there.

DJ Mydas: i write whenever i can (which is never often enough) . . . not that i don't have time to write, i just can't think of sumthin to write fast enough (when u hear about jay-z writing an entire song in his head in 20 minutes, u can never write fast enough) . . . i used to take months to write sumthin . . . but since i worked on this album, i've been able to start and finish a poem within a few weeks or even days . . . it all depends on how angry/ depressed/ in love/ charged i am

i usually write at work, as it's one of the few times where i don't have sumthin else distracting me . . . but i also like to write at home when it's past 12 . . . or in class when i'm tired of listening and ready to give my opinion . . .

the way i write might sound kind of strange, but i've never really known anyone else that writes rhymes, so i have nuthin to compare it to . . . i get an idea for sumthin (a couplet, a phrase, maybe just a topic idea) and write it in my rhyme book . . . when i have time to figure out the math problem, i sit down and write that phrase with other words/ phrases that rhyme together . . . then i do my "Beautiful Mind" thing, moving words and phrases around, adding words and phrases so they all make sense and form whut most people would call a "poem" . . . make sense? . . . that makes one of us . . .

and why . . . i could give a million reasons . . . i even devoted an entire poem to these reasons once . . . but new reasons keep popping up . . . but i'm finding more and more . . . that i write . . . because i can . . . doesn't evryone? . . . wouldn't u write rhymes if u could?

Amy: Ack, right now I'm not doing much writing. I had the beginning of a poem in my head just before sleep last night, and now I can't remember it. I compose poems best in my head, usually when I'm doing something like walking or hiking and I'm not dwelling on mundane things like getting my taxes done. Being a newlywed is infringing on my poetry brainspace a great deal. Still trying to figure out that balance. You'd think it would give me lots to write about, the inability to find the time and space to write!

As for the why, well . . . When you have these words and images dancing in your brain and you can't think of anything else, it's best for you and the words to put them down on paper quickly so they can live their life and you can live yours.

What audience(s) do you most hope to reach?

Scott: Horny women. It doesn't seem to be working though. My wife won't read my work at all, so it's no help getting laid at home.

zoEy: Most of my poetry is for Navajos. I am defining my reality as a Navajo woman who grew up in a border town at the juncture of the 20th & 21st century. I am defining my reality and not accepting the definitions imposed upon me—noble savage, drunk indian, conquered people.

Tish: Don't really have an audience in mind.

DJ Mydas: it always varies poem to poem . . . sometimes i'm speaking to the world . . . sometimes i'm speaking to the upper class . . . the lower class . . . latin people . . . white people . . . my people . . . young people . . . old people . . . people that suck at writing rhymes . . . people that think I suck at writing rhymes . . . lately i've been speaking to that girl that i wanted to listen . . . but mostly i try to speak to those people like me, who feel like no one is speaking for them . . .

Amy: Right now I'm wondering what the Caribbean audience, locals and expats, would be like. I know there's a rich tradition of Caribbean poetry, but social and cultural events aren't always mixed, at least on my small island (Nevis). Meaning, the locals do their thing and the expats do theirs.

I write primarily for myself. When I send poems to friends or do a reading in front of strangers, I hope to reach people who can get something out of it. I hope to express something that the audience wanted to but couldn't put their finger on it.

For years my grandmother had the hardest time reading my poetry. Now she shows them to a psychologist friend of hers, and I think she's finally starting to get something out of them.

What makes a poem great?

Scott: My name at the bottom.

zoEy: Being true to your art. Believing in your art.

Tish: Feeling it evokes, invokes.

DJ Mydas: just saying sumthin different that people can relate to . . . i've seen too many

people talk about the same shit . . . and too many people talk about shit and no one knows whut the fuck they're talking about . . . it's a thin line . . . but, honestly, as long as u can speak to someone . . . as long as one person understands, it's a great poem to at least one person . . .

Amy: When you hear it or read it and it feels like your spirit is leaving your body or you're levitating towards the ceiling or you want to get up and start dancing or if you cry no matter who's looking. If you still remember a line several years later, that's a great poem.

What's the role of sound in a great poem?

Scott: Every poem has two magical lives: one in the breath, and one in the dance of the eye. Without attention to both, a poem is never truly complete.

zoEy: Sound is really cool because it can help others almost hear how you heard the poem in your own head.

Tish: Helps with the generation of feeling.

DJ Mydas: if YOU don't believe whut you're saying, how can expect anyone else to? . . .

Amy: Once you've got the "facts" down, the words that convey meaning and the images, you go through letter by letter, reading it aloud as much as possible, rewriting everything and making sure the poem is music. Otherwise you're just writing an essay.

What does the term "poetic voice" mean to you?

Scott: Ever since I read Ron Padgett's famous (and hysterical) poem on the subject, I have never been able to take poetic voice seriously. I suppose I have a sort of voice, but I am completely happy leaping between radically different forms: concrete poetry, pseudo-tribal, science fiction haiku, slam, avant-garde epic, that it would be hard to retain one voice. I am not really interested in finding one style and exploiting it, but in constantly pushing the boundaries of what I can do and say, and I am happy to imitate other forms and styles for various effects. My poetic biography will be written in Hell by Mario Puzo and entitled *Steal This Voice*.

zoEy: Not really sure.

Tish: I think how the words fall into the blending of the world around one and set the mood in that realm. Not really an aura but that concept.

DJ Mydas: well, there's always that generic poetic voice that people tend to use when they can't think of any other way to articulate themselves, but i'm sure that's not whut u were getting at . . .

i always thought poetic voice was when someone spoke from their heart . . . when a person is able to express exactly whut is in their mind through words, they r using their poetic voice . . . but i don't know . . . i've never really studied poetry . . . i deal with mathematics . . .

Amy: That's sort of the trance state my brain sinks into when a poem is being composed. It feels different from inside my skull. It's the opposite of the voice I use when writing library policies or teaching medical database techniques or talking to my mom.

Have you ever composed poetry collaboratively?
If not, why not? If so, describe the experience.

Scott: Yes. I have worked with musicians and comic book artists. I have developed team poems, sometimes contributing to the words, other times only to the blocking and other performative elements. I once organized what was probably the first science fiction renku. And of course all poetry is really a collaboration between the poet and the audience, not in some realm of abstract theory, but simply in the sense of sharing and exchange. There's no escaping that in performance. In a successful performance, one engages the audience and their responses become part of the poem. Poets who don't acknowledge the responsibility of collaboration with their audience should probably be taken out and whipped by the Ogre Katcina with yucca fronds or something equally educational.

zoEy: Yes. We composed a group piece for Telluride. Tish, Rich (non-poet), and I composed another group piece that we didn't use. Collaborative poetry is more fun to create than solo poetry. I like the adrenaline rush of collaborative poetry. Collaborative poetry creation is hilarious and exhilarating. Collaborative poetry is like the nerd slam, but better.

Tish: I think of conversations with friends and that is like collaborative poetry, when we expound and fly off on tangents. It is highly charged and ideas come so fast with the banter, all we need is the background music and a few key movements to call it dance.

DJ Mydas: honestly, no . . . i don't work well with others . . . i am an asshole (in the Denis Leary sense) . . . plus, i've never known anybody else that wrote rhymes, so my poetry style never really fit well with everyone else's

Amy: Never a 50/50 collaboration. I've done lots of exercises with an old writing group I was in. Exquisite corpses, or picking out various words from envelopes, yelling out words (Tourette's) at random times during the writing process.

I've always wanted to do more writing collaboration. I've done tons of performing collaboration with group pieces. I guess with writing people get in their own trance-state, and if you're actively interacting with another person it's harder to get there.

NOTES

Introduction

1. Severin's *Poetry off the Page*, focusing on British women poets during the entire century, is one of the only comparative studies of poetry performance. Morris and Rubin construct histories of poetry's aural reception in this period; acoustical technologies, progressive education, and economic pressures all play a role. The central chapters in Middleton's *Distant Reading* include some attention to modernism along with performance practices in the nineteenth century and the second half of the twentieth (25–103). Examinations of particular scenes and circles, such as London's Poetry Bookshop, also illuminate the field. These studies parallel efforts by McGann, Morrisson, and many others to examine publishing practices—especially involving the book and the little magazine—during the same period. While Bernstein's *Close Listening* does not focus on modernism, the essays collected there are enormously helpful in illuminating the general theoretical concerns.

2. Domestic readings can verge on the salon model discussed below, although they tend to be smaller and more fully private; see, for instance, Kramer on Floyd Dell's poetry circle in Chicago (114–15).

3. See also Davey (231) on how black voices are ventriloquized by white elocutionists.

4. Nor were college audiences always responsive to work or artists that violated their expectations, as Williams found when he began delivering lectures and readings in those settings in the late thirties (Mariani 391, 438–39, 459).

5. Morrisson observes that the "major" Victorian poets did not take to the platform, although a good number of popular poets did, and contrasts this to America. I disagree with his statement that poetry readings were "more common" in the United States (77 n. 228).

6. See Bode, Reiser, and Warren on these phenomena.

7. Stevens possessed oratorical talents (Richardson 1.54, 2.181, 300) and Eliot, as Coyle describes in "'This rather elusory broadcast technique': T. S. Eliot and the Genre of the Radio Talk," worked on the latter as a distinct oral form. Cullen was much in demand for lectures and readings, although, facing the Depression, he came to prefer the steadier earnings of a teaching engagement.

8. See Gray, *Race and Time* (144) on Harper's negotiations among dialects and audiences.

9. See Strong-Boas and Gerson (100–134) and Barrett and Markowitz (235) as well as Leighton's illuminating article. Also thanks to Janet Gray, whose anthology *She Wields a Pen* is rich in references to nineteenth-century women poets who also lectured and recited.

10. Although she seems not to have recited her own poetry in public, Adah Isaacs Menken was another important nineteenth-century woman author-performer. Renée Sentilles argues that for "the Menken," as she was called, poetry served as a counterbalance to her notoriety as an actress. "As long as Menken seemed pathetic and sincere in print, she could push the parameters of respectability on stage" (69).

11. In London, Edith Sitwell was also experimenting with poetry as theater. Severin describes a 1923 performance of *Façade* at Aeolian Hall in which "Sitwell read behind a curtain with small openings, at most slightly visible, her voice projected through a sengerphone, a form of megaphone" (47). Thanks also to Marsha Bryant for sharing ideas as well as a draft of her essay, "Sitwell Beyond the Semiotic" (forthcoming in *Tulsa Studies in Women's Literature*).

12. The same folder also contains an illustrative list of his public appearances in 1926.

13. Dodge's salon was by no means the first in the United States, though it was a particularly famous one. See Loeffelholz, for example, on Annie Fields in Boston (162–75).

14. Rampersad cites an early twenties reading at this branch organized by Ernestine Rose (63–64).

15. Eric W. White, however, tells an evocative story about H.D.'s spontaneous poetic recitation at the Berlin apartment of Lotte Reiniger and Carl Koch in 1931 (16–17).

16. See Niven on how *Poetry* fostered community in Chicago; Lindsay, for example, recited poems in its offices (244). "The Little Room," an informal social club, also gathered Chicago writers in the teens (Williams 9).

1. Sounding Poetic Voice

1. Sharon Cameron, for example, uses the word "choral" in reference to Emily Dickinson's work (207).

2. Key sources on the meanings of voice for narrative are Gennette's "Voice," in *Narrative Discourse* (212–62), Bakhtin's "Discourse in the Novel," in *The Dialogic Imagination* (259–422), Booth's *Rhetoric of Fiction* (voice is a controlling metaphor throughout the book), and Lanser's "Towards a Feminist Poetics of Narrative Voice," in *Fictions of Authority* (3–24). In narrative studies, voice possesses a com-

plex array of possible meanings related to strategies of narration, the relationship between author and audience, and grammar itself (verb tense, passive versus active voice).

3. Ong cites Havelock's work frequently; in a subsequent book, *The Muse Learns to Write*, Havelock addresses the transition from orality to literacy in ancient Greece in a way that supports Ong's argument.

4. See Foley's *How to Read an Oral Poem* for specifics on what strategies and vocabularies might be appropriate to oral art.

5. See Barbara Johnson and Mary Jacobus as well as recent books by William Waters and Ann Keniston.

6. See Garrett Stewart on the "'phonophobia' generated in the wake of the Derridean attack on the logos" (3).

7. In *Victorian Soundscapes* (2003), Picker stresses the nineteenth-century science of sound and Victorian awareness of the sonic environment, while Yopie Prins's "Voice Inverse" speculates that a "historical prosody" might better inform how we listen to Victorian verse (52–55). Two anthologies that focus primarily on the twentieth century have also been important to this study. Morris' *Sound States* (1997) argues against "consigning orality to a preliterate past" and emphasizes how "the acoustical technologies that grew up with modernism also prepared the swerve toward the postmodern" (3, 8). The title of Bernstein's *Close Listening* provides a resonant phrase for the scholarly activity of attending to poetry performance. Also see Schweighauser's more recent book on American fiction as noise and on fiction's interaction with the sounds of modern life.

8. Susan Stewart, in *Poetry and the Fate of the Senses* (2002), includes chapters on sound and voice as well as discussions of the other senses in relation to poetry. Like Garrett Stewart, Susan Stewart is concerned *not* with real soundings of poems by their authors but with their silent resonances. She suggests that the status of voice hovers between medium and figure, and that poems constitute both speech-acts and images of speech (104, 109). Also see Kahn and Whitehead's anthology concerning radio and the avant-garde.

9. On the adjacent issue of sound's relationship to meaning in poetry, see Shoptaw's "Lyric Cryptography."

10. *An Exaltation of Forms*, edited by Finch and Varnes, contains a range of excellent practical essays on subjects ranging from "Dactylic Meter" to "The Metrics of Rap"; "Performance Poetry" (by Bob Holman) stands among them.

11. I am tremendously grateful to Courtney Harrison, then an undergraduate senior preparing for medical school, who researched these questions for me, and taught me what the answers meant, as an independent study during the winter of 2006. My thanks, too, to Dr. Robert Stewart at Washington and Lee University for suggesting and supporting this project.

12. In an e-mail to the author, Harrison notes a potential problem with these findings: "A confounding factor must be considered, but is not often discussed with this methodology: Increased blood flow indicates elevated activity. However, there is no way, through these procedures, to determine whether that increased activity is excitatory or inhibitory. In the nervous system, there are a variety of neurotransmitters or chemical substances that one neuron releases, binding it to the next neuron.

This action either stimulates the next neuron or inhibits it. However, blood flow increases to an area of the brain in which a neuron is activated (i.e., by a released neurotransmitter). However, ultimately there is no way via this methodology to determine whether the neurotransmitter that the activated neuron released is excitatory or inhibitory."

13. For related results, see Price et al.

14. Tsur asks, "What makes sound patterns expressive?" in his book of that title, comparing the "intuitions" (1) of literary criticism to linguistic and psychological research. His essay "Rhyme and Cognitive Poetics" explores how rhyme affects memory and even causes "acoustic confusion," sometimes dominating the sensory information a poem provides (61). Cognitive poetics, in fact, may have an important influence on literary study generally. Stockwell's *Cognitive Poetics: An Introduction* (2002) provides a helpful list of key readings and outlines this field's preoccupations with the conceptual structures of language, its persuasive patterns, and the nature of metaphor. Other writers bring science to bear on literature without the imprimatur of an established methodology. For example, in "The Neural Lyre," Turner and Pöppel try to put metrical poetry into a neuroscientific context. They find that the three-second unit or "buffer" of auditory processing corresponds to the three-second metered line (arguing that this is a cross-cultural constant). As a result, they theorize that metered poetry might have a profound effect on the brain, tuning the right and left hemispheres as meditation seems to do.

15. In April 2006 I posted a query about Jaynes on a women's poetry listserv founded by Finch. I received lively and curious responses, full of helpful references, from several poets intrigued by Jaynes, including Finch herself, Katherine Marie Drabek, Patricia Hagge, Julie Kane, Laura Kennelly, and Ann White. Also see Weissman's *Of Two Minds: Poets Who Hear Voices*, which explains poets' auditory hallucinations through evolutionary biology, and Daniel B. White's *Muses, Madmen, and Prophets*.

16. See http://poets.org/page.php/prmID/87. I accessed this lesson plan on 25 July 2006.

17. See Jordan's *Poetry for the People* for a book that does similar work.

18. I use the labels "composition studies," "composition," and "rhetoric and composition" interchangeably, but these common names for the field do possess different nuances.

19. For another extremely helpful foray into defining voice, see Elbow's introduction to *Landmark Essays on Voice and Writing* (xi–xlvii).

20. Berlin refers to Macrorie, Elbow, and others as delegates from "the moderate wing of the expressionist camp" (485); more recent writings use the term "expressivist" to designate this approach to composition teaching, which emphasizes the development of individual self through writing as well as resistance to authority and conformity.

21. My account of the evolution of creative writing is deeply indebted to Myers's sometimes defensive but very helpful book, *The Elephants Teach*. Also see Adams (73–74) and Mayers (8–17, 40).

22. See Mayers and Ritter and Vanderslice on these phenomena.

23. For a more recent example, see Webb's essay on voice and personality. Unlike deNiord, Webb writes with straightforwardness—"A good poem, like a good friend, is a pleasure to be with"—and roots poetry in personality rather than spirit. Like the former author, however, Webb defines voice both as the origin of poetry and as the condition of its cohesive, communicative power. There are many more essays and poems on voice by poets who work inside and outside of creative writing's institutions, including Louise Glück, Alice Notley, Ron Padgett, and Robert Pinsky. Also see Charles Bernstein's *A Poetics*, especially "Artifice of Absorption"; Denise Levertov's "Some Notes on Organic Form"; and Joy Harjo's "Writing with the Sun."

24. In 2003 I worked with a student research assistant, John Rumin, to survey these materials. We counted advertisements in the 2002 issue of *Poets & Writers*; Rumin also identified the top twenty-five programs nationwide and assessed their web pages and brochures. I am very grateful to him and to the Robert E. Lee Program for Undergraduate Research for their assistance.

25. Rumin solicited such materials from all twenty-five schools and counted ten instances of the word voice within them.

26. See Moore on the intersections of feminism and composition studies as well as an argument for the continuing relevance of voice as a term (194); Carlton also discusses the intersections between feminism and composition in "Voice and the Naming of Woman." On the development of creative writing as a discipline for women students, see Adams (74).

27. See also Whitehead on "coalitional voice" (xxi). There is more to say about the importance of collective voice for various literary communities than I can address here. For example, McAdams argues that American Indian poets are "reinventing 'voice'" as "a site of play between individual and collective expression" (11–12).

28. Rasula, for example, remarks on the pervasive equation of poetry with voice in *The American Poetry Wax Museum* (38). This study does not analyze poetry by the deaf, but this would be an interesting case for questions of sound, voice, and lyric. See Klima and Bellugi's "Poetry without Sound," Rée's *I See a Voice* (356–75), and Albertini, Meath-Lang, and Harris.

29. Diepeveen focuses in part on Marianne Moore, whose investigations of voice and lyric I find particularly provocative; see chapter 2 in my *Poetics of Enclosure* (41–63).

30. Also see Noland on how advocates for lyric resistance to postmodern life "have created a false vision of the poetic genre" (4), and Dorothy M. Nielsen on the "ecological subject" of some postmodern poetry (128).

31. See DuPlessis's oft-cited "'Corpses of Poetry,'" which describes a "cluster of foundational materials with a gender cast built into the heart of the lyric" (71), and its revision in her 2001 book-length study.

32. Longenbach makes a similar point in a more sweeping manner when he observes that "no poem extends the illusion of an individual speaker without challenging that illusion" (67).

33. For a more recent example, see Marshall Brown on lyricism as "haunting" and "magical" (132).

2. Edna St. Vincent Millay's Performance of Presence

1. See Steven Connor on radio ventriloquism (*Dumbstruck* 22, 402).

2. Millay's jingle echoes a well-known verse by writer and progressive educator Hughes Mearns, "Antigonish" (Baker 326).

3. McLuhan's theories define "participation" differently than I do in this passage; he argues that print is a "cooler" medium than radio, for instance, because readers must work harder than broadcast listeners to fill in the minimal sensory detail (36–37). I refer not to the process of making meaning as much to immediate interaction—as when, for example, a poet changes her presentation in response to verbal and non-verbal audience responses.

4. I thank curator Don Share and Josephine Packard, whose 2005 presentations at the Modernist Studies Association meeting alerted me to the richness of this archive.

5. I abbreviate Millay's *Collected Poems* throughout as CP.

6. See Warren.

7. I use the terms "read," "recite," and "perform" interchangeably in this chapter for variety, but in fact they suggest different approaches to sounding poetry. A "reading" implies a written text voiced with little or no stagecraft; "recitation" suggests memorized or at least highly practiced intonations. "Performance," finally, invokes theatrical comparisons, the prominence of a gesturing body, and displays of identity.

8. See Bradshaw, "Remembering Amy Lowell" on the cultural meanings of Amy Lowell's obesity.

9. In addition to Middleton and Rubin, discussed above, see Rasula on "the unique soundscape of Victorian poetics" (247).

10. For accounts of Millay's performance style, see Milford (259–61, 270–74, 307, 419–23); Gould (73–74, 231–34); Eastman (80); Wilson (749–50); Sprague (137–38); Thesing (12–13).

11. Millay's highly gendered performances are especially interesting in light of public anxieties about women's disembodied voices on the radio, although these prohibitions applied to women announcers more often than to women performers; see Hilmes (136–41).

12. Hubbard describes how Millay's poems exercise "feminine sexuality as masquerade, a show or showing in which the woman gives herself, without ever quite giving herself away" (18). Her live readings seemed to share this quality with her printed poems.

13. See Clark, *Sentimental Modernism* (3–26); Gilbert, "Female Female Impersonator" (293–312), and "Directions for Using the Empress" (163–81); Nina Miller (16–40); Walker (85–99).

14. This fundamental tension between poetry's visual and aural dimensions has been described by different theorists in different terms. See Frye on "babble" versus "doodle," which he also calls "melos" and "opsis" (274), for instance, or, more recently, Stewart on "the phonic and the graphic" (24).

15. See Barnouw (284) on FDR's fireside chats. Smulyan argues for radio's illusion of sincerity and naturalness (77–78).

16. Hilmes' *Radio Voices* focuses on radio as a social practice with particular attention to its culture-building potential and its participation in shaping gender roles (14–17).

17. Saerchinger's memoir describes his efforts to persuade the literary lights of Britain to broadcast to American audiences. His success was limited. The conditions of British radio during this period are somewhat different than in the United States, but across the Atlantic some writers were issuing their own rousing calls to poets. For instance, George Orwell, in "Poetry and the Microphone," investigates "the possibilities of the radio as a means of popularising poetry" (76).

18. As Barnouw observes, Kreymborg, Benet, Auden, and Millay did subsequently produce verse plays for radio (2.69). Also see Barnouw on the laws regulating copyright permissions on broadcast poetry performances (2.100).

19. McLuhan also writes about the radio "[giving] us back the poet's voice as an important dimension of poetic experience" (53).

20. See Barnouw (191) on the history of the "red" and "blue" networks.

21. I listened to these recordings at the Library of Congress during the summer of 2004. Excerpts are available commercially through the *Voice of the Poet* series.

22. The Library of Congress bibliographic entry describes the originals as "1930s instantaneous discs"—this probably means 78rpm shellac discs. The original recording exists on two discs, each containing a maximum of four-and-a-half minutes per side; sometimes comments or the beginning of a poem are cut off.

23. Orwell posits that this separation of poet from audience in fact benefits broadcasting, praising "the special advantage of the radio, its power to select the right audience, and to do away with stage fright and embarrassment" (76). Broadcasting cannot offer immediate connection, which means for the poet that "the audience *has no power over you*" (77).

24. As Steven Connor writes, "the radio studio or theatre was often enough portrayed in photographs to be immanent in the listening eye of the audience" (*Dumbstruck* 402).

25. Milford quotes a friend of Margaret Cuthbert's: "'You know, Edna did not want to record her voice, Margaret persuaded her to do it in the name of posterity. I can still hear her talking to Edna, telling her what it would mean someday, in the future'" (368). Furr investigates this gap between how Millay sounded to her contemporaries and how she sounds now in "Listening to Millay."

26. Millay's remarks evoke the casual intimacy of many professional announcers. For instance, Kaplan quotes an opening ramble by Ted Malone, who started reading poetry on the air in 1928: "I see you are alone. . . . Now I'll just take this rocker here by the radio and chat awhile . . ." (208).

27. Hubbard argues that Millay characteristically elongates the time for love in her printed sonnets, in contrast to the *carpe diem* pressures exerted by some male sonneteers (110, 115). Hubbard does not mention elongation as a performance tactic, but the parallel is striking.

28. Both printed and audio versions of the poem also manifest Millay's complex understanding of poetic voice. While Millay has so often been called a songbird, as if her lyrics are natural and instinctive, this sonnet mimics two

"tortured voice[s]," distinct in tone both on the page and on the air. The only bird present is a seagull's chick, metaphorically representing the "love" or relationship rather than the poet. This creature is "hushed," because his life depends on silence and surrounded by the "hiss" of a dangerous ocean. Millay thereby emphasizes the conditions framing poetic sounds. An uneasy gap exists between the performed and printed sonnet, resembling the parallel divide between the sonnet and the voices it may conjure.

29. See Hayles, who describes the additional distance recording creates between presence and voice—temporal as well as spatial (76). Radio itself creates only spatial distance.

30. Some poems also occur in a hypothetical future; time is of particular concern in how Millay refers to nature.

31. Furr finds such "embarrassment" rooted in a high culture reaction against sentimentalism (107).

32. See Furr, whose essay features other telling examples from the Millay archives at Vassar (98–101).

33. See chapter 5. Contemporary exceptions in United States broadcasting include HBO's *Def Poetry Jam* as well as occasional public radio features. For contemporary comments on the real and possible intersections between radio and poetry, see Breiner and Spinelli in *Communities of the Air*, ed. Squier (2003). Video and sound recordings are more common; university libraries are stocked with documentaries such as *Voices and Visions* and the Lannan Foundation series. Slam poets, unsurprisingly, sell their CDs at performances, but Amazon.com also carries many recordings by mainstream writers, for example, former poet laureate Billy Collins.

3. Voice and the Visual Poetry of Langston Hughes

1. Hodge's "Taking Shape: The Art of *Carmina Figurata*" in Finch and Varnes's *An Exaltation of Forms* offers a helpful introduction to that term (198–205). Higgins uses the term "pattern poetry" to refer to visual poetry published before 1900 (vii, 3–4).

2. See Jones, "Jazz Prosodies" (66–71), Nielsen (9–36).

3. Nelson analyzes the integration of illustration and text in Hughes's work (94, 190, 219), noting that reprinting of modernist work in general tends to "reduce our sense of the interrelationships between writing and the visual arts" (280n). A few other exceptions: Bolden argues for "film techniques" in *Montage* (99–100), and other scholars briefly discuss the evolving layout of that sequence and how it contributes to meaning, especially Hokansen (67). Ostrom identifies "visual patterns analogous to those in collages, mosaics, quilts, and textiles" (254).

4. See, for example, Badaracco (14) and her chapter on Imagism (30–66), Bohn (19–20).

5. See Jones, "Listening to What the Ear Demands," on Hughes's collaborations with musicians (1158–63). See Davey on the Golden Stair Press.

6. Also see Borshuk (21–90).

7. See also Michlin, who refers to poems in blues form as "transcriptions" (241).

8. In "These Old Writing Paper Blues," Ford focuses on the blues as the muse of African American poetry and teases out their complicated relationship to literary poetry. Ponce's "Langston Hughes's Queer Blues" hinges on the contrast between media; he addresses the fluctuating distances between poet and persona in Hughes's work, which parallels the variable gaps between blues music and blues poetry. More briefly, Ramazani reads "The Weary Blues" specifically as "an intricate meditation on the simultaneous distance and proximity between Hughes's blues poetry and his blues song" (144). Also see McGee on Hughes's blues as "an explosion of meanings latent in the gaps between spoken and written word" (508–09).

9. Also see Goodblatt on Hughes's use of heteroglossia (33–34) and McGee on the poet's interest in "linguistic multiplicity" (502).

10. Van Vechten loaned them the funds to begin the press; see Rampersad (1.220–23).

11. Rampersad notes that the delayed pamphlet reached Hughes after his American reading tour ended, as he left for Russia (1.241). See Thurston's analysis of the pamphlet's text and illustrations (105–14).

12. See Ford, "Making Poetry Pay," on Hughes's marketing strategies.

13. *The Big Sea* reprints nearly all of the poem, without illustrations, on pages 321–23. Hughes deletes, however, the rousing call to revolution in the poem's final section, "Christmas Card."

14. Not only did Van Vechten publish in *Vanity Fair*, but his protégé Miguel Covarrubias, who designed the cover for *The Weary Blues*, also published cartoons in that and other fashionable magazines.

15. For an illuminating discussion of Hughes's attitude towards musicians as collaborators, see Tracy (178).

16. See Thurston on how Hughes offers a "rearticulation of Jesus as a figure of revolution" (94).

17. Moglen observes that "this passage deploys a commonplace misogynist trope of the 1930s Marxist Left" (1196).

18. See Mitchell on the debate over the spatial aspects of poetry.

19. See Lemke for more on the complex relationship between modernism and primitivism among white and black artists. Chinitz addresses Hughes's relationship to primitivism, emphasizing his prose, in "Rejuvenation through Joy."

20. These include "Number" (536), "Go Slow" (537–38), and "Stokely, Malcolm, and Me," all of which end with rows of questions marks (CP 561). The signs for dollars and cents are also part of *Ask Your Mama* (CP 498–99).

21. The numbers in parentheses, here and in later portions of this chapter, refer to box and folder numbers of the Langston Hughes papers at the Beinecke library.

22. Hughes's poem appeared in the June 1940 issue of *Unquote* (1.2), which describes itself as "published here and there, now and then." The primitive publication, composed of 8-1/2×11 sheets stapled together, lists more editors than contributors. "Elderly Leaders" appears as "Public Dignitaries," the first piece in the issue, and "master's" has been changed to "golden." Hughes did not keep these changes when he anthologized the poem later.

23. Hokanson, discussing the "speakerly play of a variety of voices in a commu-nal context," locates an "authorial or 'poetic' voice" in the long poem, noting that "the poet's voice is distinct from the multitude of other voices in the poem but not divorced from or condescending toward them" (72–75).

24. "The 'finding of the voice' of the speaking subject in a language in which blackness is the cardinal sign of absence" (Gates 40n) constitutes a paradox for *Montage*, as it does for other African American texts. This may be partly why so many of Hughes's readers note his reserve, or personal absence, in many poems and the autobiographies. Most treatments of *Montage* stress its polyvocal nature, examine the binding motifs of music and frustrated dreams, and cast the author as a director of the sort of "ritual drama" Jemie describes.

25. Hughes's sexuality seems highly relevant here. See Schwarz on how Hughes uses ambiguity to open up spaces for "gay readings" (72) and Ponce on Hughes's pronouns (throughout but especially 527–30). Harlem itself may also be speaking: Jarraway argues that Hughes often identifies Harlem as female (827).

26. Nielsen also emphasizes the "movements between scripting and voicing" that characterize this work (22).

27. These reviews are collected by Dace. For more on Hughes as a folk poet, see "The Negro Artist and the Racial Mountain," in *Collected Works*, vol. 9, in which Hughes stresses his commitment to the "common element" (32); "My Adventures as a Social Poet" echoes this dedication to a racial art. Also see Nicholls on how a fan-tasy of the folk "as the authentic voice of the unconscious of the race" (4) has under-written some African American literary criticism. Hughes instead articulates a more complicated vision of black America: "Hughes's folk are quite literally all over the map, formally and ideologically" (Nicholls 16).

28. The meaning of "montage" in American English began to extend beyond film in the 1930s. For example, I came across the word in a collection of radio jar-gon published in 1945 (Cuthbert); it was defined as "a succession of brief scenes, usually one or two speeches bridged by a phase of music or a unifying sound effect" (277).

29. Hughes's composite portrait of Harlem resembles Gwendolyn Brooks' han-dling of Chicago's South Side in *A Street in Bronzeville* (1945), which Hughes re-viewed enthusiastically. Critics have noted Hughes's influence on Brooks, but the influence could have been mutual.

30. A student writes his now-famous "Theme for English B," and one poem consists wholly of a son's letter home to his mother. A string of newspaper head-lines concludes "Ballad of the Landlord," and several poems quote urban signs from cigarette machines and nightclubs.

31. See Lowney, who argues that Hughes presents "an insider's counterpublic perspective on Harlem nightlife" (373).

32. See Rampersad and Roessel's notes to the *Collected Poems* in which they de-scribe ellipses in an earlier, unprinted version (665).

33. See Hokansen, who parallels the two visual parts of this poem to boogie-woogie in which the same musician plays different parts with each hand: a bass rhythm and a treble variation (68). Tracy calls this poem "a twelve-line, twelve-bar, boogie-woogie poem annexing an exclamatory tag" (229).

34. Also see Tracy on this poem's resemblance to boogie-woogie lyrics (227–30).

35. This Library of Congress recording is commercially available from Random House Audio under the series title *The Voice of the Poet*.

4. Lyric Collaborations

1. For books on literary collaboration, see Koestenbaum (1989), Stillinger (1991), Laird (2000), London (2000), Rios and Sands (2000), York (2002), Karell (2002). Within composition theory, Ede and Lunsford (1990) are central figures, but see notes 3 and 5 in their piece "Collaboration" for a fuller bibliography (364–65). Also see edited collections by Leonard (1994), Woodmansee and Jaszi (1994), Chadwick and de Courtivron (1996), Peck and Mink (1998).

2. "By James Merrill" is a contested phrase in this chapter. I use it only in reference to "The Book of Ephraim" as a published artifact.

3. Laird's own book, *Women Coauthors*, addresses a wide scope of collaborative practices. According to Ede and Lunsford, definitions of group or collaborative writing may strictly require joint responsibility for the published document, or cover any the processes preceding composition (*Singular Texts / Plural Authors* 14–15). See also Ede and Lunsford, "Collaboration" (355); London (18–20, 23); and Karell's introduction. Stillinger uses the term "multiple authorship" (v, 22–24) to construct an inclusive model.

4. See Laird, "'A Hand Spills,'" (346) and *Women Coauthors* (1–13) and throughout; Doane and Hodges; York (3–37); Peck and Mink.

5. See Jackson's interview with McClatchy (37–42).

6. An entire essay collection, *Significant Others*, edited by Chadwick and de Courtivron, treats only pairs of authors with sexual attachments to each other.

7. Yu gives a helpful overview of the argument that *Sandover* is a poem of gay marriage (179–88).

8. Koestenbaum's focuses on male collaborative texts from the end of the nineteenth and beginning of the twentieth century. While he does not explore *Sandover* at length, "The Book of Ephraim" resonates with his paradigms. "Men who collaborate engage in metaphorical sexual intercourse," Koestenbaum asserts, and "the text they balance between them is alternately the child of their sexual union, and a shared woman" (3). Published fifty years later than the objects of Koestenbaum's analysis, "The Book of Ephraim" is relatively well-informed about psychoanalytic theory and much less evasive about homosexual love. In fact, these poems wittily mock the repressed anxieties Koestenbaum finds in earlier works, such as "castratory violence" and "a wish to usurp female generative power" (4). As Leonardi and Pope put it in 1994, "The unspeakable is more speakable now, although there's still a price to pay for speaking it" ("Screaming Divas" 261).

9. Laird notes that couples may "pivot on a partially excluded third person" (*Women Coauthors* 10); this is a particularly interesting observation in light of "Ephraim's" spirit guide, the title character.

10. See York (119–20).

11. Collaboration has also been an important subject for early modern studies; see Masten, Hirschfeld.

12. For another perspective on this "isolationist paradigm," see Leonard and Wharton, "Breaking the Silence."

13. It interests me that Merrill's most illuminating comments on poetics appear in the interview format. Interviews are conversations about books and writing that have been transcribed into print, often with considerable editing; the process evokes the written voices of Ouija-based work.

14. Merrill's entire interview with Sheehan clarifies his ideas about sound and voice in poetry. For instance, "The best writers can usually be recognized by their rhythms" (*Recitative* 30). Also see "The Education of the Poet" (*Collected Prose* 9–20).

15. See Donaldson on Merrill's "poetics of echo" (44) and Kalaidjian on *The Changing Light at Sandover*'s "choral polyphony" (102). Johnston also argues that Merrill is "above all else, a poet of voice" (105) and Halpern analyzes Merrill's oscillation between prophetic and everyday voices; neither defines poetic voice as a term, and Johnston in fact emphasizes voice as a "novelistic" strategy (107).

16. Holly Laird's seminar on literary collaborations at the 2001 Modernist Studies Association meeting deeply enriched my understanding of collaboration's nuances; I contributed a preliminary version f my work on "The Book of Ephraim" to that seminar.

17. It makes sense to refer to the historical person as James Merrill and reserve the Ouija abbreviation JM for the poem's character, but Jackson alternates here between "JM" and "Jimmy" in a fascinating way.

18. Lurie's memoir entertains contradictions of its own. On the question of belief, for instance, Lurie alternately characterizes the séances as dangerous, remarking on the one hand that "I sometimes had the feeling that my friend's mind was intermittently being taken over by a stupid and possibly even evil alien intelligence" (63) and suggesting on the other that Jackson and Merrill were surely too sophisticated to believe in such "imaginary beings" (97). Also, while Lurie laments anti-Semitism in the Ouija transcripts, she herself seems inordinately worried by the race of some of Jackson's lovers (140–47).

19. Bauer 98–100. The issue of Merrill's belief or skepticism in the Ouija board's revelations is a major subject of *Sandover* criticism. For example, Materer observes that "the firmness of his belief in the reality of these sessions varies with the skepticism of the interviewer" (*Modernist Alchemy* 2).

20. Merrill tells Vendler that he read Jaynes' book on the origins of human consciousness as he finished writing *Mirabell* (*Recitative* 52). Jaynes, a biologist, posits that verbal hallucinations issue from the speech center in our right brains, and that these verbal hallucinations played a crucial role in human evolution.

21. Other critics also note how the Ouija board facilitates Merrill's exploration of "the paradoxes of poetic authority" (Sword 134). Keller observes that its "rituals allow an expanded perception of the self as multiple, ambiguous, fluid" (248). McHale describes it as a "prosthetic device for writing" and notes its kinship to other procedural approaches to poetry (45–47). Even the word "ouija" is polyvocal, fusing the words for "yes" in two languages.

22. Also see Merrill's *Collected Prose*, 172.

23. See Sacks.

24. Merrill also incorporates other voices via allusion. Yenser observes a revealing allusion in the same passage to Euclid's golden section (240). For Merrill's comments on allusion see his *Collected Prose* (23 and 30–31).

25. Thanks to my colleague Jim Warren for help with this reference.

26. See Shetley on how Merrill negotiates audience. Merrill's comments on the "clever polysyllabic rhymes" in the songs of his childhood may also cast his own rhyming in a different light, as more populist than experimental (*A Different Person* 260).

27. Speaking to McClatchy, Jackson wonders whether Ephraim's visit really contained an "invitation to suicide" (30).

28. This scene resonates with Koestenbaum's argument that "men who collaborate engage in metaphorical sexual intercourse." However, while the modernists whom Koestenbaum treats conceal the erotics of the enterprise, Merrill more often foregrounds them. See also Laird, who observes that collaborative relationships may pivot on a partially excluded third person (*Women Coauthors* 10).

29. According to Kuberski, "Merrill's poem dramatizes poetic influence" (244). Keller also notes "*Sandover*'s frank dependency on the voices and works of Merrill's literary forebears" (214).

30. Also see Richards on the "phantom voice" of Poe.

31. MacDonald observes the relative infrequency of female poetic collaborators (1).

32. For more detail on their collaborative process, including "The Ten Commandments of Collaboration," how they handle disputes, and the use of collage and other techniques, see Seaton's interview with Mazur and Ryal.

33. I draw on "A Short History of Pearl & the Editors," available at http://www .pearlmag.com/editors.html.

34. E-mail dated 7/25/2005. Thalo now lives and works in Pennsylvania. Her web site is www.motherchaosstudios.com.

35. MacDonald reports the following about the writing process for this poem: "They wrote 'a bunch of questions and a bunch of answers (in Olive's voice) that didn't have anything to do with each other,' Duhamel says. They questioned each other and tried to fit the answers, cutting and pasting as necessary" (4). The dialogic format, in other words, mirrors a dialogic method, although it does not record it precisely.

36. See Hicok, unpaginated.

5. Voice Activated

1. See Stern on academic readings as voicings or "presentations" rather than as performances (73–75).

2. See Wojahn (266).

3. *The KGB Bar Book of Poems*, edited by Lehman and Black, is a particularly rich source of such reminiscences.

4. See http://www.sfsu.edu/~poetry/aboutUs.html

5. Also see Stern as on the increasing popularity of readings in the sixties (73).

6. An unpublished history of Washington and Lee by Ollinger Crenshaw describes the lively influence of student literary societies on this campus throughout the nineteenth century. Students had the option of joining one of these literary fraternities, whose members pooled funds to buy books and held weekly debates; their existence complemented the classical curriculum by focusing on contemporary literature and pressing social questions. These groups died out by the 1920s (1.429–41, 2.172–73).

7. Correspondence concerning these seminars and some programs are archived in Special Collections at Leyburn Library at Washington and Lee (the "English Department / Special Seminars" box).

8. Graff describes how enrollments shift toward twentieth-century literature courses in the sixties (196).

9. I draw on several sources concerning the Glasgow series, including an unpublished interview with Professor Emeritus Severn Duvall (2 May 2006), the Glasgow files archived in Special Collections at Washington and Lee, and miscellaneous later records kept by R. T. Smith in the *Shenandoah* offices.

10. I concur here with Lazer, who remembers that "at one time, perhaps from 1956–1976, poetry readings did have a revolutionary (or at least a disruptive) force to them," since dissipated—only Washington and Lee, as usual, is a good ten years behind the game (65).

11. Also see Rubin on Robert Pinsky's Favorite Poem Project, an important recent mode of poetry readings by non-authors (385–404).

12. See http://www.cavecanempoets.org/ (accessed 11 May 2006).

13. See http://www.awpwriter.org/aboutawp/index.htm (accessed 25 April 2006).

14. For a poet's perspective on the AWP, see Nin Andrews' "Poets on Poets" in Lehman and Black (2–3).

15. See Beau Sia, for example, on the advantages and dissatisfactions of college bookings for slam poets (Glazner, *How to Make a Living as a Poet* 115–17).

16. Damon links slam to the "dozens," rap, and European oral traditions (333–36); Holman mentions dada, futurism, the performance art movement of the 1980s, dub poetry, cowboy poetry, and other practices as relatives of slam (342–43); Beach compares it to populist, proletarian poetries as well as to musical forms (128); Gioia, writing about popular poetries including slam, rap, and cowboy poetry, links them to New Formalism and New Narrative (11).

17. See Damon's helpful account of who opposes slam and why (326–28) and Crown's comments on the oppositions between contemporaneous movements, spoken word and "experimentalist" or Language poetry (216–17). Strongly worded denunciations of spoken word continue to proliferate.

18. Oral poetry performance generally tends to be neglected by literary critics; recent books by Severin and Middleton are welcome exceptions. Also, slam poets did, in fact, perform at the 2006 AWP in Austin, Texas; one of them, Somers-Willett, wrote her recent dissertation on slam. Tyehimba Jess was the only tenure-track professor among the AWP slammers.

19. See Medina, Glazner, Anglesey, Eleveld, and others for examples of spoken word anthologies. Spoken word poets who have a significant presence in the print world include Patricia Smith, Tyehimba Jess, Paul Beatty, Tracie Morris, Jeffrey McDaniel, and Maggie Estep.

20. Somers-Willett organized a panel for the 2006 AWP called "Slam Poetry and the Academy," asking, "What purposes does the tension serve?" She also pointed out that the tension between performance and text is a "venerable" one going back at least as far as Vachel Lindsay. One audience member wondered if universities might assimilate performance poetry the way they assimilated creative writing.

21. Others have chosen to focus on national slams for the same reasons I have—because they offer a coherent way to sample a range of local styles. See Somers-Willett (57) and the film *SlamNation*. Alternatively, Beach focuses on one slam venue, the Nuyorican Café, stressing continuities of space and performers rather than the cross-section of nationals.

22. On this point, Nicolay comments, "In this way, slam is inherently tribal—tribal poetries are always performative, both ancient and ephemeral, and exist only in the cumulative minds of the tribe's members" (e-mail to the author 7 March 2006).

23. See Somers-Willett on the whiteness and youth of slam audiences (58–59).

24. Hair, clothing, jewelry and shoes offered every non-corporate style option imaginable (an occasional business suit appeared on a poet, but the wearers tended to look hot and scruffy enough to seem distinctly unbusiness-like). A post-grunge casualness constituted the norm, as many poets wore jeans and solid colors, seeking attention primarily through their voices. A few teams wore matching tee shirts and one duo performed a piece about romantic conflict in shadow outfits of black and startling white. Others appeared in symbolic or provocative attire, including camouflage, low-slung peasant skirts with thong straps winking above the waistlines, man-skirts, African prints, baseball caps, and untucked button-down shirts in various colors, prints, and wrinkle-formations. A few poets performed barefoot like modern dancers, while others wore sneakers, flip-flops, Birkenstocks, wedgie sandals, and spiked heels. Piercings and tattoos abounded, and many poets had words and designs inked onto their forearms with permanent marker. Black and white people sported fat dreadlocks, men wore their facial hair carved into every conceivable design, women had shaved heads or elaborate coiffures. Hair dye and makeup ranged from subtle tints to gothic ebony, with jewel-hues in streaks. Some slammers were impressively large, a few tautly muscled, many voluptuous, others with the wiry physiques of the underfed and over-caffeinated. Perfumes, essential oils, and defiantly unwashed smelliness permeated every site.

25. "I like the word 'pouty' and the word 'sibilance.' I'm a pouty, sibilant boy," one emcee pronounced with slight variations as he moved across the stage, speaking into each of five microphones.

26. Slams also require a timekeeper and accountants, also chosen from the audience. If any piece exceeds three minutes, points are deducted from its final score. When the piece concludes, judges record a number on a small yellow pad with bold black marker; when all are ready they raise the pads and the emcee

reads off the scores, lowest to highest. Two or three other people, speedy mathematicians preferred, record the five scores, drop the lowest and the highest, and add the remainder, which is quickly announced to the audience. For instance, a 7.9, 8.1, 8.6, 8.9, and 9.3 would result in a score of 25.6. Five teams compete in each bout at nationals, sending up one individual or group piece in each round, and accumulate three scores; the team with the highest total score in each bout proceeds to Friday's semi-finals. Each team competes twice, once on Wednesday and once on Thursday, once each in the early and late slots, to compensate for inevitable local irregularities in judging.

27. I view judging as a kind of audience participation, but Harrington argues that it "reinforces the distinction between artist and audience" (174). For a brief essay on the perils of slam judging, see Duhamel in Lehman and Black (64–65).

28. This showcase, titled "Grassroots Austin: The Hottest Acts in Slam Poetry" occurred at the Austin, Texas convention center on 11 March 2006 as part of the Associated Writing Programs meeting.

29. This web site purports to expose corruption in the world of literary contests; it has received national press.

30. The slam family meeting is open to all; I attended in 2005 and was even permitted to vote. One significant alteration from the early days: it now adheres to Robert's Rules of Order.

31. See http://saaniidotcom.blogspot.com/2005_08_01_saaniidotcom_archive.html.

32. See Foley on the complexities of scoring oral poetry (97–102).

33. See Somers-Willett on racial dynamics in slam for a related point: "Rewarding such writing and performance can benefit a white liberal audience: reward displaces them from being the subject of the black poet's protest" (63).

34. Its delivery into print, however, doesn't solve all ambiguities, given that the printed version is nearly unpunctuated, full of sentence fragments, and the principles of lineation are unclear. The way the poem veers towards sentiment, especially at the end, would also invite workshop critique. I mean this as an observation concerning the esthetic priorities of different communities, not as a criticism; judging a slam poem as a printed or visual object would be beside the point.

35. The "rules" underlying many editorial decisions are too various to enumerate here and differ widely from press to press. A few examples, none of them universal, none of them listed in "submissions guidelines": coauthored poems are hard to publish in prestigious magazines, as are poems with centered lines, poems that straightforwardly advocate a political point of view, poems that eschew all capital letters, poems that employ nonsense syllables, etc.

Afterword

1. Thanks to Peter Potter, NPS 2005 organizer Danny Solis, and unofficial NPS photographer Granma Dave (Dave Schein II) for presenting, and helping me sort through, various potential cover images.

2. See Morgan (411), Schumacher (446–48), and Miles (372).

3. This parallels Davidson's point in "Technologies of Presence": while "technology is capable of separating voice from speaker, conversation from community,"

the tape recorder can be "an accomplice in the recovery of more authentic speech" (103). In Ginsberg's poetry, "a voice has seized the means of reproduction and adapted it to oppositional ends" (206).

Appendix A

1. Rexroth held Thursday night soirees at his home, for example (Campbell 160, Ferlinghetti and Peters 167–68); several articles gathered in *The Literary Review* 32, no. 1 (Fall 1988) are also enormously helpful in illuminating the artistic scene that spawned the Six Gallery event. A few retellings of the Six Gallery reading occur in Campbell (178–83), Davidson (3–4), Ginsberg (*Howl* 165), Joyce Johnson (119–21), McClure (11–30), and Middleton (61–65). *Literary San Francisco*, one of the most encyclopedic treatments of that city's poetic history, gives it relatively little attention (180).

2. Thanks to Julia Spicher Kasdorf, Bruce Morrow, Herbert Kohl, and Nancy Shapiro for filling me in on the history of the Teachers and Writers Collaborative. Also see *Journal of a Living Experiment*, edited by Lopate.

3. Poet-scholar Alicia Ostriker remembers "Judy Grahn reading in workclothes and boots, reading without 'style' or affectation of any sort—standing there in front of the microphone straight and solid as an oak—and feeling I was looking at a woman who WAS a tree. That this was what a dryad would look like" (Women's Poetry List, 10 May 2006). Diane Middlebrook adds that there also occurred a "memorable public spat between Denise Levertov and Adrienne Rich regarding the role of lesbianism in conceptualizing women's poetry" (e-mail, 12 December 2006). I am extremely grateful to them for informing me about this event.

4. I am again indebted to the Wom-Po listserv for its members' collective memory and insight—they helped me build this list. Also thanks to Marsha Bryant, Janet Gray, Deborah Miranda, and Scott Nicolay.

5. See www.favoritepoem.org and Rubin (385–404).

WORKS CITED

Adams, Katherine H. *A History of Professional Writing Instruction in American Colleges: Years of Acceptance, Growth, and Doubt.* Dallas: Southern Methodist University Press, 1993.

Albertini, John A., Bonnie Meath-Lang, and David P. Harris. "Voice as Muse, Message, and Medium: The Views of Deaf College Students." In *Voices on Voice: Perspectives, Definitions, Inquiry,* edited by Kathleen Blake Yancey, 172–90. Urbana: NCTE, 1994.

Altieri, Charles. *Self and Sensibility in Contemporary American Poetry.* Cambridge: Cambridge University Press, 1984.

Anglesey, Zoë. *Listen Up: Spoken Word Poetry.* New York: One World, 1999.

Association of Writers & Writing Programs. 24 April 2006. George Mason University, Fairfax, VA. http://www.awpwriter.org/

Aviv, Rachel. "Save the Beatniks!" *Poetry Foundation Archives,* 12 May 2006. http://poetryfoundation.org/archive/feature.html?id=178113

Badaracco, Claire. *Trading Words: Poetry, Typography, and Illustrated Books in the Modern Literary Economy.* Baltimore: Johns Hopkins University Press, 1995.

Baker, Russell, ed. *The Norton Book of Light Verse.* New York: Norton, 1986.

Bakhtin, M. M. *The Dialogic Imagination: Four Essays.* Edited by Michael Holquist, translated by Caryl Emerson and Michael Holquist. Austin: University of Texas Press, 1981.

Banich, M. T. *Neuropsychology: The Neural Bases of Mental Function.* New York: Houghton Mifflin, 1997.

Barksdale, Richard K. "Hughes: His Times and His Humanistic Techniques." In *Langston Hughes,* edited by Harold Bloom, 137–50. New York: Chelsea House, 1989.

Barnouw, Erik. *A History of Broadcasting in the United States.* 3 vols. New York: Oxford University Press, 1966–70.

Barrett, Carole, and Harvey Markowitz, eds. *American Indian Biographies*. Rev. ed. Hackensack, NJ: Salem Press, 2005.

Bauer, Mark. "Between Lives: James Merrill Reading Yeats' Prose." *Contemporary Literature* 43, no. 1 (Spring 2002): 85–119.

Beach, Christopher. *Poetic Culture: Contemporary Poetry between Community and Institution*. Evanston: Northwestern University Press, 1999.

Bear, Mark F., Barry Connors, and Michael Paradiso. *Neuroscience: Exploring the Brain*. 2d ed. Baltimore: Lippincott Williams & Wilkins, 2001.

Belenky, Mary Field, et al. *Women's Ways of Knowing: The Development of Self, Voice, and Mind*. New York: Basic Books, 1986.

Benston, Kimberly W. *Performing Blackness: Enactments of African-American Modernism*. London: Routledge, 2000.

Benvenuto, Richard. *Amy Lowell*. Boston: Twayne, 1985.

Berger, Charles. "*Mirabell:* Conservative Epic." In *James Merrill*, edited by Harold Bloom. New York: Chelsea House Publishers, 1985.

Berlin, James. "Rhetoric and Ideology in the Writing Class." *College English* 50, no. 5 (Sept. 1988): 477–94.

Bernard, Emily, ed. *Remember Me to Harlem: The Letters of Langston Hughes and Carl Van Vechten, 1925–64*. New York: Knopf, 2001.

Bernstein, Charles, ed. *Close Listening: Poetry and the Performed Word*. New York: Oxford University Press, 1998.

——. Introduction to *Close Listening: Poetry and the Performed Word*. New York: Oxford University Press, 1998.

Berry, Francis. *Poetry and the Physical Voice*. New York: Oxford University Press, 1962.

Bettermann, Henrik, Dietrich von Bonin, et al. "Effects of Speech Therapy with Poetry on Heart Rate Rhythmicity and Cardiorespiratory Coordination." *International Journal of Cardiology* 84, no. 1 (2002): 77–88.

Blasing, Mutlu Konuk. "Rethinking Models of Literary Change: The Case of James Merrill." In *Critical Essays on James Merrill*, edited by Guy Rotella, 99–115. New York: G. K. Hall, 1996.

Bloom, Harold. "The Year's Books." In *A Reader's Guide to James Merrill's* The Changing Light at Sandover, edited by Robert Polito, 133. Ann Arbor: University of Michigan Press, 1994.

Bode, Carl. *The American Lyceum: Town Meeting of the Mind*. New York: Oxford University Press, 1956.

Bohn, Willard. *Modern Visual Poetry*. Newark: University of Delaware Press, 2001.

Bolden, Tony. *Afro-Blue: Improvisations in African American Poetry and Culture*. Chicago: University of Illinois Press, 2004.

Bontemps, Arna. "The Awakening: A Memoir." In *Harlem Renaissance Remembered*, edited by A. Bontemps, 1–26. New York: Dodd, Mead, 1972.

Booth, Wayne C. *The Rhetoric of Fiction*. Chicago: University of Chicago Press, 1961.

Borshuk, Michael. *Swinging the Vernacular: Jazz and African American Modernist Literature*. New York: Routledge, 2006.

Bradshaw, Melissa. "'Let Us Shout It Lustily': Amy Lowell's Career in Context." In *Selected Poems of Amy Lowell*, edited by Melissa Bradshaw and Adrienne Munich. New Brunswick, NJ: Rutgers University Press, 2002.

——. "Remembering Amy Lowell: Embodiment, Obesity, and the Construction of a Persona." In *Amy Lowell: American Modern*, edited by Adrienne Munich and Melissa Bradshaw, 167–84. New Brunswick, NJ: Rutgers University Press, 2004.

Breiner, Laurence A. "Caribbean Voices on the Air: Radio, Poetry, and Nationalism in the Anglophone Caribbean." In *Communities of the Air: Radio Century, Radio Culture*, edited by Susan Merrill Squier, 93–108. Durham: Duke University Press, 2003.

Brooker, Peter. "Modernism Deferred: Langston Hughes, Harlem and Jazz Montage." In *Locations of Literary Modernism: Region and Nation in British and American Modernist Poetry*, edited by Alex Davis and Lee M. Jenkins, 231–47. Cambridge: Cambridge University Press, 2000.

Brown, Fahamisha Patricia. *Performing the Word: African American Poetry as Vernacular Culture*. New Brunswick, NJ: Rutgers University Press, 1999.

Brown, Marshall. "Negative Poetics: On Skepticism and Lyric Voice." *Representations* 86 (Spring 2004): 120–40.

Brown, Robert J. *Manipulating the Ether: The Power of Broadcast Radio in Thirties America*. Jefferson, NC: McFarland, 1998.

Burke, Carolyn. *Becoming Modern: The Life of Mina Loy*. New York: Farrar, Straus & Giroux, 1996.

Campbell, Joseph. *This Is the Beat Generation: New York—San Francisco—Paris*. Berkeley: University of California Press, 1999.

Cameron, Sharon. *Lyric Time: Dickinson and the Limits of Genre*. Baltimore: Johns Hopkins University Press, 1979.

Campion, Peter. "Grasshoppers: A Notebook." *Poetry* (June 2005): 234–42.

Carlton, Susan Brown. "Voice and the Naming of Woman." In *Voices on Voice: Perspectives, Definitions, Inquiry*, edited by Kathleen Blake Yancey, 226–241. Urbana, IL: NCTE, 1994.

Carpenter, Margaret Haley. *Sara Teasdale: A Biography*. New York: Schulte, 1960.

Chadwick, Whitney, and Isabelle de Courtivron. *Significant Others: Creativity and Intimate Partnership*. London: Thames and Hudson, 1993.

Charters, Ann. *The Beats: Literary Bohemians in Postwar America. Dictionary of Literary Biography*. Vol. 16. Detroit: Gale Research, 1983.

Chinitz, David. "Literacy and Authenticity: The Blues Poems of Langston Hughes." *Callaloo* 19, no. 1 (1996): 177–92.

——. "Rejuvenation through Joy: Langston Hughes, Primitivism, and Jazz." *American Literary History* 9, no. 1 (Spring 1997): 60–78.

Clark, Suzanne. *Sentimental Modernism: Women Writers and the Revolution of the Word*. Bloomington: Indiana University Press, 1991.

——. "Uncanny Millay." In *Millay at 100: A Critical Reappraisal*, edited by Diane P. Freedman, 3–26. Carbondale: Southern Illinois University Press, 1995.

Clarke, Cheryl. *"After Mecca": Women Poets and the Black Arts Movement*. New Brunswick, NJ: Rutgers University Press, 2005.

Connor, James. A. "Radio Free Joyce: *Wake* Language and the Experience of Radio." In *Sound States: Innovative Poetics and Acoustical Technologies*, edited by Adalaide Morris, 17–31. Chapel Hill: University of North Carolina Press, 1997.

Connor, Steven. *Dumbstruck: A Cultural History of Ventriloquism*. New York: Oxford University Press, 2000.

Coyle, Michael. "'This Rather Elusory Broadcast Technique': T. S. Eliot and the Genre of the Radio Talk." *ANQ* 11, no. 4 (Fall 1998): 32–42.

——. "T. S. Eliot on the Air: 'Culture' and the Challenges of Mass Communication." In *T. S. Eliot and Our Turning World*, edited by Jewel Spears Brooker, 141–54. New York: St. Martin's Press, 2001.

Crenshaw, Ollinger. *General Lee's College: The Rise and Growth of Washington and Lee*. Vol. 1. New York: Random House, 1961.

Crown, Kathleen. "'Sonic Revolutionaries': Voice and Experiment in the Spoken Word Poetry of Tracie Morris." In *We Who Love to Be Astonished: Experimental Women's Writing and Performance Poetics*, edited by Laura Hinton and Cynthia Hogue, 213–26. Tuscaloosa: University of Alabama Press, 2002.

Culler, Jonathan. "Changes in the Study of the Lyric." In *Lyric Poetry: Beyond New Criticism*, edited by Chaviva Hošek and Patricia Parker, 38–54. Ithaca: Cornell University Press, 1985.

——. *Structuralist Poetics: Structuralism, Linguistics, and the Study of Literature*. Ithaca: Cornell University Press, 1975.

Cuthbert, Margaret, ed. *Adventure in Radio*. New York: Howell, Soskin, 1945.

Dace, Tish. *Langston Hughes: The Contemporary Reviews*. Cambridge: Cambridge University Press, 1997.

Damon, Maria. "Was That 'Different,' 'Dissident,' or 'Dissonant'? Poetry (n) the Public Spear: Slams, Open Readings, and Dissident Traditions." *Close Listening: Poetry and the Performed Word*, edited by Charles Bernstein, 324–42. New York: Oxford University Press, 1998.

Davey, Elizabeth. "Building a Black Audience in the 1930s: Langston Hughes, Poetry Readings, and the Golden Stair Press." In *Print Culture in a Diverse America*, edited by James P. Danky and Wayne A. Wiegand, 223–43. Urbana: University of Illinois Press, 1998.

Davidson, Michael. *The San Francisco Renaissance: Poetics and Community at Mid-century*. New York: Cambridge University Press, 1989.

——. "Technologies of Presence: Orality and the Tapevoice of Contemporary Poetics." In *Sound States: Innovative Poetics and Acoustical Technologies*, edited by Adalaide Morris, 97–125. Chapel Hill: University of North Carolina Press, 1997.

de Man, Paul. "Lyrical Voice in Contemporary Theory: Riffaterre and Jauss." In *Lyric Poetry: Beyond New Criticism*, edited by Chaviva Hošek and Patricia Parker, 55–72. Ithaca: Cornell University Press, 1985.

——. *The Rhetoric of Romanticism*. New York: Columbia University Press, 1984.

Demonet, J-F., et al. "The Anatomy of Phonological and Semantic Processing in Normal Subjects." *Brain* 115 (1992): 1753–68.

deNiord, Chard. "The Nature of Voice." *AWP Chronicle* 24, no. 2 (October/November 1991): 7–10.

Derrida, Jacques. *Of Grammatology*. Translated by Gayatri Spivak. Baltimore: Johns Hopkins University Press, 1976.

——. *Speech and Phenomena, and Other Essays on Husserl's Theory of Signs*. Translated by David B. Allison. Evanston: Northwestern University Press, 1973.

Diepeveen, Leonard. *Changing Voices: The Modern Quoting Poem*. Ann Arbor: University of Michigan Press, 1993.

Dietz, N. A. E., et al. "Phonological Decoding Involves Left Posterior Fusiform Gyrus." *Human Brain Mapping* 26 (2005): 81–93.

Doane, Janice, and Devon Hodges. "Writing from the Trenches: Women's Work and Collaborative Writing." *Tulsa Studies in Women's Literature* 14, no. 1 (1995): 51–57.

Donaldson, Jeffery. "The Company Poets Keep: Allusion, Echo, and the Question of Who Is Listening in W. H. Auden and James Merrill." *Contemporary Literature* 36, no. 1 (1995): 35–57.

Donoghue, Denis. *Ferocious Alphabets*. Boston: Little, Brown, 1981.

Doreski, William. *The Modern Voice in American Poetry*. Gainesville: University Press of Florida, 1995.

Drucker, Johanna. *The Visible Word: Typography and Modern Art, 1909–1923*. Chicago: University of Chicago Press, 1994.

Duberman, Martin B. *Black Mountain: An Exploration in Community*. New York: Dutton, 1972.

Dubrow, Heather. *Genre*. New York: Methuen, 1982.

——. *The Star Spangled Banner*. Carbondale: Southern Illinois University Press, 1999.

Duhamel, Denise, and Maureen Seaton. *Exquisite Politics*. Chicago: Tia Chucha Press, 1997.

——. *Oyl*. Long Beach, CA: Pearl Editions, 2000.

——. "Thoughts on the Collaboration of 'Ecofeminism in the Year 2000.'" *Mid-American Review* 13, no. 2 (1992): 130–33.

DuPlessis, Rachel Blau. "'Corpses of Poetry': Some Modern Poets and Some Gender Ideologies of the Lyric." In *We Who Love to Be Astonished: Experimental Women's Writing and Performance Poetics*, edited by Laura Hinton and Cynthia Hogue, 69–95. Tuscaloosa: University of Alabama Press, 2002.

——. *Genders, Races, and Religious Cultures in Modern American Poetries, 1908–1934*. New York: Cambridge University Press, 2001.

Eastman, Max. *Great Companions: Critical Memories of Some Famous Friends*. New York: Farrar, Straus and Cudahy, 1959.

Economou, George. "Some Notes Towards Finding a View of the New Oral Poetry." *boundary 2* 3, no. 3 (Spring 1975): 653–64.

Ede, Lisa, and Andrea A. Lunsford. "Collaboration and Concepts of Authorship." *PMLA* 116, no. 2 (March 2001): 354–69.

——. *Singular Texts / Plural Authors: Perspectives on Collaborative Writing*. Carbondale: Southern Illinois University Press, 1990.

Edfeldt, Åke W. *Silent Speech and Silent Reading*. Chicago: University of Chicago Press, 1960.

Elbow, Peter, ed. *Landmark Essays on Voice and Writing*. Davis, CA: Hermagoras Press, 1994.

————. *Writing with Power: Techniques for Mastering the Writing Process.* New York: Oxford University Press, 1981.

Eleveld, Mark. *The Spoken Word Revolution: Slam, Hip-Hop, and the Poetry of the New Generation.* Naperville, IL: Sourcebooks, 2003.

Eliot, T. S. "The Three Voices of Poetry." *On Poetry and Poets.* New York: Farrar, Straus and Cudahy, 1957.

Ferlinghetti, Lawrence, and Nancy J. Peters. *Literary San Francisco: A Pictorial History from Its Beginnings to the Present Day.* San Francisco: City Lights and Harper & Row, 1980.

Finch, Annie, and Kathrine Varnes, eds. *An Exaltation of Forms: Contemporary Poets Celebrate the Diversity of Their Art.* Ann Arbor: University of Michigan Press, 2002.

Foley, John Miles. *How to Read an Oral Poem.* Chicago: University of Illinois Press, 2002.

Ford, Karen Jackson. "Making Poetry Pay: The Commodification of Langston Hughes." In *Marketing Modernisms: Self-Promotion, Canonization, Rereading,* edited by Kevin J. H. Dettmar and Stephen Watt, 275–96. Ann Arbor: University of Michigan Press, 1996.

————. "These Old Writing Paper Blues: The Blues Stanza and Literary Poetry." *College Literature* 24, no. 3 (October 1997): 84–104.

Foster, R. F. *W. B. Yeats: A Life.* Vol. 1. New York: Oxford University Press, 1997.

Freisinger, Randall R. "Voicing the Self: Towards a Pedagogy of Resistance in a Postmodern Age." In *Voices on Voice: Perspectives, Definitions, Inquiry,* edited by Kathleen Blake Yancey, 242–74. Urbana: NCTE, 1994.

Furnas, J. C. *Fanny Kemble: Leading Lady of the Nineteenth-Century Stage: A Biography.* New York: Dial Books, 1982.

Furr, Derek. "Listening to Millay." *Journal of Modern Literature* 29, no. 2 (2006): 94–110.

Frye, Northrop. *Anatomy of Criticism.* Princeton: Princeton University Press, 1957.

Gates, Henry Louis, Jr. *The Signifying Monkey: A Theory of African-American Literary Criticism.* New York: Oxford University Press, 1988.

Genette, Gérard. *Narrative Discourse: An Essay in Method.* Translated by Jane E. Lewin. Ithaca: Cornell University Press, 1980.

Gilbert, Susan. "Directions for Using the Empress': Millay's Supreme Fiction(s)." In *Millay at 100: A Critical Reappraisal,* edited by Diane P. Freedman, 163–81. Carbondale: Southern Illinois University Press, 1995.

————. "Female Female Impersonator: Millay and the Theatre of Personality." In *Critical Essays on Edna St. Vincent Millay,* edited by William B. Thesing, 293–313. New York: G. K. Hall, 1993.

Gilligan, Carol. *In a Different Voice: Psychological Theory and Women's Development.* Cambridge: Harvard University Press, 1993.

Ginsberg, Allen. *Collected Poems, 1947–1997.* New York: HarperCollins, 1997.

————. *Howl: Original Draft Facsimile. . . .* Edited by Barry Miles. New York: Harper & Row, 1986.

Gioia, Dana. *Disappearing Ink: Poetry at the End of Print Culture.* St. Paul, MN: Gray Wolf Press, 2004.

Glazner, Gary Mex. *How to Make a Living as a Poet.* New York: Soft Skull Press, 2005.

——. *Poetry Slam: The Competitive Art of Performance Poetry.* San Francisco: Manic D Press, 2000.

Goodblatt, Chanita. "In Other Words: Breaking the Monologue in Whitman, Williams, and Hughes." *Language and Literature* 9, no. 1 (2000): 25–41.

Gordon, Lyndall. *T. S. Eliot: An Imperfect Life.* New York: W. W. Norton, 1999.

Gould, Jean. *Amy: The World of Amy Lowell and the Imagist Movement.* New York: Dodd, Mead, 1975.

Graff, Gerald. *Professing Literature: An Institutional History.* Chicago: University of Chicago Press, 1987.

Grant, Joy. *Harold Monro and the Poetry Bookshop.* Berkeley: University of California Press, 1967.

Gray, Janet, ed. *She Wields a Pen: American Women Poets of the Nineteenth Century.* Iowa City: University of Iowa Press, 1997.

Gray, Janet. *Race and Time: American Women's Poetics from Antislavery to Racial Modernity.* Iowa City: University of Iowa Press, 2004.

Greenblatt, Stephen. "Presidential Address 2002." *PMLA* 118, no. 3 (May 2003): 417–26.

Gregory, Horace. *Amy Lowell: Portrait of a Poet in Her Time.* New York: T. Nelson, 1958.

Griffiths, Eric. *The Printed Voice of American Poetry.* Oxford: Clarendon, 1989.

Groff, David. "The Peril of the Poetry Reading: The Page Versus Performance." *The Academy of American Poets* (21 July 2005). <http://www.poets.org/viewmedia.php/prmMID/5913>

Hall, Donald. "The Poetry Reading: Public Performance/Private Art." *The American Scholar* 54, no. 1 (1985): 63–77.

——. "The Vatic Voice." In, *Goatfoot Milktongue Twinbird: Interview, Essays, and Notes on Poetry, 1970–1976,* 1–5. Ann Arbor: University of Michigan Press, 1978.

Halpern, Nick. *Everyday and Prophetic: The Poetry of Lowell, Ammons, Merrill, and Rich.* Madison: University of Wisconsin Press, 2003.

Harrington, Joseph. *Poetry and the Public Sphere: The Social Form of Modern U.S. Poetics.* Middletown, CT: Wesleyan University Press, 2002.

Havelock, Eric A. *The Muse Learns to Write: Reflections on Orality and Literacy from Antiquity to the Present.* New Haven: Yale University Press, 1986.

Hayles, N. Katherine. "Voices out of Bodies, Bodies out of Voices: Audiotape and the Production of Subjectivity." In *Sound States: Innovative Poetics and Acoustical Technologies,* edited by Adalaide Morris, 74–96. Chapel Hill: University of North Carolina Press, 1997.

Heilman, K. M., R. Scholes, and R. T. Watson. "Auditory Affective Agnosia: Disturbed Comprehension of Affective Speech." *Journal of Neurology, Neurosurgery, and Psychiatry* 38 (1975): 69–72.

Heintz, Kurt. "An Incomplete History of Slam: A Biography of an Evolving Poetry Movement." *E-Poets Network* (1994; 2 March 2006). <http://www.e-poets.net/library/slam/index.html>

Hicok, Bob. *Caffeine Destiny*. <http://www.caffeinedestiny.com/hicok.html>

Higgins, Dick. *Pattern Poetry: Guide to an Unknown Literature*. Albany: State University of New York Press, 1987.

Hilmes, Michele. *Radio Voices: American Broadcasting, 1922–1952*. Minneapolis: University of Minnesota Press, 1997.

Hirschfeld, Heather. "Early Modern Collaboration and Theories of Authorship." *PMLA* 116, no. 3 (May 2001): 609–22.

Hodge, Jan C. "Taking Shape: The Art of *Carmina Figurata*." In *An Exaltation of Forms: Contemporary Poets Celebrate the Diversity of Their Art*, edited by Annie Finch and Kathrine Varnes, 198–205. Ann Arbor: University of Michigan Press, 2002.

Hoffman, Tyler. "Treacherous Laughter: The Poetry of Slam, Slam Poetry, and the Politics of Resistance." *Studies in American Humor* 3, no. 8 (2001): 49–64.

Hokanson, Robert O'Brien. "Jazzing it Up: The Be-Bop Modernism of Langston Hughes." *Mosaic: A Journal for the Comparative Study of Literature* 31, no. 4 (1998): 61–82.

Holman, Bob. "Performance Poetry." In *An Exaltation of Forms: Contemporary Poets Celebrate the Diversity of Their Art*, edited by Annie Finch and Kathrine Varnes, 341–51. Ann Arbor: University of Michigan Press, 2005.

Hooks, Bell. *Talking Back: Thinking Feminist, Thinking Black*. Boston: South End Press, 1989.

Hubbard, Stacy Carson. "Love's 'Little Day': Time and the Sexual Body in Millay's Sonnets." In *Millay at 100: A Critical Reappraisal*, edited by Diane P. Freedman. Carbondale: Southern Illinois University Press, 1995.

Hughes, Langston. *The Big Sea: An Autobiography*. New York: Hill and Wang, 1940.

———. *The Collected Poems*. Edited by Arnold Rampersad and David Roessel. New York: Knopf, 1994.

———. *Collected Works*. Vol. 9. Edited by Christopher C. De Santis. Columbia: University of Missouri Press, 2002.

———. *Montage of a Dream Deferred*. New York: Holt, 1951.

———. *Selected Poems*. New York: Knopf, 1959.

Inge, M. Thomas. "Collaboration and Concepts of Authorship." *PMLA* 116, no. 3. (May 2001): 623–30.

Izenberg, Oren. "Language Poetry and Collective Life." *Critical Inquiry* 30 (Autumn 2003): 132–59.

Jackson, David. "DJ: A Conversation with David Jackson." Edited by J. D. McClatchy. *Shenandoah* 30, no. 4 (Winter 1979): 23–44.

———. "Lending a Hand." In *James Merrill: Essays in Criticism*, edited by David Lehman and Charles Berger, 298–305. Ithaca: Cornell University Press, 1983.

Jacobus, Mary. "Apostrophe and Lyric Voice in *The Prelude*." In *Lyric Poetry: Beyond New Criticism*, edited by Chaviva Hošek and Patricia Parker, 167–181. Ithaca: Cornell University Press, 1985.

Jared, D., and M. S. Seidenberg. *Journal of Experimental Psychology* 120 (1991): 358–94.

Jarraway, David R. "Montage of an Otherness Deferred: Dreaming Subjectivity in Langston Hughes." *American Literature* 68, no. 4. (1996): 819–47.

Jaynes, Julian. *The Origin of Consciousness in the Breakdown of the Bicameral Mind.* Boston: Houghton Mifflin, 1977.

Jeffreys, Mark. *New Definitions of Lyric: Theory, Technology, and Culture.* New York: Garland, 1998.

Jemie, Onwuchekwa. *Langston Hughes: An Introduction to the Poetry.* New York: Columbia University Press, 1976.

Johnson, Barbara. *A World of Difference.* Baltimore: Johns Hopkins University Press, 1987.

Johnson, Joyce. *Minor Characters.* New York: Washington Square Press, 1983.

Johnston, Devin. *Precipitations: Contemporary American Poetry as Occult Practice.* Middletown: Wesleyan University Press, 2002.

Jones, Meta DuEwa. "Jazz Prosodies: Orality and Textuality." *Callaloo* 25, no. 1 (2002): 66–91.

——. "Listening to What the Ear Demands: Langston Hughes and His Critics." *Callaloo* 25, no. 4 (2002): 1145–75.

Jordan, June. *Poetry for the People.* New York: Routledge, 1995.

Kahn, Douglas, and Gregory Whitehead, eds. *Wireless Imagination: Sound, Radio, and the Avant-Garde.* Cambridge: MIT Press, 1992.

Kalaidjian, Walter. *Languages of Liberation: The Social Text in Contemporary American Poetry.* New York: Columbia University Press, 1989.

Kalstone, David. "Persisting Figures: The Poet's Story and How We Read It." In *James Merrill: Essays in Criticism,* edited by David Lehman and Charles Berger, 125–44. Ithaca: Cornell University Press, 1983.

Kane, Julie. "Poetry as Right-Hemispheric Language." *Journal of Consciousness Studies* 11, nos. 5–6 (2004): 21–59.

Kaplan, Milton Allen. *Radio and Poetry.* New York: Columbia University Press, 1949.

Karell, Linda K. *Writing Together, Writing Apart: Collaboration in Western American Literature.* Lincoln: University of Nebraska Press, 2002.

Keller, Lynn. *Re-Making It New: Contemporary American Poetry and the Modernist Tradition.* New York: Cambridge University Press, 1987.

Keniston, Ann. *Overheard Voices: Address and Subjectivity in Postmodern American Poetry.* New York: Routledge, 2006.

Kent, George E. "Hughes and the Afro-American Folk and Cultural Tradition." In *Langston Hughes,* edited by Harold Bloom, 17–36. New York: Chelsea House, 1989.

Kerouac, Jack. *The Dharma Bums.* New York: NAL, 1958.

Kinnahan, Linda. *Lyric Interventions: Feminism, Experimental Poetry, and Contemporary Discourse.* Iowa City: University of Iowa Press, 2004.

Klima, Edward S., and Ursula Bellugi. "Poetry without Sound." In *Symposium of the Whole: A Range of Discourse Toward an Ethnopoetics,* edited by Jerome Rothenberg and Diane Rothenberg, 291–302. Berkeley: University of California Press, 1983.

Koestenbaum, Wayne. *Double Talk: The Erotics of Male Literary Collaboration.* New York: Routledge, 1989.

Kramer, Dale. *The Chicago Renaissance: The Literary life in the Midwest, 1900–1930.* New York: Appleton-Century, 1966.

Kuberski, Philip. "The Metaphysics of Postmodern Death: Mailer's *Ancient Evenings* and Merrill's *The Changing Light at Sandover*." *ELH* 56, no. 1 (1989): 229–54.

Laird, Holly A. "'A Hand Spills from the Book's Threshold': Coauthorship's Readers." *PMLA* 116, no. 2 (March 2001): 344–53.

———. *Women Coauthors*. Chicago: University of Illinois Press, 2000.

Langston Hughes Papers. James Weldon Johnson Collection in the Yale Collection of American Literature, Beinecke Rare Book and Manuscript Library.

Lanser, Susan S. *Fictions of Authority: Women Writers and Narrative Voice*. Ithaca: Cornell University Press, 1992.

Larkin, Philip. *Required Writing: Miscellaneous Pieces, 1952–1982*. New York: Farrar, Straus, Giroux, 1982.

Lazer, Hank. "Poetry Readings and the Contemporary Canon." *American Poetry* 7, no. 2 (Winter 1990): 64–72.

Lehman, David, and Charles Berger, eds. *James Merrill: Essays in Criticism*. Ithaca: Cornell University Press, 1983.

Lehman, David, and Star Black. *The KGB Bar Book of Poems*. New York: Perennial, 2000.

Leighton, Mary E. "Performing Pauline Johnson: Representations of 'the Indian poetess' in the Periodical Press, 1892–95." *Essays on Canadian Writing* 65 (Fall 1998): 141–64.

Lemke, Sieglinde. *Primitivist Modernism: Black Culture and the Origins of Transatlantic Modernism*. New York: Oxford, 1998.

Leonard, James S., and Christine E. Wharton. "Breaking the Silence: Collaboration and the Isolationist Paradigm." In *Authority and Textuality: Current Views of Collaborative Writing*, edited by James S. Leonard et al., 25–40. West Cornwall, CT: Locust Hill Press, 1994.

Leonard, James S., et al., eds. *Authority and Textuality: Current Views of Collaborative Writing*. West Cornwall, CT: Locust Hill Press, 1994.

Leonardi, Susan J., and Rebecca A. Pope. "(Co)Labored Li(v)es: or, Love's Labors Queered." *PMLA* 116, no. 3 (May 2001): 631–37.

———. "Screaming Divas: Collaboration as Feminist Practice." *Tulsa Studies in Women's Literature* 13 (1994): 259–70.

Levy, Andrew. *The Culture and Commerce of the American Short Story*. New York: Cambridge University Press, 1993.

Loeffelholz, Mary. *From School to Salon: Reading Nineteenth-Century American Women's Poetry*. Princeton: Princeton University Press, 2004.

London, Bette. *Writing Double: Women's Literary Partnerships*. Ithaca: Cornell University Press, 1999.

Longenbach, James. *The Resistance to Poetry*. Chicago: University of Chicago Press, 2004.

Lowney, John. "Langston Hughes and the 'Nonsense' of Be-Bop." *American Literature* 72, no. 2 (2000): 357–85.

Lurie, Alison. *Familiar Spirits: A Memoir of James Merrill and David Jackson*. New York: Viking, 2001.

Macdonald, Nikki. "Sharing the Muse: A Collaborative Voice Emerges." *Painted Bride Quarterly* 63 (Spring 2000): 1–6. <www.webdelsol.com/pbq/issues/63/mcdonald.html>

Machan, Katharyn Howd. "Breath into Fire: Feminism and Poetry Readings." *Mid-American Review* 12, no. 2 (1992): 120–26.

MacLeish, Archibald. *The Fall of the City: A Verse Play for Radio.* New York: Farrar and Rinehart, 1937.

Masten, Jeffrey. *Textual Intercourse: Collaboration, Authorship, and Sexualities in Renaissance Drama.* New York: Cambridge University Press, 1997.

Materer, Timothy. *James Merrill's Apocalypse.* Ithaca: Cornell University Press, 2000.

——. "James Merrill's Polyphonic Muse." *Contemporary Literature* 67, no. 2 (2006): 207–35.

——. *Modernist Alchemy.* Ithaca: Cornell University Press, 1995.

Mayers, Tim. *(Re)Writing Craft: Composition, Creative Writing, and the Future of English Studies.* Pittsburgh: University of Pittsburgh Press, 2005.

McAdams, Janet. "We, I, 'Voice,' and 'Voices': Reading Contemporary Native American Poetry." *Studies in American Indian Literatures* 7, no. 3 (Fall 1995): 8–17.

McClure, Michael. *Scratching the Beat Surface.* San Francisco: North Point Press, 1982.

McDaniel, Jeffrey. "Almost Like Church." *Poetry Foundation Archive* (12 May 2006). <http://poetryfoundation.org/archive/feature.html?id=177180>

McGann, Jerome. *The Textual Condition.* Princeton, NJ: Princeton University Press, 1991.

McGee, Daniel T. "Dada Da Da: Sounding the Jew in Modernism." *ELH* 68 (2001): 501–27.

McHale, Brian. *The Obligation toward the Difficult Whole: Postmodern Long Poems.* Tuscaloosa: University of Alabama Press, 2004.

McLuhan, Marshall. *Understanding Media: The Extensions of Man.* McGraw Hill, 1964.

Medina, Tony, and Louis Reyes Rivera, eds. *Bum Rush the Page: A Def Poetry Jam.* New York: Three Rivers Press, 2001.

Merrill, James. *The Changing Light at Sandover.* New York: Alfred A. Knopf, 1998.

——. *Collected Prose.* Edited by J. D. McClatchy and Stephen Yenser. New York: Knopf, 2004.

——. *A Different Person.* New York: Alfred A. Knopf, 1993.

——. *Recitative: Prose by James Merrill.* Edited by J. D. McClatchy. San Francisco: North Point, 1986.

Meyer, Kinereth. "Speaking and Writing the Lyric 'I.'" *Genre* 22 (1989): 129–49.

Michlin, Monica. "Langston Hughes's Blues." In *Temples for Tomorrow: Looking Back at the Harlem Renaissance*, edited by Geneviève Fabre and Michel Feith, 236–53. Bloomington: Indiana University Press, 2001.

Middleton, Peter. *Distant Reading: Performance, Readership, and Consumption in Contemporary Poetry.* Tuscaloosa: University Press of Alabama, 2005.

Miles, Barry. *Ginsberg: A Biography.* New York: Simon and Schuster, 1989.

Milford, Nancy. *Savage Beauty: The Life of Edna St. Vincent Millay*. Random House, 2001.

Mill, John Stuart. *Collected Works of John Stuart Mill*. Vol. 1. Edited by John M. Robson and Jack Stillinger. Toronto: University of Toronto Press, 1981.

Millay, Edna St. Vincent. *Collected Poems*. New York: Harper Collins, 1956.

———. [Edna St. Vincent Millay reads several of her poems.] Rec. 193–? Audiotape. Brander Matthews Dramatic Museum Collection (Library of Congress). RXA 5652 B1–4.

———. *Letters of Edna St. Vincent Millay*. Edited by Alan Ross Macdougall. New York: Harper, 1952.

———. *The Voice of the Poet: Five American Women*. Series editor, J. D. McClatchy. Random House, 2001.

Miller, Cristanne. *Cultures of Modernism: Marianne Moore, Mina Loy, and Else Lasker-Schüler: Gender and Literary Community in New York and Berlin*. Ann Arbor: University of Michigan Press, 2005.

Miller, Nina. *Making Love Modern: The Intimate Public Worlds of New York's Literary Women*. New York: Oxford University Press, 1999.

Miller, R. Baxter. "The Art and Imagination of Langston Hughes." Lexington: University Press of Kentucky, 1989.

Moglen, Seth. "Modernism in the Black Diaspora: Langston Hughes and the Broken Cubes of Picasso." *Callaloo* 25, no. 4 (2002): 1189–1205.

Monroe, Harriet. "Comment: The Radio and the Poets." *Poetry* 36, no. 1 (April 1930): 32–35.

Moore, Cindy. "Why Feminists Can't Stop Talking about Voice." In *Rhetorical Women: Roles and Representations*, edited by Hildy Miller and Lillian Bridwell-Bowles. Tuscaloosa: University of Alabama Press, 2005.

Morgan, Bill. *I Celebrate Myself: The Somewhat Private Life of Allen Ginsberg*. New York: Viking, 2006.

Morris, Adalaide. Introduction to *Sound States: Innovative Poetics and Acoustical Technologies*. Chapel Hill: University of North Carolina Press, 1997.

———. "Sound Technologies and the Modernist Epic: H. D. on the Air." In *Sound States: Innovative Poetics and Acoustical Technologies*, 32–55. Chapel Hill: University of North Carolina Press, 1997.

Morrisson, Mark. *The Public Face of Modernism: Little Magazines, Audiences, and Reception, 1905–1920*. Madison: University of Wisconsin Press, 2001.

Mullen, Harryette. "African Signs and Spirit-Writing." In *African American Literary Theory: A Reader*, edited by Winston Napier, 623–42. New York: New York University Press, 2000.

Murr, Naeem. "Poetry Readings: A Field Guide." *Poetry* (June 2004). <http://www.poetrymagazine.org/magazine/0604/comment_1782.html>

Myers, D. G. *The Elephants Teach: Creative Writing since 1880*. Englewood Cliffs: Prentice Hall, 1996.

National Poetry Festival: Proceedings. Washington, D.C.: Library of Congress, 1964.

Nelson, Cary. *Repression and Recovery: Modern American Poetry and the Politics of Cultural Memory, 1910–1945*. Madison: University of Wisconsin Press, 1989.

Nicholls, David G. *Conjuring the Folk: Forms of Modernity in African America*. Ann Arbor: University of Michigan Press, 2000.

Nielsen, Aldon Lynn. *Black Chant: Languages of African-American Postmodernism*. New York: Cambridge University Press, 1997.

Nielsen, Dorothy M. "Ecology, Feminism, and Postmodern Lyric Subjects." In *New Definitions of Lyric: Theory, Technology, and Culture*, edited by Mark Jeffreys, 127–50. New York: Garland, 1998.

Niven, Penelope. *Carl Sandburg: A Biography*. New York: Charles Scribner's Sons, 1991.

Noland, Carrie. *Poetry at Stake: Lyric Aesthetics and the Challenge of Technology*. Princeton: Princeton University Press, 1999.

Norris, Kathleen. *The Virgin of Bennington*. New York: Riverhead, 2001.

Notley, Alice. *Coming After: Essays on Poetry*. Ann Arbor: University of Michigan Press, 2005.

Olson, Charles. *Collected Prose*. Edited by Donald Allen and Benjamin Friedlander. Berkeley: University of California Press, 1997.

Olson, Stanley. *Elinor Wylie: A Life Apart*. New York: Dial Press, 1979.

Ong, Walter J. *Orality and Literacy: The Technologizing of the Word*. Methuen, 1982.

Orwell, George. "Poetry and the Microphone." In *I Belong to the Left*, vol. 17 of *The Complete Works of George Orwell*, edited by Peter Davison, 74–80. London: Secker & Warburg, 1998.

Ostriker, Alicia. E-mail to the Women's Poetry List. 6 May 2006. <http://lists.usm.maine.edu/archives/wom-po.html>

Ostrom, Hans. *A Langston Hughes Encyclopedia*. Westport, CT: Greenwood Press, 2002.

Padgett, Ron. *The Straight Line: Writings on Poetry and Poets*. Ann Arbor: University of Michigan Press, 2000.

Parini, Jay. *Robert Frost: A Life*. New York: Holt, 1999.

Parker, Patricia. Introduction to *Lyric Poetry: Beyond New Criticism*, edited by Chaviva Hošek and Patricia Parker. Ithaca: Cornell University Press, 1985.

Peck, Elizabeth G., and JoAnna Stephens Mink, eds. *Common Ground: Feminist Collaboration in the Academy*. Albany: State University of New York Press, 1998.

Perloff, Marjorie. *The Dance of the Intellect: Studies in the Poetry of the Pound Tradition*. New York: Cambridge University Press, 1985.

——. *Differentials: Poetry, Poetics, Pedagogy*. Tuscaloosa: University of Alabama Press, 2004.

——. *The Poetics of Indeterminacy: Rimbaud to Cage*. Princeton, NJ: Princeton University Press, 1981.

——. "A Response." In *New Definitions of Lyric: Theory, Technology, and Culture*, edited by Mark Jeffreys, 245–55. New York: Garland, 1998.

Picker, John M. *Victorian Soundscapes*. New York: Oxford University Press, 2003.

Polito, Robert. *A Reader's Guide to James Merrill's* The Changing Light at Sandover. Ann Arbor: University of Michigan Press, 1994.

Pollitt, Katha. Untitled essay. In *The KGB Bar Book of Poems*, edited by David Lehman and Star Black. New York: Perennial, 2000.

Ponce, Martin Joseph. "Langston Hughes's Queer Blues." *Modern Language Quarterly* 66, no. 4 (December 2005): 505–37.

Posner, David M. "Rhetoric, Redemption, and Fraud: What We Do When We End Books." *Profession* (2005): 179–82.

Price, C. R., et al. "Brain Activity during Reading: The Effects of Task and Exposure Duration." *Brain* 117 (1994): 1255–69.

Prins, Yopie. "Voice Inverse." *Victorian Poetry* 42, no. 1 (2004): 43–59.

"PSI Poetry Slams Inc. FAQ: Poetry Slams." *Poetry Slam, Inc.* (7 March, 2006). <http://www.poetryslam.com/modules.php?name=MainPage>

Rajan, Tilottama. "Romanticism and the Death of Lyric Consciousness." In *Lyric Poetry: Beyond New Criticism*, edited by Chaviva Hošek and Patricia Parker, 194–207. Ithaca: Cornell University Press, 1985.

Ramazani, Jahan. *Poetry of Mourning: The Modern Elegy from Hardy to Heaney.* Chicago: University of Chicago Press, 1994.

Rampersad, Arnold. *The Life of Langston Hughes.* 2 vols. New York: Oxford University Press, 1988.

Rasula, Jed. *The American Poetry Wax Museum: Reality Effects, 1940–1990.* Urbana: NCTE, 1996.

Rée, Jonathan. *I See a Voice: Deafness, Language, and the Senses—A Philosophical History.* New York: Henry Holt, 1999.

Reiser, Andrew C. *The Chautauqua Moment: Protestants, Progressives, and the Culture of Modern Liberalism.* New York: Columbia University Press, 2003.

Reynolds, David S. *Walt Whitman's America: A Cultural Biography.* New York: Vintage, 1995.

Richards, Eliza. "Lyric Telegraphy: Women Poets, Spiritualist Poetics, and the 'Phantom Voice' of Poe." *Yale Journal of Criticism* 12, no. 2 (1999): 269–94.

Richardson, Joan. *Wallace Stevens.* 2 vols. New York: Beech Tree Books, 1986.

Rifkin, Libbie. "Making It / New: Institutionalizing Postwar Avant-Gardes." *Poetics Today* 21, no. 1 (Spring 2000): 129–50.

Rios, Theodore, and Kathleen Mullen Sands. *Telling a Good One: the Process of a Native American Collaborative Autobiography.* University of Nebraska Press, 2000.

Ritter, Kelly and Stephanie Vanderslice. "Teaching Lore: Creative Writers and the University." *Profession* (2005): 102–12.

Rosenstone, Robert A. "Mabel Dodge." In *Affairs of the Mind: The Salon in Europe and America from the 18th to the 20th Century*, edited by Peter Quennell, 131–52. Washington, D.C.: New Republic Books, 1980.

Rothenberg, Jerome. "New Models, New Visions: Some Notes toward a Poetics of Performance." In *Performance in Postmodern Culture*, edited by Michael Benamou and Charles Caramello. Madison, Wisconsin: Coda Press, 1977.

Rubin, Joan Shelley. *Songs of Ourselves: The Uses of Poetry in America.* Cambridge, Harvard University Press, 2007.

Sacks, Peter. "The Divine Translation: Elegiac Aspects of *The Changing Light at Sandover*." In *James Merrill: Essays in Criticism*, edited by David Lehman and Charles Berger, 159–85. Ithaca: Cornell University Press, 1983.

Sadoff, Ira. "Hearing Voices: The Fiction of Poetic Voice." *New England Review* 14, no. 4 (1992): 221–32.

Saerchinger, César. *Hello America!: Radio Adventures in Europe*. Boston: Houghton Mifflin, 1938.

Sáez, Richard. "'At the Salon Level': Merrill's Apocalyptic Epic." In *James Merrill: Essays in Criticism*, edited by David Lehman and Charles Berger, 211–45. Ithaca: Cornell University Press, 1983.

Schmid, Julie. "Spreading the Word: A History of the Poetry Slam." *Talisman: A Journal of Contemporary Poetry and Poetics*, vols. 23–26 (2001–2002): 636–45.

Schulman, Robert. *The Power of Political Art: The 1930s Literary Left Reconsidered*. Chapel Hill: University of North Carolina Press, 2000.

Schultz, Susan. "Hawai'i's Local Vocals: Pidgin Literature, Performance, and Post-coloniality." In *Close Listening: Poetry and the Performed Word*, edited by Charles Bernstein, 343–59. New York: Oxford University Press, 1998.

Schumacher, Michael. *Dharma Lion: A Critical Biography of Allen Ginsberg*. New York: St. Martin's Press, 1992.

Schwarz, A. B. Christa. *Gay Voices of the Harlem Renaissance*. Bloomington: Indiana University Press, 2003.

Schweighauser, Philipp. *The Noises of American Literature, 1890–1985: Toward a History of Literary Acoustics*. Gainesville: University Press of Florida, 2006.

Seaton, Maureen. "An Interview by Neil de la Flor." *Scene 360: The Film and Arts Online Magazine* (2005). <http://www.scene360.com/STORYboard_interview_seaton.html>

——. "The Singular and Plural of Poet: An Interview with Maureen Seaton," conducted by Estee Mazur and Richard Ryal. *Gulfstream!ng* 2 (Spring/Summer 2002): 1–7. <http://w3.fiu.edu/gulfstrm/SeatonInterview.htm>

Sentilles, Renée M. *Performing Menken: Adah Isaacs Menken and the Birth of American Celebrity*. New York: Cambridge University Press, 2003.

Severin, Laura. *Poetry Off the Page: Twentieth-Century British Women Poets in Performance*. Burlington, VT: Ashgate Press, 2004.

Shetley, Vernon. *After the Death of Poetry: Poet and Audience in Contemporary America*. Durham: Duke University Press, 1993.

Shoptaw, John. "Lyric Cryptography." *Poetics Today* 21, no. 1 (2000): 221–62.

Shulevitz, Judith. "The Close Reader: Sing Muse . . . Or Maybe Not." *New York Times Book Review* (December 1, 2002): 34.

Silliman, Ron. "Afterword: Who Speaks: Ventriloquism and the Self in the Poetry Reading." In *Close Listening: Poetry and the Performed Word*, edited by Charles Bernstein, 360–78. New York: Oxford University Press, 1998.

Sivier, Evelyn M. "English Poets, Teachers, and Festivals in a 'Golden Age of Poetry Speaking,' 1920–50." In *Performance of Literature in Historical Perspectives*, edited by David W. Thompson, 283–300. Lanham, MD: University Press of America, 1983.

——. "Penny Readings: Popular Elocution in Late Nineteenth-Century England." In *Performance of Literature in Historical Perspectives*, edited by David W. Thompson, 223–30. Lanham, MD: University Press of America, 1983.

SlamNation: The Sport of Spoken Word. Dir. Paul Devlin. Slammin' Entertainment, 1998.

Smethurst, James. *The Black Arts Movement: Literary Nationalism in the 1960s and 1970s*. Chapel Hill: University of North Carolina Press, 2005.

———. *The New Red Negro: The Literary Left and African American Poetry, 1930–1946*. New York: Oxford University Press, 1999.

Smulyan, Susan. *Selling Radio: The Commercialization of American Broadcasting, 1920–1934*. Washington, DC: Smithsonian Institution Pres, 1994.

Somers-Willett, Susan B. A. "Slam Poetry and the Cultural Politics of Performing Identity." *Journal of the Midwest Modern Language Association* 38, no. 1 (Spring 2005): 51–73.

Spinelli, Martin. "Not Hearing Poetry on Public Radio." In *Communities of the Air: Radio Century, Radio Culture*, edited by Susan Merrill Squier, 195–216. Durham, NC: Duke University Press, 2003.

Sprague, Rosemary. *Imaginary Gardens: A Study of Five American Poets*. Philadelphia: Chilton, 1969.

Squier, Susan Merrill, ed. *Communities of the Air: Radio Century, Radio Culture*. Durham, NC: Duke University Press, 2003.

Stern, Frederick C. "The Formal Poetry Reading." *Drama Review* 35, no. 3 (Autumn 1991): 67–84.

Sterne, Jonathan. *The Audible Past: Cultural Origins of Sound Reproduction*. Durham, NC: Duke University Press, 2003.

Stewart, Garrett. *Reading Voices: Literature and the Phonotext*. Berkeley: University of California Press, 1990.

Stewart, Susan. *Poetry and the Fate of the Senses*. Chicago: University of Chicago Press, 2002.

Stillinger, Jack. *Multiple Authorship and the Myth of Solitary Genius*. New York: Oxford University Press, 1991.

Stockwell, Peter. *Cognitive Poetics: An Introduction*. New York: Routledge, 2002.

Strong-Boas, Veronica and Carole Gerson. *Paddling Her Own Canoe: The Times and Texts of E. Pauline Johnson (Tekahionwake)*. Toronto: University of Toronto Press, 2000.

Sword, Helen. *Ghostwriting Modernism*. Ithaca: Cornell University Press, 2002.

Thesing, William B. *Critical Essays on Edna St. Vincent Millay*. New York: G. K. Hall, 1993.

Thomas, Lorenzo. *Extraordinary Measures: Afrocentric Modernism and Twentieth-Century American Poetry*. Tuscaloosa: University of Alabama Press, 2000.

———. "Neon Griot." In *Close Listening: Poetry and the Performed Word*, edited by Charles Bernstein, 300–323. New York: Oxford University Press, 1998.

Thurston, Michael. *Making Something Happen: American Political Poetry Between the World Wars*. Chapel Hill: University of North Carolina Press, 2001.

Tracy, Steven C. *Langston Hughes and the Blues*. Chicago: University of Illinois Press, 1988.

Tsur, Reuven. "Rhyme and Cognitive Poetics." *Poetics Today* 17, no. 1 (Spring 1996): 55–87.

———. *What Makes Sound Patterns Expressive?* Durham, NC: Duke University Press, 1992.

Tucker, Herbert. F. "Dramatic Monologue and the Overhearing of Lyric." In *Lyric*

Poetry: Beyond New Criticism, edited by Chaviva Hošek and Patricia Parker, 226–43. Ithaca: Cornell University Press, 1985.

Turner, Frederick, and Ernst Pöppel. "The Neural Lyre: Poetic Meter, The Brain, and Time." In *Expansive Poetry: Essays on the New Narrative and The New Formalism*, edited by Frederick Feirstein, 209–54. Santa Cruz, CA: Story Line Press, 1989.

Turner, Victor. "A Review of 'Ethnopoetics.'" In *Symposium of the Whole: A Range of Discourse toward an Ethnopoetics*, edited by Jerome Rothenberg and Diane Rothenberg. Berkeley: University of California Press, 1983.

Vendler, Helen. "Divine Comedies." In *A Reader's Guide to James Merrill's* The Changing Light at Sandover, edited by Robert Polito, 134–43. Ann Arbor: University of Michigan Press, 1994.

Von Hallberg, Robert. *American Poetry and Culture, 1945–1980*. Cambridge: Harvard University Press, 1985.

Walker, Cheryl. "The Female Body as Icon: Edna Millay Wears a Plaid Dress." In *Millay at 100: A Critical Reappraisal*, edited by Diane P. Freedman, 85–99. Carbondale: Southern Illinois University Press, 1995.

Waters, William. *Poetry's Touch: On Lyric Address*. Ithaca: Cornell University Press, 2003.

Warren, James Perrin. *Culture of Eloquence: Oratory and Reform in Antebellum America*. University Park: Pennsylvania State University Press, 1999.

Webb, Charles Harper. "The Pleasure of Their Company: Voice and Poetry." *Cortland Review* (Spring 2006). <www.cortlandreview.com>

Weissman, Judith. *Of Two Minds: Poets Who Hear Voices*. Middletown, CT: Wesleyan University Press, 1993.

Wetzsteon, Ross. *Republic of Dreams: Greenwich Village, the American Bohemia, 1910–1960*. New York: Simon and Schuster, 2002.

White, Daniel B. *Muses, Madmen, and Prophets: Rethinking the History, Science, and Meaning of Auditory Hallucination*. New York: Penguin, 2007.

White, Eric W. *Images of H.D./from* The Mystery. London: Enitharmon Press, 1976.

Whitehead, Kim. *The Feminist Poetry Movement*. Jackson: University of Mississippi Press, 1996.

Whitman, Walt. *Walt Whitman: Complete Poetry and Collected Prose*. New York: Library of America, 1982.

Williams, Ellen. *Harriet Monroe and the Poetry Renaissance*. Urbana: University of Illinois Press, 1997.

Willis, Elizabeth. "The Arena in the Garden: Some Thoughts on the Late Lyric." In *Telling it Slant: Avant-Garde Poetics of the 1990s*, edited by Mark Wallace and Steven Marks, 225–36. Tuscaloosa: University of Alabama Press, 2002.

Wills, Clair. "Contemporary Women's Poetry: Experimentalism and the Expressive Voice." *Critical Quarterly* 36, no. 3 (Autumn 1994): 34–52.

Wilson, Edmund. *The Shores of Light: A Literary Chronicle of the Twenties and Thirties*. New York: Farrar, Straus and Young, 1952.

Wise, R., et al. "Distribution of Cortical Neural Networks Involved in Word Comprehension and Word Retrieval." *Brain* 114 (1991): 1803–17.

Wojahn, David. "'A Kind of Vaudeville': Appraising the Age of the Poetry Reading." *New England Review and Bread Loaf Quarterly* 8, no. 2 (1985): 265–82.

Woodmansee, Martha, and Peter Jaszi, eds. *The Construction of Authorship: Textual Appropriation in Law and Literature.* Durham, NC: Duke University Press, 1994.

Yancey, Kathleen Blake, ed. *Voices on Voice: Perspectives, Definitions, Inquiry.* Urbana: NCTE, 1994.

Yenser, Stephen. *The Consuming Myth: The Work of James Merrill.* Cambridge: Harvard University Press, 1987.

York, Lorraine. *Rethinking Women's Collaborative Writing: Power, Difference, Property.* Toronto: University of Toronto Press, 2002.

Yu, Christopher. *Nothing to Admire: The Politics of Poetic Satire from Dryden to Merrill.* New York: Oxford University Press, 2003.

INDEX